France and the Maghreb

Florida A&M University, Tallahassee
Florida Atlantic University, Boca Raton
Florida Gulf Coast University, Ft. Myers
Florida International University, Miami
Florida State University, Tallahassee
University of Central Florida, Orlando
University of Florida, Gainesville
University of North Florida, Jacksonville
University of South Florida, Tampa
University of West Florida, Pensacola

France and the Maghreb

Performative Encounters

Mireille Rosello

University Press of Florida

Gainesville · Tallahassee · Tampa · Boca Raton

Pensacola · Orlando · Miami · Jacksonville · Ft. Myers

Copyright 2005 by Mireille Rosello
Printed in the United States of America on recycled, acid-free paper
All rights reserved

10 09 08 07 06 05   6 5 4 3 2 1

A record of cataloging-in-publication data is available from the Library of Congress.
ISBN 0-8130-2853-1

France and the Maghreb: Performative Encounters is to be published in French
as *France-Maghreb: Poétique d'une Encontre méditerranéenne* by L'Harmattan, Paris.
It is part of the series Etudes transnationales, francophones et comparées (Transnational,
Francophone, and Comparative Studies), series editor Hafid Gafaïti.

The University Press of Florida is the scholarly publishing agency for the State
University System of Florida, comprising Florida A&M University, Florida Atlantic
University, Florida Gulf Coast University, Florida International University, Florida State
University, University of Central Florida, University of Florida, University of North
Florida, University of South Florida, and University of West Florida.

University Press of Florida
15 Northwest 15th Street
Gainesville, FL 32611-2079
http://www.upf.com

To Geneviève and Pierre Vidal-Naquet

Contents

Acknowledgments

I wish to thank the following colleagues and institutions for organizing conferences or research days and for enabling many of us to present the early stages of texts that were subsequently published. Their intellectual energy provided us with the opportunity to engage in fruitful debates and to improve our work in progress: Ieme van der Poel, Inge Boer, Patricia Pisters, Ginette Verstraete, and the Amsterdam School for Cultural Analysis; Francesca Sautman, Thomas Spear, and the Graduate Center at CUNY; Michael Dash and New York University; Charles Bonn and the Université Lumière, Lyon 2; Alain Montandon and the Centre de Recherches sur les Littératures Modernes et Contemporaines at the University Blaise Pascal in Clermont-Ferrand; Farid Laroussi, Chris Miller, and Yale University; Michèle Vialet, Catherine Raissiguier, and the University of Cincinatti; Hafid Gafaïti, Patricia Lorcin, and Texas Tech University at Lubbock; Marc Brudzinski, Sabrina Draï Wengier, and the University of Miami; Alec Hargreaves and the Winthrop-King Institute for Contemporary French and Francophone Studies; Vinay Swamy and the University of Washington at Seattle; Dominic Thomas, Ali Behdad, and the University of California at Los Angeles; Stamos Metzidakis, Seth Graebner, and the Washington University in Saint Louis, Olivier Clarinval, Ramon Foukoue, Vanesa Garcia Velasco, Chris Picicci, Tom Regele, Christina Vander Vorst, Enrico Vettore, Gina Psaki, Karen McPherson and the University of Oregon at Eugene; Soraya Tlatli and the University of California at Berkeley. Your hospitality and intellectual support are much appreciated. I also want to thank the editors of journals and collected volumes for providing me with exciting reasons to start exploring some of the issues developed in this book: Pit Ruhe, Cilas Kemedjio, Alec Hargreaves, Abigail Descombes, Patricia-Pia Célérier, Patricia Lorcin, Françoise Lionnet, and Dominic Thomas. I thank all the authors whose fascinating work I read while writing this book and especially Assia Djebar and Fouad Laroui. They have inspired and moved me; they also made me laugh.

I am grateful to the Northwestern University doctoral students and research assistants who were closely involved in the preparation of the manuscript: Chris Hogarth, Fran Hutchins, Brad Reichek, and Amy Settergren.

A special note of gratitude goes to the two anonymous readers who agreed to comment on the manuscript and who took the time to write encouraging and detailed reports. I don't know who you are, but I know what you did and I hope that the final version of the book convinces you that you have not wasted your breath. I wish to thank Amy Gorelick, my acquisitions editor, and Jacqueline Kinghorn Brown, project editor, who accompanied this project from beginning to end at the University Press of Florida; and thanks are also due the copy editor, Catherine Nevil Parker, for her thoughtful and exceptionally thorough work on the transcript. I am grateful to Bill Cloonan for introducing us, as well as for his constant support, friendship, and exceptional sense of hospitality.

As always, Françoise Lionnet, Pit Ruhe, Colin Davis, Jean-Xavier Ridon, and Jean Mainil inhabit these pages in intangible and indispensable ways.

Introduction

What Are "Performative Encounters"?

The phrase "performative encounters" is not meant to be immediately transparent or understandable, and if the expression is greeted with a slight moment of hesitation, if a second look is required, I welcome my readers' hesitation as a desirable reticence. Although my goal is not to disconcert, if the unknown combination of words creates a second of discomfort, this moment of friction is not due to a lack of previous knowledge or a difficulty in understanding. On the contrary, it is the beginning of a new process that resembles the type of encounters that the phrase would like to describe.

One of the hypotheses tested in this book is that the violence of some historical contexts makes any initial encounter with another subject almost impossible. No first encounter can ever take place when history, language, religion, and culture exert such pressures upon the protagonists of the encounter that their desire to speak or be silent is trapped by preexisting, prewritten dialogues and scenarios. This is often the case for subjects that we assign to one of the shores of the Mediterranean (to France or the Maghreb, for example). We think of them as either Maghrebi or French. We call them Algerians or Europeans and sometimes Arabs or Berbers. They are confined to the imaginary, physical, or administrative boundaries of one nation, one culture, one language, and one religion.

By performative encounters, I mean a type of encounter that coincides with the creation of new subject-positions rather than treating preexisting (pre-imagined) identities as the reason for, and justification of, the protocol of encounter—whether it is one of violence or trust, respect or hostility. When we assume that we can identify the Mediterranean subjects who will be the ordinary heroes of this book, if we already know what to call them (*pieds-noirs* or *harkis*, Arabs or Berbers, *roumis* or settlers, terrorists or politico-financial mafia), the encounters that we imagine are already overdetermined by our narratives. A preestablished script will prevent the encounter from becoming performative because it will impose the language of the encounter, the subject-positions from which each protagonist meets the other, and therefore the protocol of the encounter will force itself upon the subjects. They will be expected to choose their camp, to protect or defend themselves, to accuse, to defy.

A performative encounter would be this exceptional moment when, in spite of an international or national conflict, in spite of the violence that reigns and imposes its rules, an unknown protocol replaces the script. A performative encounter is a multidimensional event that creates subjects because a protocol of exchange suddenly functions as the precondition of the emergence of the encounter. New subject-positions, a new language, and a new type of engagement appear at the same time, none of the elements depending on the preexistence of the others.

The obvious and perhaps mythical legacy invoked by the adjective "performative" is the classic encounter between what John L. Austin called "things" and "words" (1962). Just as a speech act is necessary for a "promise" to exist, for a war to start, for a ceremony to be celebrated, a performative encounter may retrospectively be read as the point of discontinuity between a before and an after. It is certainly no coincidence that when observers seek to describe the relationship between Algeria and France, one of the most frequent and unexamined metaphors is the image of a wedding (or a divorce). As if Austin's very first example of performative statements—the "I do . . . uttered in the course of the marriage ceremony" between a man and a woman (or more accurately, in the text, by a man who "takes this woman to be [his] lawful wedded wife")—forever imposed its exemplary power upon any collective encounter, forcing it into a mold whose social, religious, and (hetero)sexual premises and consequences are later on ignored (1962: 5).

But if performative encounters could be reduced to Austin's explanation of what goes on during such ceremonies, his definitions would lead us to the pessimistic reenactment of preexisting rules and subject-positions through the articulation of the same memorized set-phrases and formulas, which is the opposite of a performative encounter.

Even Austin's theoretical texts are narratives capable of haunting (rather than describing) each performative encounter during which new words must be invented to do new things. No "I do" comes ready to use, and the rules that govern the union and the shape of the relationship thus inaugurated do not exist yet. A performative encounter must invent both the words for the thing and the thing through the words, thus creating the context that would supposedly produce verifiable and predictable effects. A study of performative encounters needs to emphasize what Austin's critics deemed most inadequate, or perhaps what, in the original theories, proves to be fuzzy and unpredictable.

Austin himself starts his second chapter on "misfires" with an example that involves the difference between "Christians" and "Mohammedans" and troubles the issue of a legal union and disunion between two individuals who may not belong to the same national or religious community: "Consider 'I divorce you,' said to a wife by her husband in a Christian country, and both being Christians rather than Mohammedans" (27). In this context, Austin admits, witnesses may "reject what may be called a whole code of procedure" and class the utterance as "a misfire . . . because the procedure invoked is not accepted" (27). And the encounter between subjects whose groups accept different "procedures" is precisely what this book is about. The supposedly problematic situation will be the norm rather than the exception, which makes the so-called norm hypothetical and unpredictable.

The subjects created at the moment of the performative encounter have to find a solution to the dilemma caused by a situation where all the elements of what Austin describes as a presumably unproblematic public ceremony are absent. What is most useful here about two Christians trying to performatively repudiate each other on Muslim soil is the large number of unresolved hypotheses that Austin himself must include in his prose: "*If*," he starts, "the utterance is classed as a misfire" or "it is *presumably* persons other than the speaker who do not accept" or "In this case it *might* be said. . ." (27, my italics). For the protagonists who emerge during a performative encounter, the most interesting consequences of Austin's models are concentrated in the areas of latitude that he concedes in the "presumably," the "ifs," and the "might." Besides, the situations invoked as "examples" of a supposedly extratextual referent are offered to us as stories: their presence is made of words that tell stories, and the fictional encounters that they imagine belong to the type of discourse that famously triggered the most interesting discussions of Austin's theories. The little fable about Christians in a Muslim world reminds me of the fact that Austin's lectures were originally delivered in 1955, at the beginning of what was not yet, performatively, the Algerian war. It also signals itself as the type of text that John Searle identified as problematically "parasitical" to the theory of performativity: like "citations," like "promises made by actors on stage in the course of a play or statements made in the novel by novelists about characters in the novel" (1977: 204).

If Austin's parameters had not have been rewritten and modified to the extent that the intellectual heritage is a complex web of arguments and counterarguments, it would probably not be interesting to invoke him here. The successive amendments and reformulations proposed by the post-deconstruction rewritings of Austin's models problematize any analogy between a purely linguistic speech act and the encounters studied in this book (Butler 1990a & b; 1997a & b; Derrida 1972; Felman 1983; Searle 1969, 1977, 1979).

The encounters studied here are precisely not the equivalent of legal contracts and it would be impossible to find a community of judges willing to agree that something was "done." The encounters are (inscribed in) narratives and stories that are typically described as fiction. Here, words are of the type that most definitions will consider not binding, and therefore not serious. In the order of the Real, they may well be perceived as parasitical or at least tangential to politics and history. They belong to the categories of language that Austin originally wished to exclude, a gesture that Derrida famously criticized in "Signature Event Context" (1972). The narrative, fictional, and literary quality of the written encounters described here may lead some readers to doubt that they will ever have a performative effect.

Rather than assuming that a performative encounter is a case of performative speech act, let's imagine the relationship between citations, dramatic language, and all the instances of what we treat like serious discourse as the equivalent of the multiple and problematic areas of distinction and overlap between fiction and history. In other words, the point is not to deconstruct the distinction between "parasitical" utterances and others or between fiction and nonfiction, but to concentrate on fiction because it is assumed to be parasitical and will therefore function as the forgotten text of the original procedure. We can only meet the other if we have already internalized stories about the other and about ourselves in the presence of that other. Narratives are both the norm and the formulation of the norm although they are precisely constructed to give us the illusion that they describe rather than perform. Consequently, it will be both necessary and implausible to argue that only stories can have an effect at the very moment when they are being told. Only the performance of a new narrative can inaugurate a new scene that will, however, be perceived as having already happened, thus becoming the old narrative that we use as a reference to meet the other.

In order to imagine performative encounters, it is useful to question the way in which the relationship between the context and the word relate to each other in terms of power. Following Derrida, focusing on gender and even more specifically drag as an exemplary case study, Judith Butler started arguing in the 1990s that identities need the force of iterability and citationality in order to be convincingly performed (1990, 1993). Performative encounters are aware of their own temporal duplicity: they call into question the assumed preexistence of the law that guarantees their power and produce their fragile and uncertain effect by reference to the simultaneous invention of the code and of its performance. The code is a language; the performance is the protocol of the encounter; and a third element paradoxically appears as both the precondition and the aftereffect: a new embodied subject.

At the beginning of *Touching Feeling*, Eve Sedgwick writes: "both deconstruction and gender theory seem to have an interest in unmooring Austin's performative from its localized dwelling in a few exemplary utterances or kinds of utterance and showing it instead to be a property of language or discourse much more broadly. You could caricature Derrida as responding to Austin's demonstrating of explicit performatives by saying, 'But the only really interesting part of it is how all language is performative'; and Judith Butler as adding, 'Not only that, but it's most performative when its performativity is least explicit—indeed, arguably, most of all when it isn't even embodied in actual words'" (2003: 6).

If performatives are not "embodied in actual words," what kind of embodiment is Sedgwick thinking about to account for Butler's position? The return of the "body" in this scenario is a compelling vision in the case of performative encounters where gender is only one of the preinscribed stereotypical scripts to be questioned. The body, its perceived gender and its ethnic identity as well are what is performed and reembodied as a result of the performative encounter. In that sense, performative encounters are not only about identification but about subjectivization and the construction of the subject as author of the encounter with the new othered self. For the "I" of the stories to appreciate the iterability of the encounter with the other, a new subject must first have emerged.

Theoretically, all encounters are performative in the sense that they are the perfect crucible where subjectivization emerges. As Sara Ahmed puts it at the beginning of her *Strange Encounters,*

> The others cannot be simply relegated to the outside: given that the subject comes into existence as an entity only through encounters with others, then the subject's existence cannot be separated from the others who are encountered. As such, the encounter itself is ontologically prior to the question of ontology (the question of the being who encounters). (2000: 7)

But the point of my argument is that the encounter between "others" is disallowed by certain contexts. History is one of the possible ways of naming objections to a deconstructive theoretical position: in an ideal (theoretical and philosophical) world, all encounters are performative. And yet, an encounter also implies that some sort of dialogue and engagement is going to take place between the (supposedly) newly emerged subjectivities. And I would argue that as soon as we move from the realm of ontology to an exploration of the type of conversations that occur between historically situated protagonists, a long list of preexisting constraints troubles the theoretical possibilities of creative encounters. Most encounters rely on previously established subjectivities that function as authoritarian scripts. For example, in 1957, if a subject positioned himself as a member of the French military, any meeting with a *fellagha* (Algerian rebel) was a confrontation with the enemy. Conversely, anyone living in Algiers' Casbah who saw a paratrooper would have had an encounter with a possible torturer, even if that man was carrying a basket of bread: *timeo Danaos et dona ferentes.* After all, what other scenarios could have been written?

Forty years after the Evian accords, the positions of "*fellagha*" and "paratroopers" have lost some of their immediate performative force. They no longer function as a mandatory script. But other scenarios have gained strength and relevance. We may wonder why, today, when a French citizen meets a

French citizen (although even that description erases other possibilities), one of them sees and therefore meets an "Arab-looking woman wearing a *hijab*," although that man will probably not be able to represent himself as, say, "a Breton who does not wear a little crucifix around his neck." The unlikelihood of the second self-portrayal and the difficulty entailed in trying to craft a perfectly symmetrical pair of identificatory statements underlines what is missing when encounters are generated by petrified historical narratives that impose stereotypical subject-positions. It also reveals the cultural and linguistic agility required by performative encounters.

For the new subjects created by the encounter will also need to invent a *logos* adapted to their situation. The creativity required to invent and sustain a performative encounter goes together with a certain type of language and a certain type of narrative. All the stories collected in this book have a specific tonality: sometimes, they are comical, but most of the time, they flirt with tragedy and sadness. The language of performative encounters will always be close to laughter or poetry. That is, it will always constitute some sort of translation within and between languages, oscillating between what Gilles Deleuze calls "stuttering" in one's own language and various forms of screams (1987: 116). It will be a sort of Khatibian "love in two languages" (Khatibi 1983a) or what Jacques Derrida calls a "politics of friendship" (1994a). It is never neutral, because it names a radical unknown.

From the outside, a performative encounter will look like an unexpected meeting between people that we normally assume to be incompatible. Without realizing that our identification patterns are precisely what are being questioned and redefined by the new protocol of encounter, we marvel at the existence of an extraordinary alliance or friendship (that we interpret as transnational), of a love story (that we perceive as an encounter between two religions), or of a business deal (that we read as transgressing ethnic boundaries). Here, however, the performative encounter is characterized by the fact that the subjects who came into existence at the same time as the encounter have already reconfigured those identification markers that we perceive as predating the exchange and that we impose upon them. Performative encounters invent new protocols of cohabitation and coexistence rather than new identities. They are less about "ways of being" than about "ways of being with" ("fréquentage," as some sociologists put it) [Curnier 1999: 28].

What types of stories are required for such a task? Are some narrative genres better equipped to describe performative encounters? If some subjects are capable of meeting the other for the first time because they accept being radically othered by the experience, will they not speak a new language? At the very least, we can expect a slight difference, an accent, a tone, or an inflection to color their voices. The "overture" of Assia Djebar's collection of short stories, *Women of Algiers in their Apartment* (1980; 1992), ends on a passage that I would like to propose as emblematic of this type of voice. Written after ten years of relative silence during which the author turned to a collection of lost images and lost testimonies, *Women of Algiers* is the culmination of a long period of reflection on what it means to use the *"qalam."*[1] The end of the first short story makes a proposal that the reader can interpret as a double contract between writer and reader: this is how the narrator wants to write, this is how we should read. This type of listening would help us transcend identification patterns constructed from double negations (neither/nor) or double inclusions.[2] Here is the narrative pact offered by the end of the story: "Ne pas prétendre 'parler pour,' ou pire 'parler sur,' à peine parler *près de* et si possible *tout contre*" (Djebar 1980: 8) ["Don't claim to 'speak for,' or, worse, to 'speak on,' barely speaking next to, and if possible *very close to*"] (Djebar 1992: 2).

This oft-quoted sentence takes on a new meaning if we listen to its suggestion in the context of performative encounters. If, instead of concentrating exclusively on its meaning,[3] we pay attention to the marginal or extrasemantic apparatus embedded in the writing, we will notice the abundance of supplementary markings (quotation marks, italics, reformulations) which signal that language is in difficulty, that language itself is being talked about. We will also appreciate the quasi impossibility of translating the echoes generated by the word "contre." In the original, the "tout contre" means "very close to" (as the translator suggests), but the other meaning of "contre" ("counter," "against" as in "speak up against") disappears from the English version. We can hear the narrator's recommendation (to us and to herself) to speak "tout contre" as an invitation to embrace, simultaneously, the two sides of the French word "contre" which is itself an encounter between proximity and hostility, between "close" and "counter." Speaking "tout contre" is a way of inventing the space where a subject is both "against" and still capable of tenderness and intimacy ("very close to"). In that sense, it resembles the moment of performative encounters during which subjects must learn the art of combining contact and opposition.

Performative encounters can therefore be "felicitous" without referring to the subject's happiness, especially if we systematically associate happiness and a state of peacefulness. Of course, the ghosts of the Algerian war, who haunt the relationship between France and the Maghreb, invite us to take the shortcut from peace to happiness: the misery caused by war and conflicts make it difficult not to. But empires have so often abused the concept of "pacification" that it may be worth questioning any systematic equation between a happy encounter and a peaceful encounter. Peace, when imposed by armed colonial forces, is a rhetorical *coup de force*. As Michael Waltzer reminds us, it is prudent to distinguish between what he calls different "regimes of toleration" (1997: 15). The *Pax Romana* promoted multiculturalism, but it was a kind of multiculturalism that parodied the harmonious diversity imagined by classical democratic and egalitarian thinkers. Colonial rulers may trick us into fetishizing peace and cohabitation:

> Imperial rule is historically the most successful way of incorporating difference and facilitating (requiring is more accurate) peaceful coexistence. But it isn't, or at least it never has been, a liberal and democratic way ... settled imperial rule is often tolerant—tolerant precisely because it is everywhere autocratic (not bound by the interests or prejudices of any of the conquered groups), equally distant from all of them. (Waltzer 15)

Colonialism is "distant from all" rather than "close to" everyone, and it has a vested interest in peace and political stability because its goal is to maximize the economic profit derived from the exploitation of the land made possible by the war of conquest. But just as peace cannot be the only goal or evidence of a performative encounter, performative encounters cannot be equated with confrontation either. The type of revolutionary violence advocated by Frantz Fanon is not a form of performative encounter. Whether we agree or not that his project was the only viable way out of colonization in Algeria, his script is based on a counterviolence which inverts the course of history but does not modify the relationship between individuals and communities. Neither war nor peace constitutes, in and of themselves, the preconditions of performative encounters.

Similarly, the difference between a harmonious or a confrontational relationship may be irrelevant to the performative force of an encounter. Encounters that we encode as "unhappy" or even "tragic" can be felicitous because they produce an imaginative way out of an historical, individual, or cultural impasse if they invent a new grammar or theoretical model that goes beyond the distinction between harmony and happiness, tragedy, and conflict.

Unhappy encounters are frequent in Djebar's fictional texts. One particularly moving account of such encounters appears in the story entitled "Annie and Fatima" in *Oran, langue morte* (1997b: 219–34). Like many of Djebar's characters, Fatima is the child of an interracial Franco-Maghrebi couple: her father is Berber and her mother is French. After a painful and acrimonious divorce, the father leaves, taking the little girl to Kabylia without her mother's consent. When the story begins, Annie has finally negotiated a visit and is hoping to see Fatima again for the first time after ten years. She has just told her story to the first-person narrator, with whom she is staying for a few days on her way to Kabylia. The narrator is amazed to discover that the mother has been learning a Berber language because she is under the impression that this is her only chance of communicating with her child:

Vois-tu, quand elle m'a dit qu'elle apprenait le berbère pour pouvoir un jour communiquer avec sa fille, j'ai été frappée, bouleversée même par cette évidence: on parle toujours, quant à nous, de la "langue maternelle" perdue et à réacquérir (Et dans mon cas, c'est cela, le berbère, le parler enfin comme ma grand-mère, puisque ma mère s'en est coupée!), mais Annie, vois-tu, elle va, elle à la rencontre de la "langue de la fille!" Une langue non plus de l'origine mais de son avenir et tout désormais s'est remis, en elle, à bouger! (1997b: 228)

[You see, when she told me that she was learning a Berber language in order to be able to communicate with her daughter some day, I was struck, even overwhelmed, by this obvious fact: we always talk about the "mother tongue" that we lost and must relearn (in my case, that is what Berber is, I wish I could speak it like my grandmother, since my mother was cut off from it!). But you see, Annie must reach out and encounter the "daughter's tongue!" Not the tongue of the origin but the language of her future and, within herself, everything has started moving once more!]

In order to have an encounter with the daughter, the mother must literally learn a new language. Her own attempt counteracts the movement of separation that the father's family had almost completed. She refuses to let her divorce become the symbol of an ever-widening gap between two communities, two lifestyles, two languages, and two cultures. But no "maternal instinct," no "mother nature" can account for the relationship between the two characters. They only share the desire to speak to one another.

As for the little girl, she does not have a mother tongue anymore, although one of the surprises that awaits Annie is the discovery that just as she has learned the daughter's tongue, the little girl knows some of hers. Fatima cannot be assigned to the new place of linguistic origin that symbolizes once and for all the father's culture, the father's law. She does speak some French, but her mother notices that it is "scolaire, emprunté" (229). *Scolaire* obviously means that Fatima's French was learned at school, but in French saying that a creative or analytical text is "*scolaire*" would also mean that it is derivative or imitative. The way in which the little girl uses French does not allow her spontaneous creation. And while *emprunté* means "gauche" and "clumsy," it also means, literally, "borrowed" (i.e., Fatima's French does not belong to her; it is not hers; she uses it and gives it back).

The encounter is performative because the two subjects must abandon the comfort of positions that could dictate the form of their dialogue. Instead of witnessing a daughter-mother relationship and a conversation in the mother tongue, the story presents us with the emergence of a new subject who speaks a new tongue. When Annie talks to her daughter—when she manages to articulate the sentence in Berber that must encapsulate and put an end to ten years of separation—she discovers that her voice seems to emanate from another "I," a subject different from herself that is brought into existence at the very moment of the encounter:

> —C'est vrai, ce fut soudain comme si j'avais une autre voix, comme si c'était une autre en moi, une étrangère et pourtant moi, ou une morte d'avant ressuscitée à travers moi, une autre voix donc en moi—une voix de petite fille perdue—débita la phrase berbère apprise la veille. (1997b: 231)

> [—And truly, suddenly, it was as if I had another voice, as if someone else in me, a stranger, and yet it was me, or a dead person, someone from before who was resurrected, another voice within me—the voice of a lost little girl—who recited (*débita*) the sentence that I had memorized the day before.]

The word *débiter* [to reel off] evokes a pupil reciting a lesson without necessarily understanding its contents; it is a verb used to describe a poor acting job. Literally, it also means chopping, cutting into pieces, or the debit that has to do with debts and borrowing. Just as the little girl's French is *emprunté* [borrowed], the mother's Berber is *débité* [debited]. The text knows that it cannot pacify this exchange: the speaker's performance cannot simply be reduced to benevolent or hostile intentions (the meaning of words is not all that counts). The encounter expresses the intricate mixture of violence and love that transcends the subject's desire and agency. Annie is conscious of a dislocation, of the intervention of another voice, and of the intrusion of another "I."

She would like her sentence to connote love. She wants it to be a "petite phrase d'amour" [a little love sentence] (232), but the story refuses to erase the violence of the situation, to erase years of separation and absence. The performative encounter remains an emblematically incomplete process that is both felicitous and tragic. The narrator suggests that the daughter is *hurt* by the sentence. The little girl receives, perceives the sentence as "une avalanche, un torrent, un lancer de petites pierres, pas des caresses, non" [an avalanche, a torrent, a rain of little stones, but not caresses, oh no] (231). The story describes the words as natural disasters or even weapons meant to harm. This is not because the mother wants to hurt, but because neither nature (maternal love) nor culture (mother tongue) are enough to pacify the dialogue. The conflictual dimension of the situation is preserved by the text even if both subjects are providing us with a hopeful model of mutual reaching out beyond one's language. In other words, this story is not about the poetry of minor languages that even Deleuze warns us against idealizing (1987).

This moment of the performative encounter is another specific example of the different types of performativity that have been studied in recent gender studies and postcolonial theories. The text suggests that the mother's words "do things," but unlike traditional performative statements, their effectiveness is not the result of her intention to transform them into acts that go beyond language. Of course, it is possible to read the whole passage figuratively and to argue that the stone-like quality of the words is not able to have an effect outside of the realm of language. But I am not arguing here that linguistic stones cannot hurt. I am interested instead in the peculiar situation created by the encounter between two subjects who do not wish to hurt each other but whose performance is hijacked by historical violence, that is, by a force that is not unconscious but not controlled by the speaker's agency either.

Recent analyses of the power of words tend to be suspicious of discourses that assume that language can transcend its own boundaries, or rather of the agenda that gets mobilized around the question of whether or not certain types of utterances that a group agrees are capable of hurting (hate speech for example) should be banned and deemed unlawful. Yet, if we agree that language may, in certain conditions, inflict injury, should it necessarily follow that the best way of handling hate speech is the passing of new laws or even the intervention of a legal authority?[4]

In *Excitable Speech*, where she analyzes the power or lack of effectiveness of certain types of racial insults and verbal abuse, Butler examines the consequences of such logic and continues her reformulations of performativity in the context of hate speech (1997a). We may accept, in principle, that it is possible for a sentence to kill (or at least to constitute bodily harm). But Butler points out that even if we demonstrate that language has been used for the very purpose of hurting another subject, this is in no way the equivalent of saying that each statement will be the equivalent of a weapon that reaches its target.

> I wish to question for the moment the presumption that hate speech always works, not to minimize the pain that is suffered as a consequence of hate speech, but to leave open the possibility that its failure is the condition of a critical response. If the account of the injury of hate speech forecloses the possibility of a critical response to that injury, the account confirms the totalizing effects of such an injury. Such arguments are often useful in legal contexts, but are counter-productive for the thinking of nonstate-centered forms of agency and resistance. (1997: 19)

Like a weapon, a racial insult can always lose its way, misfire, or fail to reach its victim (Butler 1997: 19). The performative effect of such sentences is always difficult to predict, and they are guaranteed neither by the speaker's malevolence nor by the presence of a favorable context. In other words, if a victim is "missed" by hurtful words, it is not simply because he or she has chosen to ignore the insult. Butler does not describe rational speakers who decide not to consider themselves as insulted. Her study involves situations where, should the word have reached its target, it would have indeed wounded the protagonist. The context of the "misfiring," especially in the case of racial insults, has to be analyzed case by case, with the type of attention to details required by Austin himself when he discussed the research that led to the writing of his books.[5]

The story of Annie and Fatima's encounter, however, is slightly different. It is about the power of words, and the mother's sentence is indeed described as a type of language that can either reach its goal or miss its target. But the originality of the scenario is that the sentence is not meant to have a negative effect; it is not an insult or threat. Theorists who warn us against a simple equation between verbal abuse and physical abuse tend to emphasize the possibility for words to misfire, but present the margin of error as a desirable window of opportunity because, in their examples, the statements that may miss their human targets happen to be malevolent racial slurs or sexual insults. A series of shifts occurs between that type of situation and Djebar's story.

In the case of the sentence that ends up functioning like a "lancer de petites pierres" [throwing of little stones], it is important to keep in mind that the desire to speak was not intentionally aggressive. The mother meant to "caress"; she wanted the sentence to be a "love sentence," as when we talk about love stories. The "stones" and the "avalanche" are accidental. They are not weapons used to destroy or hurt. At the same time, the violence of the performance cannot simply be dismissed as a misunderstanding: the little girl cannot be said to have badly interpreted, nor can the mother be accused of Freudian slips. We cannot interpret the element of violence as the hidden truth that a careful analysis would reveal in its simplicity.

The "stones" and the "avalanche" are the traces of the historical violence that separates the two subjects. It would disappear if they simply refused to talk to each other, but peace would amount to capitulation. Djebar does not wish to hide the "torrential" energy of Annie's desperate need to talk to her daughter, but the possibly devastating consequences of this avalanche of love are preferable to the absence of a performative encounter. This is no cordial and polite meeting. It is motivated by a violent desire to go beyond the constraints imposed by the conditions of the encounter.

Any attempt to talk about such encounters will bear the trace of this violence, and this has incalculable consequences not only for the subjects who look for the most adequate "sentence" but also for the writers who want to give an account of such extraordinary meetings. On the other hand, whereas the mentioning of hate speech ends up infecting the discourse of those who want to suppress it, the telling of performative encounters could also be performative in that it will provide us with a new possible grammar of encounters. In order to write about the encounter, Djebar had to pay attention to the grain of the voice and to the transmission of the message, to the characters' tone and to the consequences of their words. Just as performative encounters coincide with the invention of a new *logos*, the storytellers who seek to relay and relate the experience will have to experiment with new genres or new ways of mixing genres. If they are successful, they will be able to add their tales to the preexisting repertoire of stories of encounters, and the presence of such texts will enrich the collective cultural canon. The telling itself may then acquire performative qualities to the extent that the addition of new possible scenarios would transform the memory of one individual performative encounter into a more plausible model of verisimilitude (whereas performative encounters tend to be read as examples of radically exceptional behaviors).

The language that emerges in the presence of performative encounters will blur the distinction between participants and public (and between reader and writer), because it will require from each subject a heightened level of attention to the storytelling practice. As we will see in the following chapters, performative encounters almost systematically become self-referential writings about writing, or stories about the authority of stories. In a nutshell, performative encounters are the history of History or force the reader to think about the mode of historiography adopted in the tale. Many of the heroes of the primary texts studied here are fascinated by history and are either professional or amateur, self-reflexive historiographers who are in the process of rewriting the century-long series of encounters between France and Algeria.

In "Annie and Fatima," the first-person narrator may seem to be digressing from her story when she adopts the language of the historian, or rather of a theorist discussing the status of historical discourse. But she is only apparently going off on a tangent: the two women's tale is history in the making. As she tells their story, the first-person narrator is led to reflect on the destiny of couples whose trajectories mirror the historical directions taken by their respective nations. She characteristically interprets their situation in terms of competing narrative structures. She suggests that when two individuals meet, two narrative scenarios suddenly come into contact and sometimes clash: a double individual destiny imitates national history, the latter functioning like the scenario of a play in which the characters must perform their role according to the preexisting script. The narrator suggests that the actors are not even aware that they are characters in a play:

Au cours des vingt, trente dernières années qui ont suivi la séparation douloureuse mais consommée des deux destins collectifs, quelques individus—des Algériens là, des Françaises ici, ou l'inverse—reforment sur la sphère privée, le "couple"; sans se rendre compte qu'ils vont jouer,

malgré eux, une pièce fantomatique d'amour certes, mimant la célé-
bration du passé, chargeant ce dernier, malgré tout, d'espoir rétroactif.
(Djebar 1997b: 220)

[In the twenty or thirty years that followed the painful but final separation between two collective destinies, a few individuals—Algerian men
and French women or vice-versa—reconnect the two pieces of the
"couple" in the private sphere, not realizing that whether they wanted it
or not, they are going to be actors in a ghostly play, a love story of course,
that would mimic the celebration of the past, investing it with retroactive
hope in spite of everything.]

This pessimistic vision traces an interestingly unidirectional arrow between
individual and collective experiences: here the private couple does not model
itself on archetypal couples (such as Romeo and Juliet, for example, or even
Don Juan and his amorous conquests). The reference is a historic encounter
between two countries, France and Algeria, wedded by the multifaceted rules
of colonial policies. It is certainly significant that Djebar, who has always been
fascinated by the model of the palimpsest and the process of successive
rewritings (especially on monuments) (1995c; 1999b), should abandon that
particular image and turn, instead, to the universe of theatrical performance
where actors and mimes reenact the past.

In "Annie and Fatima" the dialogue between two individuals is thus imagined as a performance (the characters "mime" the events of the past). It is an
endless rehearsal of the same drama, because the protocol of encounter takes
the form of obsessive haunting. Today's stories are haunted or rather performed by ghosts who have been cast in "une pièce fantomatique" [ghostly
play] (1997b: 220). The narrator suggests that, one way or another, such
couples can only be reactionary, or at least backward-looking and nostalgic.
They can only replay a version of the past even if they "le chargent d'un espoir
rétroactif" [endow it with retrospective hope] (220).

The reenacting of the past resembles the reprinting of the unchanged version
of an old text. No rewriting has taken place. Unique love stories cannot be
imagined, and the singularity of the individuals who meet each other across
borders is negated by history. All couples are interchangeable, because the type
of relationship poetically summed up by Montaigne as a case of "Par ce que
c'estoit luy; par ce que c'estoit moy" [Because he was he, because I was I][6] is
made impossible by the existence of a ghostly script that seems to function like
the text's unconscious, or rather, like the lines that actors must memorize:
"Comme si une pulsion sourde se remettait à travailler, malgré le nouveau
décor, et ceux-là même qui ne se savent pas doublures du passé à la double face,
les malheureux . . ." [As if a dull drive had started to work again, in spite of the

new set, and those who do not know that they are standing in, that they are the body doubles of a double-faced past, oh woe is them] (Djebar 1997b: 221). Theatrical metaphors quickly replace one brief allusion to the psychoanalytical model of compulsive repetitions. They dominate the whole passage, saturating the text with references to the "set," placing actors on a stage and depriving their performance of what could make them original, specific, and glamorous since, after all, the heroes are mere body doubles. The narrator imagines the encounter as the layering of two narratives: new stories are "haunted" by an old script, and actors are not even aware that they are repeating old lines.

This allusion to a preexisting text that forces itself onto recent performances is both the description of the problem and the dynamic vision of a solution. If the characters who act out the old scenario want to avoid being at its mercy, if they want to avoid narratives in which "la magie ou le poison opère, généralement dans un désir de mort ou de dévoration" [magic and poison generally work through a desire for death and devouring] (Djebar 1997b: 221), we must be aware that we are not in the position of speaking subjects free to choose our words, but in the role of actors, or, even worse, of doubles whose unimportant presence on stage protects the real star's body. In French, the word *doublure* [body double] accumulates layers of important connotations that all have to do with substitution, replacement, and second-handedness: a *doublure* is a body double, but it is also the lining of a garment, the inside-out, ghostly shape that remains invisible. The verb *doubler* also means to dub and evokes the doubling of languages that takes place when performative encounters make translation and decoding necessary.

Franco-Algerian couples fail miserably, the short story tells us, not because they are composed of incompatible elements—their culture, their religion, or their language do not come in the way of some preassumed harmony—but because they do not write their own stories. Performative encounters are the exceptional situations that occur when the couple liberates itself from the script and moves to another type of storytelling practice.

> Quelques unions algéro-françaises, ou franco-maghrébines s'avèrent par chance bien appareillées. Il n'y a plus alors des victimes en proie à l'Histoire, cette vieille tragédienne hantée par des rôles en putréfaction. (Djebar 1997b: 221)

> [Luckily, a few Algerian-French or Franco-Maghrebi unions turn out to be good matches. At that point, we no longer have victims at the mercy of History, that old tragic actress, haunted by putrid roles.]

If we don't know that history, then the old tragic actress dubs our story as we speak, and we are condemned to endless forms of meaningless and violent repetition.

Why, we may ask, would Djebar, a historian herself, present us with such a negative interpretation of the effects of history? Should we carefully preserve the distinction between what the character says and refrain from collapsing the author's point of view and the overt textual content? It is a sound principle of narratological precaution, but we may also consider that the passage is warning us against a certain type of history rather than against history as a whole, as a genre. We should beware of history when it is a bad narrative, or rather bad theater. Unfortunate are those who will be haunted by its morbid ghosts. It is urgent, the narrator suggests, to switch roles and to play different parts.

To that kind of history, we may want to prefer a different type of narrative, which the postface of the collection of short stories proposes as an antidote to the danger of "putrid roles": "la fiction, cette ballerine écervelée, [qui] gambade en amont ou en avant-garde de ce théâtre" [fiction, this brainless ballerina, dancing upstream or at the avant-garde of the stage] (Djebar 1997b: 374).

Ecervelée in French evokes silliness and childish carelessness but, etymologically, it means that someone's brain has been removed. Paradoxically, the almost inaudible allusion to a violent intervention on the human body also connotes the possibility of new visions and of new forms of art, as if the dancer could not rely on previously learned patterns stored in her brain.[7] In the short story, the narrator does not choose between history and fiction, but proposes a type of text that refuses to be possessed and haunted by the "putrid" charm of the "old tragic actress" or by the ghostly power of the colonizer.

Previous attempts to deal with the colonial past (including by Djebar herself) have emphasized different textual and cultural tactics. In *L'Amour, la fantasia*, for example, readers became acquainted with the metaphor of excavation, which is symbolically opposed to other texts' attempts at imposing silence and censorship (1995a). In "Annie and Fatima," however, the narrator goes even further when she warns us against the risk of being seduced by history's "putrid roles." Her images do not celebrate the cathartic uncovering of previously hidden bodies.

Performative encounters do not take us away from the realm of lies into the pacified territories where historical truth is finally revealed. They are not about looking for a nonnarrative reality that would once and for all protect subjects from previously written scripts. They question history as a genre and look for different scenarios. And even if we accept the hypothesis that well-matched Franco-Algerian couples are few and far between, we may not have to agree with the narrator's notion that they are the result of "luck." It is not because the two members of the encounter were predisposed to be matched that they succeed in creating new positions, but because they invent a new language and a new type of narrative. The grammar of their "love in two languages," or *bi-*

langue as Abdelkebir Khatibi puts it, does not exist yet, but it is not impossible to dream that once it has been composed, their new play can then be offered to the community as a new collective script to be acted upon.

Sometimes, the words of the encounter would not be recognized by linguists as a full-fledged language. They are whispered terms of endearment or screams, an inflection, or a few sentences stuttered in another idiom. As we have seen, they can take the form of a single phrase learned over several years by a mother who is not going to be deterred by apparently insurmountable obstacles. Often, the language of performative encounters will verge on poetry, for everyday syntax and common metaphors cannot always be relied upon when someone tries to tell new stories. In some texts, the radical novelty of the encounter will be inscribed at the level of the genre, and storytellers will have to work through and displace existing literary traditions or disciplinary practices.

Performative encounters can be compared to that moment of "*mésentente*" (both mishearing and disagreement), when the members of a community understand that there is something incalculable about the very definition of the community and, more specifically, about who belongs and who can speak on its behalf. Jacques Rancière (1995) suggests there exists a "mésentente" [mishearing] about communities fundamentally built on the perpetuation of a wrong, which affects every member of the society because of the way in which the group has constituted itself. The distribution of roles and the definition of the parts of the community have always been the result of a miscalculation.

As defined by Rancière, mishearing does not occur between someone who says white and someone who says black. Instead, it is "le conflit entre celui qui dit blanc et celui qui dit blanc mais n'entend point la même chose ou n'entend point que l'autre dit la même chose sous le nom de blancheur" [the conflict between someone who says white and someone else who says white but does not hear the same thing or does not hear that the other says the same thing with the word whiteness] (12). Throughout his book, Rancière insists that this type of dissent and mishearing has nothing to do with a specific demand or with the content of a grievance. In the Franco-Maghrebi context, we could say that it is not the equivalent of demanding to be free from colonial rules or of trying to recapture the land that belonged to one's ancestors. Instead, it has to do with the way in which any given community calculates its parts within the very definition of itself as community. Depending on how the parts of the community are imagined, then a subject's voice can be heard by the community as language or as noise.

Using Athenian democracy as an example, Rancière analyzes the paradoxical status of the *demos*, the people, which is defined by a lack of any specific attribute: unlike the *oligoï*, the *demos* does not possess wealth; unlike the *aristoï,* the *demos* is not characterized by virtue. What the *demos* has, however, is freedom (no one may be enslaved for owing money, for example), but to have freedom is to be in the peculiar position of having as one's unique attribute what the others—all others—have too. Freedom, Rancière explains, occupies an asymmetrical position vis-à-vis money and moral qualities, which makes the parts of the community incommensurable. Freedom belongs to everyone but even more specifically to the people, which has nothing else but freedom.

Freedom belongs to all, but more specifically to the *demos* precisely because it has nothing but freedom and is therefore the victim of a wrong. It is the part that does not get counted, the part that does not have a part. Rancière proposes to reserve the word "political" to describe moments when this calculation is interrupted and troubled. Similarly, performative encounters correspond to those rare and defining interventions when the dialogue between those who believe that they are the only legitimate participants in the conversation is interrupted by the voice whose story the community pretends is a form of noise. Politics (as Rancière puts it) and performative encounters (as I claim here), exist when official dialogues (historical scripts) are troubled by "l'inscription d'une part des sans-parts" [the inscription of the part of those who have no parts] (169). The rest of the time, miscalculation is the norm, a miscount that affects all colonial and colonialist societies, but which exists as the precondition that must be interrupted by performative encounters.

It is therefore no coincidence that performative encounters should be most easily observed in the realm of fiction or at least during moments when discourse is used in innovative ways. Performative encounters are not plausible. They are an exception to the rules that lead to segregation between people and peoples. They will occur when subjects ignore, or rather cross, internal borders erected within cities by colonialism, conflicts of decolonization, or their post-independence consequences. Performative encounters require linguistic mediation and are best captured by the telling of a story, the invention of unexpected metaphors. They will appear in conjunction with the unusual combination of narrative techniques, the coexistence of mutually exclusive genres such as the detective novel and poetry, fiction and archival research, autobiography and history, or the emergence of supposedly impossible forms of testimonies (conversations with the dead, history written by the severed hand that a dead painter passes on to a twentieth-century female writer as in the famous passage from Djebar's *L'Amour, la fantasia*).

The following chapters are a collection of more or less successful, more or less felicitous, performative encounters. The first chapter begins with an account of the controversial football game organized immediately after September 11, 2001. The event was hailed as the first friendly game or meeting (in French "rencontre") between Algeria and France after the former became independent more than forty years ago. Apparently, the attempt was a failure: first, a large portion of the public booed the French national anthem, causing anger and resentment among political leaders, journalists, and the French population. Later, the game ended prematurely when the field was overrun by crowds of young men presented as French people of Algerian origin. But I would argue that, if we do not focus exclusively on the more visible and public aspects of the event, some elements can be identified as moments of performative encounters.

This chapter explores the alternative discourses generated on the border of this political and cultural fiasco. By listening to what the public had to say, I propose to interrupt the layer of official commentaries just as the young men interrupted the game. Their spectacular intervention forces us to rethink the composition of the two teams, of the two nations, and even the rules of the game. When we focus on the theatrical performance of those bodies who were supposed to remain away from the stage and behind the fences that marked the limits between players and spectators, we may be able to trouble the conventions that (failed to) prescribe the encounter between the two entities known as France and Algeria.

I therefore analyze the sometimes amusing comments and proposals overheard by journalists in bars and on the streets, comparing them with more theoretical discourses about the "border" between France and Algeria: the construction of "interrupted borders" (Etienne Balibar 1998), the function of "mixed memories" (Benjamin Stora 1991, 1995, 2001a), or the invention of mythic and atypical football games by Michel Serres (1991). This allows me to compare the politics and aesthetics of the official "Year of Algeria in France," or "Djazaïr 2003," to the more unpredictable and chaotic conversations gleaned in public spaces around the stadium. I suggest that an encounter between the two layers of commentary would have constituted a fruitful performative encounter.

The second chapter focuses on stories and essays that have, implicitly or explicitly, opted out of *métissage* or hybridity as a solution to the difficult relationship between France and the Maghreb. More specifically, I concentrate on Djebar's imaginative account of what happens to the categories of "Muslim" and "Christian" names when they are used as the main ingredients of performative encounters. As we have seen, Djebar's texts often rewrite the original "couple" (France-Algeria) as an encounter between two subjects whose relationship with each of the nations but also with each other is complex and ambiguous. Like Kateb Yacine's *Nedjma* (1956), her fictions can be read as allegorical constructions of a new decolonized nation. But whereas *Nedjma* has been interpreted as an allegory of Algeria, I propose to read Djebar's texts as the dynamic and forever changing representation of the encounter between France and Algeria. The characters' complex trajectories represent the unstable protocol of cohabitation that no treaty between governments and no theory of hybridity can hope to stabilize and solidify.

Djebar's intensely political fictions invent new Franco-Algerian female friendships ("Women of Algiers in their Apartment"), Franco-Algerian couples ("Félicie's Body"), and unexpected alliances wrought between French and Algerian subjects during the Algerian war (*L'Amour, la fantasia*). Her texts insist on the crucial need for imaginative protocols of encounters between historically estranged identities. For example, in "Félicie's Body," we are invited to join a family united around the mother in a Parisian hospital. In the presence of the apparently silent character, a performative encounter slowly develops between all the children, who must decide whether Félicie, the French woman who was in love with her husband Mohamed, can be buried next to her Muslim spouse. For this ritual to be acted out, she must first be performatively transformed into a Muslim after her death. The long conversation that ends in a collective decision is a complex exploration of the power of words and of the power of names. For, the children born to the Algerian man and the French woman have two names (one traditionally Muslim, one traditionally Christian). However, instead of presenting this double reference as a solution (a bicultural hybridity), Djebar views this dual identity as a starting point, as the ingredient of complex forms of encounters with the self and with others. Each child becomes the symbol of a different type of relationship *with* hybridity. The loving encounter between the parents does not erase hierarchies between the man and the woman or between the colonized and the colonizer (each parent deriving power from one of the axes). Tensions are never resolved, and the text explores the different tactics adopted by each child in different contexts: one chooses between the two names, one opts for a third one, and one constantly fights the parents' decision. This story is not about *métissage*, it is about cohabitation, about the endless continuation and reinterpretation of the supposedly original encounter.

Chapter three moves on to an analysis of the language created by performative encounters. I suggest that North African literature occupies a unique position in the debate on language in postcolonial fiction. Like sub-Saharan African authors who are concerned by the impact of europhone languages on African literature, Maghrebi authors are keenly aware of linguistic issues. Other previously colonized areas, such as Caribbean islands, have developed a creole language and a theory of hybrid expression. No such "creolization" has occurred in the Maghreb, and no manifesto urges writers to find a third way between their native tongue and the ex-colonizer's language (Bernabé et al. 1993). And yet, a specifically Maghrebi position is emerging: younger authors' performative encounters with language are highly self-conscious and inscribed into their fiction. Less interested in language in general than in the explicit, professional relationship that a writer entertains with the cultural role of words, they develop an articulate, and theorized (but also a more distanced and less paralyzing), account of the encounter between Maghrebi literature and its languages.

Recent linguistic studies on the importance of bilingualism, code switching, and multicultural street language have become a source of literary inspiration, and contemporary novelists incorporate these theories into their texts. They have also read the first generation of Maghrebi authors (Khatibi and Driss Chraïbi in Morocco, Djebar in Algeria), and these well-known classics resonate in their own fiction. But their attitude has changed: their elders' sometimes desperate passion for language has turned into an amused and distanced appreciation of how languages work, of what types of relationships authors and language develop. Rather than commenting on the *loss* of the native maternal languages Arabic or Berber (Khatibi 1983a; Bensmaïa 1985), on the *violence* done to the young colonized subjects forced to function and write in French (Khatibi 1971; Mezgueldi 1996), on the fiasco of mandatory "Arabization" in Algeria after decolonization (Grandguillaume 1983; Taleb Ibrahimi 1995), they humorously theorize the encounter between the decolonized scriptor and his or her linguistic "ratatouille" (Laroui 1998).

Chapter four continues this analysis of the *logos* of the encounter, but moves from the level of language to the level of genre. Just as the consciousness of having lost a native tongue slowly turns into a self-conscious encounter with language as an object of desire, the relationship between individuals and their past generates encounters that create new subject and object positions: new types of historians, new types of historiographies, and new encounters with history. In Europe today, it is now common knowledge that the memory of the Algerian war was repressed for almost forty years, silence becoming the preferred mode of remembrance, the telltale sign of repressed history. In Algeria, other preferred modes of memories and other types of silence prevail, as official history enshrines national heroes and forgets unglamorous episodes of the war. By differentiating between different types of silence (erasure, censorship, secrecy, shame, absence of archive, repression), I propose to distinguish between different types of historiography and to concentrate on those that have replaced silence with a creative myth about silence. The proliferation of stories about silence has replaced or displaced a missing archive with a very specific type of account that cuts across the genres of history (Stora 1995; Chaulet-Achour 1998), autobiography and documentary (Benguigui 1996, 1997; Djebar 1995b), and fiction (Sebbar 1997).

As Stora recently put it, the issue is no longer the absence of an archive or a deliberate political will to silence. Both official and literary discourses are engaged in a meticulous archeology of knowledge. According to the historian, the trouble today is that most texts are produced within one community and are addressed to that community alone, which "generates a constant sense of absence due to the non-encounter between memories" (2001a).

I would suggest that many recent narratives experiment with an alternative model, trying to imagine the encounter between memories. In this chapter, I concentrate on a historical-fictional text that precisely tries to craft a meeting point between memories: Mehdi Lallaoui's *La Colline aux oliviers* (1998). As a result of several amateur historians' quests, the definition of memory and history evolves from a traditional linear and individual narrative (a search for a missing ancestor) and turns into the equivalent of a love story that manifests itself as the complex imbrication of different types of collective archives and practices (including teaching, giving, loving, or making serendipitous discoveries). Encounters between historiographies occur, enabling us to move beyond the opposition between fiction and history or memory and history. Lallaoui's text fictionalizes the encounter between two different types of historiographies that propose radically different visions of what it means to rewrite the past within or beyond national territories and communities.

In the fifth chapter, I consider an alternative storytelling practice proposed by some authors and filmmakers whose work on encounters redefines our traditional conception of what it means to converse. Chapter five focuses on transnational dialogues whose protagonists cross the ultimate border between the dead and the living. I suggest that this corpus constitutes a new type of haunted *logos*. The fictive cemeteries that I visit in this final chapter are the places where unique types of encounters occur: there, the living come to talk to the dead. These burial places are inhabited by a not-yet-imagined nation whose unrecognized citizens are haunted by the desire to invent new forms of dialogue. They have not accepted the supposedly final and definitive fracture between France and Algeria, between the French and the Algerian people. And yet, the authors do not present them as nostalgic or reactionary forces; they are not even unrealistically optimistic. All these characters acknowledge the consequences of a bloody war of liberation between an ex-colonial power and its colonized land and still refuse to sever historical and cultural links between the two lands. Their ultimate goals and ethical positions, however, vary enormously. Some of the stories we will read introduce us to heroes who do try to invent a type of positive dialogue (that colonialism and war have always already foreclosed). Others, on the other hand, paint the portrait of individuals who do the same things for reasons that are neither humanistic nor altruistic: they have chosen to cynically exploit the fatality of historical separation between the French and the Algerians, and they use the dead to perpetuate violence.

These narratives transform the grave into a place where new words, new stories, are exchanged between the dead and the living and between the living who talk about their dead. Each visit is different: some look after a grave, others vandalize it; some offer to take care of a burial site, others exploit the sadness of an exiled population who cannot return to their parents' graves. And sometimes, the grave becomes the only possible hyphen between two mutually exclusive traditions. An Algerian song of mourning does not correspond to the ghostly side of ontology as Derrida defines it in *Specters of Marx* (1993; 1994b). My goal is not to emphasize the always elusive presence of the ghost or even to look for a metaphor for what is the always ghostly nature of any encounter between speaking subjects. By "ghosts," I mean a type of historical presence that cannot be accommodated by historical writing, that will, perforce, be excluded, foreclosed by narratives whose logic requires the taking of sides, the ratification of treatises between real political powers. They cannot replace history books, but they can help us invent the space of a realm of memory that sometimes does not exist beyond the pages of a book, the lyrics of a song, the images of a film.

Starting with Djebar's *Algerian White* (1995b; 2003a), a somber and poignant elegy written after three of her friends were assassinated in Algeria in the 1990s, the chapter moves on to Yamina Benguigui's *Inch'Allah dimanche* (2001). Set in the North of France in the 1970s, the director's first fiction film narrates the unlikely encounter between the widow of a French colonel and a recently immigrated Algerian woman, who become allies. The next primary text is a novel by Mehdi Charef, *Le Harki de Meriem* (1989), in which the author explores the fate of *harkis* who moved to France after the war. The children of those Algerians who fought on the side of France are rejected by both the French and the Algerians. The dead hero's body cannot be buried in Algeria, but his sister creates new alliances with her estranged grandmother. The chapter ends with Djebar's novel *La Femme sans sépulture* (2002), where Djebar's renewed archeological search for female historiography leads her to unexpected conclusions about a desirable absence of burial. Here the performative encounter transforms history into a dissident and scandalous discourse whose metaphor is the "fertile" body of the dead Mudjahida whose unburied corpse lies exposed to the sun. Uncomfortably poised between fiction and history, hauntologies are tormented by the ghosts that official discourse can nei- ◆ ther forget nor properly commemorate.

Finally, chapter six posits that encounters are not well served by revolutions, heroes, or dates and that a performative reading of performative encounters will emphasize specific practices. Rather than discovering performative encounters as one discovered continents, rather than looking for radically new genres or fashionably new stories, we may need, on the one hand, to trust what we name serendipity, and on the other hand, to believe in the virtue of repetitive, unspectacular, and patient critical activities such as microcomparisons and the close study of details. Both fleeting and relatively unpredictable, the perception of performative encounters paradoxically rewards the patience of those who observe without knowing exactly what they are looking for, a type of activity that readers will find reflected in the representations of Anouar Benmalek and Akli Tadjer or in Jean Plantu's acrobats, artists who transform the pain of the dislocated body into ephemeral performances of beauty.

Football Games and National Symbols

Reconfiguration of the French-Algerian Border through Philosophy and Popular Culture

The year 2003 was the "Year of Algeria in France." For a whole year, the issue of the encounter between two entities known as "France" and "Algeria" was automatically treated as culturally relevant. Reinforcing the commonplace (but rather inarticulate) sense that France and Algeria cannot be indifferent to each other because they share a long colonial past, the "Year of Algeria in France" also changed the vantage point from which the general public, as well as cultural critics, could talk about this relationship

The more or less implicit aim of such a highly publicized series of events was to improve the relationship between the two countries, to replace suspicion and mutual rancor with friendship and harmony. Such a goal can hardly be criticized, of course, and, after all, it is quite possible that the objective was reached at least in certain very limited contexts. I suggest, however, that the "Year of Algeria in France" was not necessarily less effective when it seemed to fail. It led to moments of performative encounters when it forced subjects to rethink their assumptions about what constitutes an improvement, what we mean by "France" and "Algeria," and why those two entities construct themselves as separate or intertwined, as linked or engaging in a dialogue.

The remarkable number of political and cultural events organized under the umbrella of the "Year of Algeria in France" was interpreted (and this interpretation was not an insignificant gesture) as a "dialogue" between two protagonists: "France" and "Algeria." And I continue to protect the two words with quotation marks because I would like to suggest that it is not prudent to assume that any of the elements of the equation (the "dialogue," "France" or "Algeria") came first. For the cultural critic interested in exploring protocols of performative encounters, the questions are: who spoke for whom during these more or less official interdisciplinary encounters? Which theory of delegation or representation was implicit or explicit when singers, authors, filmmakers, or political leaders spoke for Algeria-France? What running thread were we supposed to identify through such disparate events as a French president's first state visit to Algeria since the independence; a raï music concert at the Zenith in Paris; an Algerian film festival in Clermont-Ferrand (a French provincial town that many young Algerians had perhaps never heard about [Colombani 2003]); and a series of readings from Saint Augustine's work by Gérard Depardieu in the Catholic cathedral of Notre-Dame de Paris (Nouchi 2003)?

In this context, any attempt at explaining the two words "France" and "Algeria" can only perpetuate the illusion that we know, ahead of time, what they mean before the beginning of the dialogue. Such an enterprise is possible of course, but probably less productive than a willingness to postpone our desire to define. Paying attention to the choices that language forces each speaker to make to talk about the encounter would help. To begin with, I must remember that this is the year of Algeria in France and not the year of France in Algeria.[1] Then, when I write "France-Algeria," some sort of precedence is already automatically granted to the word that comes first. On the other hand, choosing "Algeria-France" over "France-Algeria" only makes the point that the alternative itself needs to be theorized if we want to avoid the simple plea-sure of binary reversals. And if the word order suggests that hidden and uncon-scious hierarchies are at work, some of the posters crafted to publicize the event also highlighted the fact that each state had to make decisions about which language to use. Suggesting that the "original" name of the countries should be preserved (France, in French and *El Djazaïr*, in Arabic, for example, rather than El-Djazaïr-Farança or France-Algérie) will only expose the fragility of such concepts as "origin" or even "official" language. Once again, each new imagined possibility uncovers new possible protocols of relationship. A desire for the original or authentic sign will reveal the existence of other layers of choices or conflicts that we may not imagine as significant problems until we test them: is there a Berber name for "El Djazaïr?" What would be respected or disrespected if we chose to write El Djazaïr rather than الجزائر. Trying to ex-plain the protocol of encounter between the two countries forces me to become aware of the type of metaphors that I mobilize when I imagine a space *between* Algeria and France. Do I visualize one of those borders that we think of as "natural" (a sea, a river), or a political line of demarcation (a state line), or an abstract linguistic sign (a hyphen for example)?[2] Paying attention to each of the images also makes me more aware of the values attached to some of the repre-sentations that we select, sometimes absentmindedly: what would a hyphen between France and Algeria signify? Would it unite the two entities as the French suggest when they translate hyphen with "trait d'union" (literally a union mark),[3] or would the hyphen signal opposition and be the equivalent of "versus" as when we talk about the France-Algeria football game?[4] Replacing the hyphen with a question mark would introduce a completely new code that would force us to stop as if an unknown obstacle had appeared on a road, something that would function less as a traditional border than as a type of roadblock.[5] If I write "France?Algeria," I renounce the comfort of conventional diacritical signs, but I also give myself a chance to postpone the description of the form of relationship that predates the encounter. I am also questioning what I know about the two elements of the binary pair that the question mark both unites and separates like a river running through a city. For performative encounters to emerge during this highly ritualized "Year of Algeria in France," a certain amount of uncertainty was needed, doubts not only about the nature of the connection but also about the definition of the two poles of the encounter. This hesitation disappears if we act and talk as if we knew what we mean when we choose France-Algeria over Algeria-France or vice-versa, and if we can assume that we all agree about the work done by the hyphen.

My search for and exploration of moments of performative encounters will not exactly coincide with the most obvious type of criticism leveled against the principle of the "Year of Algeria in France," although there will be some overlap. Many intellectuals soon suspected that it would be a governmental affair that would most likely confiscate the polyphonic richness of the words "France" and "Algeria." After all, it was clear that a binational political will backed this yearlong event and would stage a specific type of economic and cultural encounter. And yet, denouncing the process of appropriation of national symbols by governments does not tell us exactly *what* the process represses.

Looking for performative encounters means asking slightly different questions. For example, if this had not been an official encounter, would we have witnessed a dialogue between two nations, or rather between two people, or perhaps between two communities (instead of between two governments)? What difference would it have made in that case? Isn't the choice among different types of binary pairs already a dangerously simplistic duality?

The paradox of the "Year of Algeria in France" is that even if this ambiguous operation did succeed in creating new representations of Algeria and France, it first had to pretend that the meaning of the two words were more or less a given. In other words, if "El Djazaïr 2003" or the "Year of Algeria in France" generated performative encounters, we can only discover their traces in the moments when this foundational duality gave way to other questions about the relationship and about the subject-positions authorized by the framing of the debate. The performative success of these rare occurrences would be visible if some subjects were now capable not only to start a new type of conversation between two entities previously imagined as "France" and "Algeria," but also, and more radically, to rethink the very definition of the entities in question.

The old metaphors that serve to construct the encounter are gradually being displaced by other images. In the twenty-first century, it still makes cultural sense to imagine France and Algeria as the old bitter and bickering couple of Djebar's stories, but it is also legitimate to suspect that the historic "couple" is being historicized and questioned.

Clearly, as Nourredine Saadi remarks, the icon of the couple continues to dominate a certain cultural landscape: "on ne peut parler des relations franco-algériennes sans évoquer les mots de la passion, invoquer le couple, comme s'il s'agissait de personnes ou de personnages de fiction" [it is impossible to talk about Franco-Algerian relationships without using passionate language, without conjuring up images of couples as if they were real persons or characters in a novel] (2003: 170). Heterosexual couples, or at least a "fictional" rendition of such relationships, remain on the horizon of verisimilitude. As such, they remain the script that will be displaced by other images. In Djebar's work, the connections made between the elements of the couples and the abstract binational entities are already changing. Her "couples" are very different from those imagined by Kateb Yacine or Frantz Fanon, in whose earlier works the colonized nation often became an allegorical feminine figure.[6]

In this chapter, I propose to test a number of hypotheses about *which* new protocols of encounter have emerged between the two former "complementary enemies" (Tillion 1960/1961) and to ascertain what consequences such changes have had on the definition of the two parties.

The three different models of encounter that I propose to examine here are elaborated by scholars whose work belongs to three different disciplines: history, political theory, and philosophy. The first model is imagined by Stora, who deplores the absence of a "mélange des mémoires" [memorial melting pot] (2001a). We owe the second one to Etienne Balibar, who acknowledges that no paradigm of "interpenetration" has been successfully tested between the two countries, but who suggests, nonetheless, that the image of a borderline between the two states cannot exhaust the representation of the French-Algerian reality. Finally, crossing such theoretical models and so-called popular discourses, I will turn to one of Serres' philosophical tales, a curious story of football games that must end in a tie and seems, at first, to describe an inconclusive type of encounter. I will argue, however, that the story not only describes an almost perfect example of a performative encounter, but that it is also intriguingly replayed in certain layers of popular discourse in France after an unfortunate sports event.

My goal is not to choose between the three visions and to declare which one best reflects the current state of the encounter or provides us with the best chance of establishing performative encounters. Instead, I will let the three models reformulate each other and allow them to interact and dialogue with popular discourse. The following examples enable us to examine what type of encounter is made possible when an event or a series of events lead us to question the implicit notion that the mere existence of a binational "dialogue" (or any type of dialogue) necessarily constitutes an improvement of the relationship between France and Algeria.

Suggesting that "dialogues" are not, in and of themselves, a solution is not the same as preaching the virtue of discretion and forgetfulness, and it should perhaps be said that contemporary French and Algerian subjects can be expected to have internalized the value of remembering and the danger of denial. Today, one of the least authorized protocols of encounter between subjects and their past is silence. But if silence is no longer condoned by governments or individuals, the layers of historical discourses that have come to appear preferable to it are not simply replacing a vacuum. The (academic, scholarly, fictional, or popular) history of the French-Algerian past is characterized by a metadiscourse that keeps describing the causes, the effects, and the presence of silence but also reflects on historical discourse itself and on the discipline of history, even as it attempts to reveal or make sense of the past (Rosello 2002). The dialogue with the past changes the past as well as the present. It also modifies the way in which we judge our own memorial practices.

Multiple Memories Trapped behind the Barbed Wires of History

In France and in Algeria, or within the French-Algerian contemporary vision of "myself" and "the other," the war of independence often functions as a sort of mythical origin of the current dialogue, the political and ideological fracture becoming the symbol of a new beginning between the two states.[7] Yet, since 1962, each decade slightly modifies what can be immediately understood about this point of discontinuity. Both countries were traumatized, but they do not share the same narrative of the trauma. And some historians are pessimistic about the possibility of an encounter between the different (his)tories.

In France, since the beginning of the 1990s, the war between the two countries is slowly becoming a historical possibility rather than a taboo. When Stora published his famous 1991 La Gangrène et l'oubli [Gangrene and Forgetfulness], critiquing both the French and the Algerians for their handling of their national memories, it was still difficult for the French to acknowledge the existence of a war and to accept that torture had been widespread. Algeria, Stora claims, also simplified and reduced the past to a simplistic one-sided narrative. "L'histoire officielle [. . .] a institué des repères, construit sa propre légitimité, effacé toute démarche pluraliste. Elle a, en fait, fabriqué de l'oubli" [Official history [. . .] created landmarks, constructed its own legitimacy, erased any pluralistic approach. In fact, it manufactured forgetfulness] (1991: 304).

National assumptions have rapidly evolved since then. Recently, the work of international mourning and remembrance has led to the reemergence of the archetypal and tragic couple of the torturer and the victim in the French press, in bookstores, and on television. The old and unrepentant General Aussaresses admitted his responsibility in the death of one of the National Liberation Front (NLF) leaders, Ben M'Hidi, in a controversial book that Pierre Vidal-Naquet calls "an assassin's memoir" (2001), after one of his victims, Louisette Ighilahriz, accused him in *Le Monde* and in her published autobiography, *Algérienne*.[8]

In Algeria, the construction of a national history was obviously different. And the tendency to idealize the revolutionary moment and to instrumentalize liberators and heroes is also questioned. As a result, the voices of a previous generation of thinkers, whose dissident points of view were suppressed when they tried to contest certain of the military choices of the FLN, are now slowly becoming audible in a new context.[9] Recent autobiographical or fictive characters overtly object to one-sided accounts that do not include other voices, as does, for example, the narrator of one of Boualem Sansal's "Souvenirs d'enfance et autres faits de guerre" ["Childhood Memories and Other War Heroic Deeds"] (2003): "L'histoire officielle ne prend rien qui soit antérieur au 1er novembre 1954, date du déclenchement de la guerre de libération contre le colonialisme français sous la direction seule et unique du Front de libération nationale" [Official history excludes everything that predates November 1st 1954, the date when the war of liberation against French colonialism breaks out under the exclusive leadership of the National Liberation Front] (39). Furthermore, he knows that his public will decode the irony of his own apparent docility when he adds: "M'en tenant à la règle, j'ai effacé de mon cursus mes jeunes années d'avant-guerre" [I followed the rule, I erased my prewar childhood from the slate](40). The deliberate act of forgetfulness is negated by the story that talks about the process as the narrator asks: "Qui faut-il croire quand la guerre est terminée et que commence le mythe?" [Who should we believe when the war ends and when the myth begins?](45). What is supposed to be suppressed is present through the denunciation of a national imperative that the short story clearly condemns. In 2003, in Sansal's text, forgetfulness has become the theme, the topic of the narrator's reflexion. Memory and the crisis of remembering are self-referentially included in the fiction; they become a literary topos.

That phenomenon is not limited to the distant past, nor is it a way of avoiding more recent events. The wave of unspeakable violence unleashed after 1992—(when the military intervened between the two rounds of the electoral process after it became obvious that the Islamist party would be victorious), and including when the "Second Algerian War," as some commentators call it, spilled over onto French territory—is carefully documented by historians (Kepel 2000: 255–274).[10] Such was the case in 1994 when members of the Groupes Islamistes Armés (GIA) hijacked an Air France aircraft and in 1995 when bombs were planted in Paris. Moreover, the fact that many of the intellectuals and artists assassinated around 1993 were Francophone and internationally famous also attracted the media's attention, although the series of massacres perpetrated in Algerian villages was not covered as effectively. As for the French-Algerians or the Algerian-French people who refuse to choose between the two shores of the Mediterranean, they often become pawns in the games of political leaders who regularly stereotype them and reduce them to one-word fashionable cultural issues: "immigration," "*banlieues*" and, more recently, "terrorism."

In short, national and international memories are actively at work, but the dominant view that remembering is indispensable has not clarified what type of relationship each (remembering) subject can create with which (remembered) narrative. The perception that silence is no longer an option is accompanied by the knowledge that it is impossible to simply and finally reveal the "truth" that governments seek to hide from their people. The collective manifesto signed by many Non-governmental Organizations (NGOs) and published in *Le Monde* on February 6th 2003 asks, "L'Année de quelle Algérie?" [The Year of Which Algeria?].[11] When its authors worry that "L'Algérie de chair et de sang, l'Algérie mutilée, qui souffre nous restera cachée" [The Algeria made of flesh and blood, the Algeria that is mutilated, that suffers, will remain hidden], their point is clear and, at this particular historical junction, almost predictable. In fact, if any cultural accumulation of knowledge about history and memory has occurred in the last ten years in the Maghreb and in Europe, many readers will be sensitive to the limits of a text that alerts us to the existence of a secret but cannot lead to the desired encounter with this "mutilated" body. The authors tell us that a certain Algeria is "hidden" and censored, that it exists elsewhere, out of reach. My point is that an encounter with that "hidden" Algeria would indeed be desirable, necessary even, but that the work required for the encounter to be performed does not boil down to the removal of preexisting obstacles or of an ideological filter. A truer Algeria would not be suddenly revealed to a blind(ed) world if only censorship ceased.[12]

Stora acknowledges that the long period of silence that followed the Algerian war in France has now been replaced by a proliferation of testimonies, but he also suggests that this abundance of narratives is not the sign of a successful national and international process of mourning. In 2001, he stated:

Il ne suffit pas de faire des films ou d'écrire des livres pour évacuer les passages douloureux de l'Histoire: c'est plus compliqué que cela. Le problème de tous les films qui ont été réalisés depuis la fin de la guerre d'Algérie, c'est qu'ils ont été faits pour des publics qui ne se mélangent jamais. On peut voir des films pour les pieds-noirs, des films pour les Algériens, ou pour les Harkis. Mais il n'y a pas de vision d'ensemble. De ce fait, les mémoires ne se mélangent pas: quand on réalise un film, c'est un film pour soi-même ou sa propre "communauté." Cela crée un perpétuel sentiment d'absence, qui vient du fait de la non-rencontre des mémoires. (2001a)

[It is not enough to make films or write books in order to come to terms with History's painful moments: it is more complicated than that. The trouble with all the films that were made since the end of the Algerian war is that they were made for publics that never merge. Some films are made for *pieds-noirs*, others for Algerians or Harkis but there is no common vision. Consequently, memories do not mix: people make films for their own benefit or for their own "community." The result is a pervading sense of absence due to the lack of encounters between stories.]

According to Stora, there is no sign that the Algerian-French couple is about to be "reunited" or "refondé," as President Chirac put it during his speech in Algiers (Agence France Presse [AFP] 2003). The original France-Algeria couple has been replaced by a multiplicity of voices that do not add up to a coherent whole.[13]

What has changed is that narratives *do* take into account differences *within* each camp: we now know much more about the deadly internecine wars that decimated the Algerian army; we know that the Berber minority has suffered from the process of Arab algerianization; we also know about the fate that France reserved to the *harkis* and about the precarious status inherited by the children of binational couples.[14] The void left by censorship or trauma has been replaced by a "proliferation of images and texts," but they lack a protocol of encounter:

Il n'y a pas de croisement possible, on ne rentre pas dans la parole et la douleur de l'autre. Nous sommes dans une accumulation de récits dont il faut éviter à tout prix qu'ils se croisent. Le film documentaire de Tavernier, essentiel en ce qu'il restitue du vécu, ne donne la parole qu'aux appelés français et pas du tout aux harkis. Arcady va plaire aux pieds noirs, Schoendoerffer aux officiers, Boisset aux anticolonialistes. (Stora 2003a)

[There is no possible encounter, no contact with the other's story nor with the other's pain. Narratives proliferate but we make sure that they never intersect. Tavernier's documentary is essential because he talks about the experience of young French conscripts, but he does not allow the *harkis* to speak. Arcady will please *pieds-noirs*, Schoendoerffer officers, and Boisset anticolonialists.][15]

A cultural critic would argue that Stora puts too much emphasis on the directors' intended public: after all, a *pied-noir* director may wish to make a film "for his or her community" and still be greeted by a general public made up of different constituencies. Any generalization about how a given author will deal with the complexity of his or her own positioning is bound to simplify not only the work of art but also the context of its reception. Assuming that we know what will please a given public is a dangerous bet and does not consider the possibility of viewers who transgress the films' identity politics and systems of address.

And yet, the usefulness of Stora's point is to highlight the limits of a simple move from binary oppositions to more complex and nuanced multiple constructions. The Algerian war did force subjects to choose between two camps, and the present should ideally find a cure to that duality. But the passage from binary thinking to a plurality of Frances and Algerias does not necessarily solve the issue of the lack of encounters between different layers of memory.

If the proliferation of stories maintains hostile divisions or even widens the gap between preexisting communities (originally defined by the conflict), then our postindependence narratives will lead to representations of groups that coexist without interacting, without encountering each other. The picture will not be so different from the pattern that historians obtain when they observe old colonial societies. This type of multiculturalism (the coexistence of Arabs, Jews, Berbers, Spaniards, French people, etcetera depicted in exotic literature such as Elissa Rhaïs' novels or colonial films such as *Pépé le Moko*) cannot be denied. But nostalgia for that supposedly pluralistic era cannot forget that this mosaic of communities was also synonymous with misery and inequality.

The Dream of a Thick, Incomplete Border as Territory

To this vision of unhappy fragmentation between several Frances and Algerias, Balibar opposes a different imaginary model. According to him, the two members of the couple are not really two separate parts, and they are not separable. In an article provocatively entitled "Algérie, France: une ou deux nations?" [Algeria, France: One or two Nations?], Balibar suggests that "finalement la décolonisation a fait passer de la fausse simplicité du un à la fausse simplicité du deux" [ultimately, decolonization meant the passage from the false simplicity of one to the deceptive simplicity of two] (1998: 78).

The author is aware that his thesis is likely to be misinterpreted and rejected by two types of communities of readers who would normally not agree with each other: some will suspect him of "nostalgeria," that is, of a form of regression towards imperial (con)fusion. Is Balibar mourning the time when Algeria was a part of France? On the other hand, those who view the presence of a large Algerian population in France as a threat to French culture might well be angered by what they will interpret as a pro-immigration statement. Balibar clearly rejects both points of view, which is why it is so intriguing that he should continue to maintain that it is impossible to simply separate the two nations.

For if we cannot even identify two separate entities, then how could France and Algeria really meet each other? Is Balibar suggesting that no simple encounter will ever be possible because of the absence of autonomous subjects or subject-positions?

Au moment où—des deux côtés—on voudrait couper la France de l'Algérie et l'Algérie de la France, c'est-à-dire "achever" le processus de 1962 qui s'est révélé, d'une certaine façon, inachevable, on s'aperçoit que ce n'est plus possible. Moins que jamais. C'est pourquoi j'en reviens toujours à la même question: avons-nous des moyens de penser une telle situation, qui n'en fassent pas une "révision" de l'histoire: ni une décolonisation achevée, ni le retour à la fameuse thèse de l'Algérie "nation en formation," plus ou moins hantée par les fantômes de l'Empire français? (1998: 79)

[At a time when, on both sides, a tendency exists to sever all bonds between France and Algeria and between Algeria and France in order to "complete" the process started in 1962, a process that proved, in a sense, impossible to complete, we realize that it cannot be done. Now, less than ever, which is why I always keep asking the same question over and over again: are we equipped to think through such a situation in ways that do not amount to a "revision" of history? Can we stay away from the idea that decolonization was indeed accomplished but also from the well-known thesis that Algeria is an inchoate nation, more or less haunted by the ghosts of the French Empire?]

One of the important differences between Balibar's vision and more frequent descriptions of the Algerian-French relationship is his rhetorical choice. While the media or political leaders tend to privilege the metaphor of the couple, with its hardly masked sexual innuendos and references to "carnal" attachment to the land, the philosopher chooses images borrowed from chaos theory and geometry, which enables him to reconfigure the space that we normally imagine as "between" the two countries.

According to him, it is because the two governments never succeeded in "instituer l'interdépendance ou aménager institutionnellement l'interpénétration qu'on est revenu vers l'impossible isolement" [instituting interdependency or in creating institutional forms of interpenetration, that they had to regress towards an impossible isolation] (1998: 78). While the advocates of a new dialogue between France and Algeria suggest that the couple has been reconciled and that their conversation is now based on friendship, alliance, or even love, Balibar moves away from the metaphor of the encounter that would force him to renounce his model and accept that two separate entities exist.

As early as 1955, Mouloud Feraoun was aware that the "couple" was a problematic vision, and he rejected the image through a retrospective annulment of the marriage metaphor. In a November–December 1955 entry of his journal, he imagined himself answering the question of why Algerians are suddenly intent on a divorce. Why do they "prononcent ce divorce en dépit des menaces qui pèsent sur leur tête et des pires souffrances qu'ils supportent" [declare this divorce in spite of the threats that hang over their heads and of the terrible hardships that they have to endure] (1990: 25)? According to him, people who wonder about the so-called "divorce" are trying to find a solution to a problem that is incorrectly posed: "La vérité, c'est qu'il n'y a jamais eu mariage. Non. Les Français sont restés à l'écart. Dédaigneusement à l'écart. Les Français sont restés étrangers" [The truth is that there was never any marriage. No, the French stayed apart. Contemptuously far away. The French remained strangers] (1990: 25).

Balibar's invalidation of the couple metaphor is implicit rather than explicit. He views, or rather constructs, the two nations as one complex, chaotic whole that would resemble a specific type of "fractal border." In order to conceptualize what he calls "non-separation" and "non-exclusion," he privileges

la figure plus abstraite de la frontière non-entière, ce que les géomètres contemporains appellent une "fractale" [. . . .] Ce qu'il faut remettre en question c'est l'idée que les dimensions de l'appartenance nationale soient nécessairement représentables par des nombres entiers, comme un ou deux. Il faut donc suggérer, au moins à titre d'allégorie numérique, que l'Algérie et la France, prises ensemble, ne font pas deux mais quelque chose comme un et demi, comme si chacune d'entre elles, dans leur addition, contribuait toujours déjà pour une part de l'autre. (1998: 76)

[the more abstract figure of the interrupted border, what contemporary geometry calls "fractals" . . . . What we must question is the idea that numbers such as one or two can adequately help us represent national belonging. We must suggest, at least at the level of numerical allegory, that Algeria and France, taken together do not add up to two but to something like one and a half, as if each of the nations, when you look for the sum, already constituted a part of the other.]

Balibar thus gives up on images of encounter because he does not see in front of him two separate entities. Even if optimistic voices currently envisage a Franco-Algerian "dialogue" as motivated by mutual respect, Balibar knows that such friendships would always be reversible and likely to turn into hatred. The loving couple is always on the verge of hate. What Balibar proposes instead is that "l'ensemble franco-algérien lui-même est en train de devenir une 'frontière,' évidemment très épaisse et complexe, irréductible à l'image théorique de la ligne de démarcation entre des souverainetés autonomes" [the whole Franco-Algerian territory is becoming a "border," an obviously very thick and complex border that we cannot reduce to the theoretical model of the line of demarcation line between two sovereign states] (1998: 81).

Like all the discourses that propose new protocols of exchange between the two countries, Balibar's images are difficult to classify. They sound like a description and a wish or perhaps even a prescription. Or, to put it differently, he does not explain if he considers that his explicit desire of "non-exclusion" has performative effects and if or how we could verify them. The paradoxical dream of a border so thick that it ends up overlapping with the territories that it should divide probably does not correspond to the experience of those young Algerian demonstrators chanting "Des visas, des visas!" [Visas, Visas!] during President Chirac's 2003 visit to Algeria. In practice, for many French-Algerians who try not to choose between the two countries, the traditional binary divide is far from disappearing. Everyday practices are controlled by the principle of state lines and, for many ordinary citizens, the separation between France and Algeria remains a most conventional and practical hurdle.

On the other hand, Balibar's dream of an interrupted or incomplete border aptly describes new forms of Franco-Algerian literary experiments. Contemporary authors are keen on exploring the potential of interpenetration. Sometimes, the type of mixing that Stora wishes would happen between stories and between memories occurs at the most elemental level, that of the word itself. I am thinking of Djebar's creation of an imaginary "Alsagérie" in *Les Nuits de Strasbourg* (1997a) or of Danièle Maoudj's "Mon Désorient" ["My Dis-Orient"] (1996). Similarly, in *Les Rêveries de la femme sauvage* (2000), Hélène Cixous, who had already mourned her "algeriance" (obviously constructed on the model of Derridean *différance* [1997a]), describes herself as "malgérienne" (2000: 124). She also calls her Jewish father a "Bizarrab" (46) and wishes she were "inseparabic" (45). Thematically, most recent novels focus on undecidable heroes who often have triple, rather than dual, legacies. In terms of genre, the fusion between autobiography, history, detective fiction, and poetry is more and more common (Mehdi Charef, Assia Djebar, Leïla Sebbar, Yasmina Khadra).

Most typical of this recent literary trend are Sansal's novels, in which the characters cannot explain to themselves to what extent they are "Algerians" or "French" before the end of the book. For the reader, this delay involves hundreds of pages written in a baroque, almost Rabelaisian, style that does not seem at first to fulfill the narrative contract proposed by the detective story. In *L'Enfant fou de l'arbre creux* [The Mad Child in the Hollow Tree], the hero believes that he is of European origin, like his parents. But he knows that he was born in Algeria (his parents were *pieds-noirs*). The whole book is necessary for him (and us) to come to terms with the fact that he is, and has always been, "inseparabic" as Cixous would put it, opting for ultimate concision where Sansal chooses exuberantly excessive prose. The truth of the narrator's origin has to do with multiple layers of internal deceit within the two warring camps. When he was born to an Arab family, his father was killed by a corrupt NLF middleman, and his mother, to save his life, gave him away to the only woman she felt that she could trust, but who belonged to the other side, the side of European settlers or *pieds-noirs*. When Pierre, as a grown-up, comes (back) to Algeria without a visa, he is incarcerated in the infamous Lambese prison, which enables the author to write about an immobilized quest instead of constructing a more typical travel narrative. Because he is literally arrested within his (own unknown) country, the tool that Pierre can use in his search for his origins (or rather for what origins mean) is the word. As a result, an obsessive and compulsive litany fills the pages of the book. It takes the form of a dialogue with his problematic alter ego, Farid, his cell companion (both the same and the other, both the friend and the enemy), imprisoned for terrorist activities. We can imagine the cell as the space of Balibar's fractal border and also as the set of the performative encounter between the two characters, whose definition of identity will be articulated only as a result of their conversation. Only after they have given up on the illusion that they are separated by their nationality can they hope to be the subjects of their own encounter.

Balibar's fractal nonborder, delicately poised between description and hope, is therefore more likely to be present in the realm of art and literature than in the practices of immigrants and binationals or even in testimonial writings. He would be the first to agree that interpenetration or interdependency have not been imagined at the level of governments, which does not prevent him from proposing a visionary point of view where reconciliation would not be a future dream because, if we accept his model, it would already have occurred. It is also probably too early to ascertain whether the stories that adopt this vision are the emerged tip of a cultural and political iceberg (in other words if they will soon seem to us perfectly "realistic" or if, in retrospect, they will appear as a few utopian discursive islands invented by a handful of dissident literary voices).

If we move away from the world of academic or erudite publication and if we observe popular culture, other configurations appear: street culture and *banlieue* culture, and especially the universe of soccer/football games, set the stage for other modalities of encounter between the two parts of the French-Algerian couple. In this environment defined by binarism and the opposition between winning and losing, it will be more difficult to find examples of successful, or even dreamed, interpenetration. But as dualities are reinforced, other types of resistance emerge, and the world of public sports provides ample opportunity to observe moments of "mésentente" (mishearing) *à la* Rancière.

The last portion of my chapter is thus dedicated to those subjects who will continue to play the part of "les sans-parts" [those who have no part] (Rancière 1995: 169) as long as each shore continues to treat them as others precisely because they belong to both: they are young Algerian immigrants or French people of Algerian origin who often live in the much-maligned *banlieues*. I argue that, in a system that does not promote interpenetration, the emergence of performative encounters coincides with the proliferation of the seemingly haphazard and chaotic (but theoretically innovative) tactics adopted by the spectators of a 2001 soccer game that was made to symbolize the relationship between France and Algeria.

Philosophical Football Games: Towards a Tie

Let us then turn to football (or soccer) games—events that involve two teams, two groups of men united and separated by a ritual encounter. Let's consider one event in particular, keeping in mind that the game in question was referred to as "friendly," a technicality that suggests that others are not. As usual, the teams were identified by the names of the countries that they were supposed to represent (France-Algeria), although what this metaphorical or metonymical transfer between players and nations really means is rarely discussed or specified. In short, this was a "France-Algeria" game.

It was also hailed as the first of its kind: never since 1962 had such an event been organized, which added some solemnity to the occasion. In addition, if the stakes were minimized by the "friendly" quality of the encounter, the historical context had the opposite effect.

First of all, this match was perceived as the modified repetition of another sporting event that had gone down in history as an almost mythical moment of reconciliation between France and the Maghreb—the final game of the 1998

World Cup series. This match had somehow solved the issue of hyphenated identities by introducing a convenient third element into the native-foreign binary equation. At the time, the official "French" team was playing against Brazil. "Les Bleus" as they were called, had won the cup and the whole of "France" was vicariously enjoying their football team's victory.

But one of the key cultural elements of that triumph was that the group of men who were expected to represent "France" was precisely not constructed in a rigidly homogeneous way. They were defined as a mosaic of diversity, and it was almost mandatory to notice and celebrate their multicultural collective identity. Algeria, needless to say, formed a crucial component of this collective due to the presence of the team's charismatic hero, Zinedine Zidane. At the time, the most common cultural reflex was not to wonder about the relationship between France and Algeria or between the French and the Algerians. Most commentators seemed inspired by a desire to emphasize unity and harmony. "France" and a football team made up of many players of Algerian origin coincided happily.

It did not seem to matter much that a few conceptual lines between ethnicity, origin, and nationality were blurred in the process. The commercial logic of contracts that transforms players into globalized commodities and "transfers" them like banks transfer money turns the idea of a national team into a fiction but does not prevent exuberant manifestations of national pride when the supposedly "French" or "Algerian" team wins. The player's ethnicity ends up representing the whole country's multicultural diversity in ways that are perhaps even more arbitrary than when immigrants are asked to play that role.[16] The idea that other types of international cultural or political loyalties could have led the Algerian-French "couple" to reappear was repressed, forgotten, and denied. Zidane, the son of a migrant Algerian worker born in Marseilles, was catapulted to the status of national French hero. Between two commercials for a brand of bottled water, he instantly became, in spite of his shyness and modesty, the media's favorite expert on "Beurs" and integration. He also became the symbol of a French model of cultural integration (Tribalat 1998: 5; Dely 1998: 4–5).

If we think about the encounter from the point of view of the protocol of exchange that was privileged as the most relevant, however, were the national festivities not a celebration of victory rather than a celebration of integration— a victory for victory in other words? Was the joy expressed in the streets motivated by an even rudimentary consciousness of the connection between the team's success and its multicultural diversity? And if the link was made, should we rejoice? After all, if "les Bleus" had lost, and if a right-wing leader had blamed the defeat on the immigrant components of the French team, wouldn't we have (rightly) objected to this type of conceptual hijacking? Would it not have been correctly interpreted as a racist aberration? And if we can extrapolate and surmise that we would have rejected any attempt to establish a link between integration and "defeat," then is it not fair to refuse just as categorically to read a causal link between the team's success and the fact that it represents a successful multicultural encounter between native and foreign players, men of Algerian and French origin?

As always, acknowledging the danger of a highly reversible line of argument will perhaps lead us to reflect on the definition of the elements of the binary pair. We may be inclined to wonder why we establish a relationship between a team's victory and what we mean by "success" when what is at stake is the felicitous quality of the social link created by the interaction between communities. We may also wonder how that relationship is defined. Finally, we may ask why the team and the nation become indistinguishable, how we become the "we" of "we won," footballers (and thus the nation) by proxy.

More effectively than the 1998 triumph, which was drowned in a tidal wave of feel-good discourse, the second football game forced spectators and observers to reach that nodal point that Rancière qualifies as the fruitful knot of his *mésentente*. This time, the game *did* become a performative encounter because it encouraged participants to question the unanimity of the first event, to reconfigure the categories of participation and the notions of peace, harmony, and social dialogue.

That second game, intended to symbolize a moment of reconciliation between France and independent Algeria, was scheduled for October 2001. The fact that the superficial connections between a nation and a football team had not been successfully addressed before or after 1998 was clearly irrelevant. But this time, the hyphen between France and Algeria symbolized a face-to-face confrontation rather than internal diversity. Socially, the context had clearly changed since 1998, and the French social fabric had deteriorated.

Furthermore, between the time when organizers started making plans and the day when the two teams met in a Parisian stadium, September 11, 2001, had occurred and a traumatized global consciousness, sometimes prone to hasty shortcuts and amalgams, wanted to apply black and white grids to any event that could possibly be read as a meeting between the West and the Arab world. The game took place at a moment when it was practically impossible to think about anything other than the terrorist attacks in New York.

Strangely enough, I find it most relevant to comment on this supposed "first" encounter between France and Algeria since 1962, because it did not take place. The highly symbolic confrontation was displaced by marginal activities whose meaningfulness troubled the original scenario, creating moments of performative encounters that did not allow the status quo of *mésentente* to dominate the tone of the cultural conversation.

Even before the beginning of the game, things had gotten out of control (at least from a symbolic point of view). It became clear that the atmosphere was not going to be particularly amicable when a significant portion of the crowd started booing the French national anthem to the dismay of reporters, politicians, as well as other spectators. Then the game started, but was officially interrupted before its end, before it was possible to declare that one of the teams had lost or won. The players (the only bodies endowed with symbolic national values) were interrupted by a crowd of spectators who had climbed over the fence and joined them on the field, thus becoming unofficial players (but players nonetheless). They were changing the parts of the community, abandoning their role as spectators, and creating a new subject-position that would prove very difficult to categorize.

Before the organizers could claim victory for one of the camps, the whole scene had changed. The duality of the football game had been replaced by a multifaceted tragicomedy where different audiences intervened to confuse the apparent simplicity of the ludic duel. The binary dynamic of the Algeria-France dialogue exploded into a myriad of polyphonic conversations, transforming the public sphere into a complex and popular theater. A chaotic and discordant chorus of voices was suddenly audible; it was neither harmonious nor cohesive but it was also resistant to attempts at dismissing it. It could not be reduced to one of the nations—it was neither simply Algerian nor simply French. The event went beyond the boundaries of the playing field to include city streets and bars, as if the composition of the two teams had suddenly become more inclusive and more difficult to simplify. Places and positions were troubled, the encounter multiplied, and the margins came to the center (as bodies and as words). The text and the paratexts changed as journalists had to comment not only on the game itself but on what happened before, after, inside and outside, on the field, and in the audience.

The official failure of the "reconciliation" attempt coincided with the proliferation of minority voices that suggested, discreetly, that other models (of reconciliation) existed. They came up with alternatives to the principle of a game that can only end in victory or defeat and to the idea that one of the two countries would have to be the loser. Zaïr Kédadouche's *La France et les Beurs* (2002) was written right after the extraordinary football match to which he was a witness. Kédadouche, who presents himself as the president of the Intégration France association (and also as a former professional football player), was obviously scandalized by the young rioters' attitude, and he is keen to dissociate himself from their group. In an expression of his frustration, he directly addresses some of the theoretical issues raised by the encounter between two teams, their supporters, the two nations, and their representatives. Similarly, Azouz Begag and Christian Delorme, two well-known social activists whose work—the first as a sociologist, the second as a priest—echoes well beyond their native Lyon, published an article in *Le Monde* in response to the interrupted game (2001).

Curiously, no one blames the youths for misunderstanding the stakes of the encounter, that is, for overreacting to a game that stages only a symbolic victory and defeat. When their anger at the national anthem or their intrusion on the playing field is condemned or excused, it is generally in terms of their action's strategic impact. Their behavior is not presented as a failure to appreciate the playful quality of the encounter. After all, commentators could have pointed out that a match is precisely not a conflict and that "fair play" is not the same thing as loyalty to one's side in times of war. Instead, observers often collected testimonies that took very seriously the potentially violent repercussions of the encounter and questioned the premises of the game itself. Perhaps we should not dismiss them as random or improvised remarks emanating from unworthy sources. If we listen to their proposals with a critical ear, their ideas might be capable of drawing our attention to what, in the game, in the rules of the game and in the protocol of the encounter, needs changing, even if the distinction between the symbolic aspect of the sport and so-called real life is maintained and retranslated when we apply their suggestions to national and international politics.

Just as the "two" of the Algeria versus France football game was questioned by the carnivalesque cacophony, the suggestions made to redefine such encounters were multiple, incomplete, playful, and imaginative. Naturally, they had no performative effect; they could not be implemented. They belong to the genre of gossip, public rumor, and café conversations. They are popular tactics, ways of "making do" as Michel de Certeau calls them (1990). To the separation between two nations, two flags, two countries, and two football teams, they oppose forms of interpenetration that were always multigeneric, often verging on the bizarre. Interdependency and interpenetration were imagined as interventions on the timing, the flags, the players' roles, and the rules of the game. A flurry of inventive, sometimes naïve, sometimes revolutionary, proposals circulated, relayed by the press and the media.

Talking about the relationship between the flag and the teams, Kédadouche, angered by his compatriots' irreverent attitude but also capable of understanding their despair and disillusionment, hopes that the next event will bring about a change in the public's attitude: "en ce 7 octobre à Barbès, je voudrais voir les drapeaux des deux pays, ou, mieux encore, les couleurs de la France et celles de l'Algérie sur le même morceau de tissu" [on October 7, at Barbès, I would like to see the flags of both countries, or even better, the colors of France and Algeria united on the same piece of fabric](2002: 47).

In other places, different suggestions were made: why not split the match into two equal parts so that the border does not pass through Zidane's body?[17]

He could then play in both teams so that each of the two nations that he can claim to embody could equally benefit from his talent.

> Avant le match, on inventait en souriant, à Marseille, Paris, Lyon, Roubaix, de nouvelles tactiques de jeu et on retombait sur la même formule: il aurait fallu que Zidane joue une moitié de match dans chaque partie de son identité! Là, la rencontre aurait vraiment été la fête de la réconciliation. Mais les règles de la FIFA ne prévoient pas ce genre de liberté. Dommage. (Begag and Delorme 2001)

> [Before the game, in Marseilles, Paris, Lyon and Roubaix, people smilingly invented new tactics, and always came up with the same formula: Zidane should have played one half of the game in each of the parts of his identity! Then, the encounter would have been a genuine reconciliation party. But FIFA rules do not allow for that kind of freedom. Too bad.]

Remarkably, the authors and their interviewees do not suggest that Zidane should have played "for" Algeria, or "for" France, or even on one team but, rather, in one "part" of his identity. In this model, reconciliation has nothing to do with hybridity or cultural *métissage*, but with the possibility of switching sides, of moving over to the other camp—a type of activity that, in times of war, is always perceived as the traitor's behavior. Allusions to "smiles" and to the level of resignation indicated by the free, indirect style at the end of the passage ("too bad") suggest that the emotional charge of these conversations is relatively weak. The tone of the dialogue connotes amusement and serenity but also a level of engagement that is far from indifference.

All the interventions shared some of the characteristics of the paratextual and chaotic antics of the rowdy audience: they required, as Begag and Delorme are quick to point out, an important theoretical investment. The situation would have required a level of inventiveness and freedom from the system, a political imagination.[18] The symbolic and ludic function of the sports event did not fulfill its promise and did not lead to the sublimation of real violence. For, in this context, the connection established between the team and the nation was a metaphorical trap. The metonymic displacement of tension failed to produce its expected results; the logic of international tension infected the world of sports instead of allowing symbolic confrontations to express a desire for reconciliation. It was not enough to move from the real to the game, the game itself had to be changed.

And this is where the paradoxical category of the tie or of the so-called "match nul" comes in (the French use the same word for a tie as for any kind of contract that is null and void). The tie was proposed as a solution to (and as a possible transgression of) the rule of the mandatory "win or lose" dichotomy. Zidane, it is rumored, wished for such an ending. According to one journalist:

"Symbole pour symbole, le match France-Algérie en représentait un, bien lourd, avec Zinedine Zidane dans le rôle du Franco-Algérien ayant choisi son camp, au moins sur le plan sportif. Sentimentalement, le joueur vedette n'avait-il pas lui-même souhaité un score nul?" [If we were to speak about symbols, the game Algeria versus France was a heavy-duty affair, especially with Zidane cast in the role of the Franco-Algerian who had chosen his camp, at least from an athletic point of view. Sentimentally speaking, had not the star player wished for a tie?] (Bernard 2001).

What is important here is that the wish for a seemingly inconclusive ending is the exact opposite (and, more precisely, not the equivalent) of a cancelled game: a game whose result is symbolically null and void is not the same thing as a game that did not take place. That is the point of Zidane's ambivalent and apparently paradoxical position. He wishes that he could play on both sides (and not against himself), and he hopes that no one will win. A tie would not have been the equivalent of a void match; it would neither have been a form of abstention nor a refusal to play. However, the rules of the game must be changed before a player is allowed to view the tie as a desirable result and not an exception.

We could imagine a situation where a tie could become the goal of the game, something that the players work at reaching. It could be an excess of activity rather than the lack connoted by the idea of "void." Both teams could decide to play until they each have the same number of points. They could interpret their determination as a willingness to go further, further than the rules, and further than the time that was arbitrarily granted to the encounter.

Strangely, Zidane's is a vision that Serres seems to have anticipated in his *Le Tiers instruit* [*Educated Third*] as early as 1991. Like his eighteenth-century predecessors, the philosopher sprinkles his more abstract passages with short, self-contained moral tales. In one of these narrative episodes, he invents an intriguing utopia based on the reconfiguration of a soccer game. In this story, the game is not interrupted but prolonged beyond all plausible limits to reach a point that will prevent one team from monopolizing victory. The players and the spectators agree to participate in a possibly endless and deadly ritual in the name of a sort of equality that seems foreclosed by the rules of a normal match.

As the story goes, during World War II, two sailors are shipwrecked and stranded on an island called "l'île Nulle" [Void Island] or "la Tierce-Ile" [Third Island] (Serres 1991: 196). To pass the time, they teach the natives how to play soccer. In time, the sailors are rescued and conveyed back to Europe. Years later, long after the end of the war that had motivated their exile, they return to the island for a visit and discover that their hosts are still playing soccer, though with radically changed game rules to suit their own unique perspective. Now, the game can end only once both teams have scored the same number of goals. As long as this equitable result is not reached, the islanders consider that a state of barbaric inequality exists (because no victory can be shared). Instead of "partage" (sharing), a state of "départage"(parting, separation) prevails:

> Si à la fin le résultat se trouve nul, la partie s'achève sur le vrai partage. [. . .] Sinon, les deux équipes, comme vous dites, sont départagées, chose injuste et barbare. A quoi bon humilier des vaincus si l'on veut passer, comme vous, pour civilisés? Alors, il faut recommencer, longtemps, jusqu'à ce que le partage revienne. Il arrive parfois que la partie dure des semaines. On a même vu des joueurs en mourir. (200)

> [If, at the end, the game is a tie, a genuine sharing of victory occurs. . . . Otherwise, victory is not shared but split. The teams are not a part, they are torn apart, "départagées," as you put it, which is cruel and barbaric. What is the point of humiliating the losing team if we wish to be called civilized like you? Consequently we must start again and again for as long as it takes until the sharing of parts is reached. Sometimes, the game lasts for weeks. Some players have been known to die.]

Here, the type of heroism that consists of dying for the cause has nothing to do with war or revolutions. Players die of exhaustion to fulfill the dream of equity, to move from the victory of one of the parts to a victory that is the reconfiguration of the community as victorious. The stakes are far from negligible. It is, after all, a matter of life and death. The utopia is not presented as the angelic absence of violence nor is it a state of natural benevolence. It requires extreme moral and philosophical determination. In order to be fruitful and performative, the encounter that both acts to trouble the status quo and acknowledges the possibility of mishearing/*mésentente* should not be an invitation to apathy and indifference. No pacified serenity is advocated here. Serres' parable is a type of performative encounter that makes recommendations quite similar to the types of tactics imagined by Zidane or Begag. Their seemingly impractical and highly whimsical proposals bear the seeds of a radical redefinition of the encounter and deserve a closer look.

At stake is not some sort of abolition of the game; the encounter need not disappear, but it can be radically modified if participants (including spectators) disrupt all the "parts" of the community, the subject-positions that the two parties implicitly accept as values of the game. It is no longer enough to put an end to silence. The goal is to give a voice to those French-Algerians whose speech is made inaudible by a polyphonic cacophony so loud that we interpret it as noise. To do so, it is necessary to conceptualize a type of encounter that preserves the difference between a cancelled match and an apparently inconclusive match. As a performative rewriting of the rules, Serres' endless game is one option. This kind of rewriting highlights moments of mishearing and encourages us to rethink the preconditions of the encounter, even if the result is still considered a (spectacular) failure or a failure for those interested only in the spectacle.

Because dialogues (at least most officially imposed dialogues) are tautologically encoded as desirable dialogues, the staging of the refusal to be represented at the official encounter is a dangerous strategic choice. Those who fear that their position will be adulterated beyond recognition by the frame of the encounter have to take into account the obvious dangers of complete refusal: those who abstain, those who refuse to participate in the encounter, may jeopardize the agenda that they seek to promote. The fact that a potential actor in the encounter refuses the protocol of exchange can only destabilize the officially encoded subject-positions if a trace is kept of their refusal to engage.

When a group of artists from Kabylia decided to boycott the "Year of Algeria in France" (Nait-Zerrad 2003: 8), many voices bitterly regretted their absence and accused them of making irresponsible decisions. Such censures, however, sought not to preserve the illusion of a supposedly united state but were made in the name of this very same (suppressed) Algeria that both the boycotters and their critics believe in and want to share. Lahouari Addi wrote, "Boycotter l'Année de l'Algérie, c'est rendre service à la mafia politico-financière qui a mis en coupe réglée l'économie du pays" [To boycott the Year of Algeria is to serve the interests of the political-financial mafia that has monopolized the country's economy](2003: 8). On the other hand, when they publicly refused what Hervé Bourges called "la tribune qui leur était offerte" [the forum they were being offered] (qtd. in Mazouz 2003), Algerian Kabyles *did* succeed in going beyond the opposition between participation and boycott to the extent that the performance of their refusal was adequately relayed by Bourges' powerful voice. Their boycott was a carefully staged boycott. Through Bourges' account of their absence, they were proposing another type of nonencounter and were inviting us to ask the same type of questions Rancière raises. Paradoxically represented by their absence, they were staging the ghostly presence of their own exclusion.

If the Kabyles judge that the preconditions of the encounter made their voices inaudible, should we believe (or verify) that they were denied access to the very language that would have allowed them to articulate the wrong that "Algeria" was inflicting upon them at the very moment when they were speaking in its name?[19] Bourges and the absent Kabyles, who probably shared a desire to break up the illusion of a monolithic Algeria, were (perhaps strangely) positioned on the knot of *mésentente* that literally functioned as a moment of mishearing. In which case, the artists did not "raté une occasion de s'exprimer" [waste an opportunity to express themselves], as Bourges put it (in Mazouz 2003).[20] Their nonintervention did not amount to a disappearing act. On the contrary, they were named and created as dissident speaking subjects by their very absence. The success of their decision to boycott comes from the metarepresentation of their absence, which sets quotation marks around the names of the countries that meet and participate in the quest for this subaltern voice, which Spivak argues is so often already foreclosed. (1994).

Of course, we cannot hope that the rules of football are about to be changed or that it is plausible that international football associations will be willing to accommodate the dream of Serres' islanders. The principle of a game where two teams work towards perfect symmetry and equity is probably as virtual as Balibar's fractal border at this point. That level of interpenetration would only happen if the memorial melting pot wished for by Stora became a reality. We also know that it is difficult to even imagine the type of dialogue (speaking and listening practices) that would be required to put an end to the mishearing between France and Algeria. But it is already something to know that a politi- cal will to reconcile the two nations will only become a performative encounter if the rules of the game change and if a *logos* emerges at the same time as the redefinition of the two entities occurs. If the "fractal border" becomes as plausible as the line of demarcation, then the idea that we must work towards a "tie" may not be such a remote possibility. Just as the players on the mythic island know that they may have to play for a long time before reaching their goal, we may take comfort in the thought that it is normal for the quest to be imagined as interminable, never quite finished. If we accept the principle that we are now looking for a different type of conclusion, it may not be so hard to accept that there is no way to reconstruct the dialogue between France and Algeria as long as we do not entertain the possibility that the problem itself has to be framed differently. Rather than trying to reestablish friendly links between France and Algeria, we may want to ask what an encounter between France-Algeria and Algeria-France would be like today if we let it happen.[21]

2

Beyond Hybrid Identities

Endless Negotiations of Names, Religious Symbols,
and National Identities in Assia Djebar's Fiction

> . . . le problème n'est pas de s'entendre entre gens parlant, au propre ou au figuré, des langues différentes, pas plus que de remédier à des pannes de langage par l'invention de langages nouveaux. Il est de savoir si les sujets qu'il faut compter dans l'interlocution "sont" ou "ne sont pas," s'ils parlent ou s'ils font du bruit.
> **Jacques Rancière 1995: 79**

> . . . the problem is not for people to understand each other when they speak, literally or figuratively, "different languages" or to repair linguistic breakdowns by inventing new languages. The issue is to know whether the subjects that must be counted as parts of the conversation "are" or "are not," whether they speak or produce noise.

This chapter focuses on books that have implicitly or explicitly opted out of theoretical models of hybridity. In these narratives, *métissage* is not presented as a solution to the difficult relationship between *France* and the Maghreb. Assia Djebar often fictionalizes what she calls the original "couple" (France-Algeria) as an encounter between two characters whose complex trajectories represent the unstable protocol of cohabitation that no treaty between governments and no theory of hybridity can hope to stabilize and solidify. They inhabit the labyrinth that Balibar describes as a fractal frontier (1998). The protocol of their encounter will always be unstable regardless of the political situation between the two nations. Whether or not a process of decolonization can ever be achieved, the relationship between individuals whose identities are imagined as hybrid cannot be stabilized.

Djebar's fictions often paint portraits of Franco-Algerian female friendships ("Women of Algiers in Their Apartment"), Franco-Algerian couples ("Annie and Fatima," *La Disparition de la langue française*), and unexpected alliances wrought between French and Algerian subjects during the war of liberation (*Fantasia*, *Le Blanc de l'Algérie*). Her narratives insist on the crucial need for imaginative protocols of encounters between historically estranged identities.

"Yasmina-Félicie": *Vibrations* of the Given Name

In "Félicie's body," one of the short stories published in *Oran, langue morte*, Djebar creates a visionary couple capable of reinventing a script in spite of the constraints imposed by the "old tragic actress" that haunts all Algerian-French or Franco-Maghrebi unions (1997b: 221). Paradoxically, when the narrative starts, the conversation between the two heroes is over; they will no longer be able to speak to each other. Mohammed, Félicie's husband, has been dead for a long time. As for Félicie, whose "body" is displayed in the title of the story as if she were one of Djebar's "femmes sans sépulture" [unburied women], the reader learns that she is in a coma in a Parisian hospital. At the end of the tale, she will die, surrounded by her children and grandchildren, without having said a word, even to her eldest son, Karim-Armand-Titi. The two main protagonists cannot speak, but their silence provides their family with the opportunity to describe the choices that their parents had to make, over and over again. Each of the children's accounts reveals that their constructed identities are as unstable as the original couple's and that constant negotiations continued to take place between the parents, between the parents and the children, between the brothers and sisters, and also, whenever they must relate to outsiders, on both sides of the Mediterranean.

The symbol of the felicitous encounter between Félicie and her husband Mohammed is their children's names. The fictional representation of their performance is that they were able to write a new love story that gave their sons and daughter a new understanding of the connection between the name of a person, their identity, and their singular agency or desire.

Each has a double name, or, to be more exact, two given names: one traditionally Muslim and the other one Christian. And yet, this apparent duality is not the same as a double belonging that would solve, once and for all, the issue of the characters' identities. As usual, Djebar seems to resist the comfort of bicultural or binational *métissage*. On the contrary, the short story treats this permanent duality as a point of departure. Rather than codifying identity as two parts linked or bridged by the hyphen, the given names generate multiple encounters with others and with the self, and they create friction. Each character ends up developing a unique relationship to hybridity instead of becoming a hybrid.

Djebar always portrays the relationship between the parents as successful in spite of the fact that the couple is caught up in a set of violent colonial hierarchies and in the war of independence. The story does not simply define the encounter as an idealized individual exception. Love exists in spite of the fact that the heroes' sexual and ethnic identities forever put them in asymmetrical positions. They do not symbolize the individual solution to the tensions generated by the colonial situation. No resolution of the national conflict is *mise en abyme* by the couple. At first, we may assume that the short story will exploit one of the common topoi of Maghrebi literature where the characters are destroyed by a national script.

In Albert Memmi's *Agar*, the couple formed by the Tunisian narrator and her French spouse implodes when they come in contact with the man's family and community, and, as usual, it is tempting to interpret the self-destructive violence unleashed between the lovers as a prophetic vision of what will necessarily happen to the peoples of colonizing and colonized countries. In the preface of the *Portrait du Colonisé* [*The Colonizer and the Colonized*], Memmi remembers the narrative and political objective that he had set for himself when he had written *Agar*. He insists on the exemplary and even performative force with which he wishes to endow his fictional couples.

In *Portrait*, Memmi's first-person narrator is looking for a script that would enable him to break free of the colonial fatality that condemns him, whether he is alone or in a couple. But unlike the characters of "Félicie's body," he never finds a narrative capable of dislocating the protagonist's preinscribed destiny.

> J'avais écrit un premier roman, "La Statue de sel," qui racontait une vie, celle d'un personnage pilote, pour essayer de me diriger dans la mienne. Mais l'impossibilité qui m'apparut au contraire, d'une vie d'homme accomplie dans l'Afrique du Nord de l'époque, me conduisit à tenter une issue dans le mariage mixte. Cet échec fut "Agar," qui se terminait par un autre échec. Je fondais alors de grands espoirs sur le couple, qui me semble encore l'un des plus solides bonheurs de l'homme; peut-être la seule solution à la solitude. Mais je venais de découvrir également que le couple n'est pas une cellule isolée, une oasis de fraîcheur et d'oubli au milieu du monde; le monde entier au contraire était dans le couple. Or pour mes malheureux héros, le monde était celui de la colonisation; et si je voulais comprendre l'échec de leur aventure, celle d'un couple mixte en colonie, il me fallait comprendre le Colonisateur et le Colonisé et peut-être même toute la relation et la situation coloniales. (1973: 9)

> [I had written a first novel, *The Pillar of Salt*, a life story which was in a sense a trial balloon to help me find the direction of my own life. However, it became clear to me that a real life for a cultured man was impossible in North Africa at that time. I then tried to find another solution, this time through the problems of a mixed marriage, but this second novel, *Strangers*, also led me nowhere. My hopes then rested on the "couple," which still seems to me the most solid happiness of man and perhaps the only real answer to solitude. But I discovered that the couple is not an isolated entity, a forgotten oasis of light in the middle of the world; on the contrary, the whole world is within the couple. For my

unfortunate protagonists, the world was that of colonization. I felt that to understand the failure of their undertaking, that of a mixed marriage in a colony, I first had to understand the colonizer and the colonized, perhaps the entire colonial relationship and situation.] (1990: 5)

Memmi's solution is to give up on a certain type of story and to adopt another. The novel is doomed, and he turns to another genre, that of the essay. *Le Portrait du colonisé* is that essay added to the series of fictional narratives that all seem to hit a dead end.

"Félicie's body" proposes another type of solution. In the short story, the interracial couple is not separated by history. The script does not doom the characters to failure. On the other hand, the narrative as a whole does not see itself as the bearer of the kind of hope that Memmi talks about in his preface. In "Félicie's body," the lovers are never portrayed as an "isolated cell," let alone an "oasis of freshness and forgetfulness." Instead, constant friction keeps the relationship alive and in a perpetual dialectic relation to the colonial world. That universe does not destroy them but defines them. The couple is the manifestation of the performative encounter rather than what should become the exemplary solution that could modify the historical cohabitation between the colonizer and the colonized (as well as between man and woman). While Mohamed and Félicie invent their own form of encounter, they also bequeath to each of their children something far more complex than either their individual or dual legacies. Instead of receiving a prepackaged cultural patrimony that they would have to manage as best they can, they inherit their parents' will to perpetuate an encounter that exists only at the moment they both perform it.

In the story, tension manifests itself whenever the children must make a decision about their names. And whenever they do, the text suggests that their double legacy consists not only of the difficulties that plague their parents' relationship but also the rich repertoire of tactics that Moh and Félicie have accumulated as a response to such dangers.

Each responds in his or her own way to the names that they have been given, just as the members of the couple had to find a new solution to each new moment of the encounter. While the story has two principal narrators (two of the children), a few pages are reserved for other family members. The sharing of narrative voices is neither balanced nor systematic. One voice dominates throughout, that of Karim-Armand, who has lived in Paris for years. He is responsible for two long textual portions of roughly fifty pages each, and his story is not directed to the reader or to any character in particular. Rather, it is a long monologue, which addresses the mother as "tu." We hear his words, but we are not the recipients of this tale; this puts us in the position of the excluded third party, as the relatively unlikely intradiegetic addressee is the mother (who cannot speak and probably cannot hear due to her comatose state).

The daughter, Louise-Ourdia, only appears after the end of the first part and only remains present for a dozen pages. Her words are not addressed to the mother. She says "I," and her whole intervention is a long digression on the function of her name, which she links to a painful childhood memory. Finally, two other narrative levels are added to this polyphony: a short part called "Palaver" (a third-person narration whose origin is not clearly identified) and the concluding pages of the book, a long poem called "Le Rire de l'ensevelie" ["The buried woman's laughter"]. In that final portion of the story, for the first time, we hear the mother's voice saying "I." Her body, which is now the body of a Muslim woman, is being sent to Oran so that she can be buried next to her beloved husband Moh. Only then is the character whose new name is "Félicie-Yasmina" given a chance to say "I" (as if she had had to wait for the invention of that new double identity to finally accede to the status of full-blown speaking subject). She is the product of all the points of view that the story has previously developed.

The text as a whole thus presents us with a plurality of voices, though two narrators are clearly more important than all the others. They are the ones who create Félicie. One voice is female, belonging to the youngest daughter, Lousie-Ourdia; the other one is male and is that of the eldest son, Karim-Armand.

When all the elements are present, "Félicie's body" becomes a complex and composite ensemble that can teach us *how* to maintain a delicate and precarious positioning where one can be (or has a right to be) opposed to something, *contre*, without losing the right to be "tout contre" (the right to tenderness and affection, to physical intimacy). This "tout contre" is a way of speaking and a way of listening at the same time, a practice that has everything to do with vibration. The encounter is not a form of communication or of translation if, by translation, we mean the passage from one language to another or the search for words that would mean the same thing in different contexts. In the story, words are very powerful but their effectiveness and performative force are not related to their meaning, at least not directly. Their vibration matters more, which suggests that comprehension between subjects is not the primordial issue. "Félicie's body" gives us at least three examples of performative encounters generated by the beneficial vibration of speech. Each time, the meaning of words could have resulted in incomprehension or could have worsened the level of violence that was already present.

The Power of the Sacred Word

The first example has to do with several interpretations of what it means for a word to have power. And, as is characteristic in the case of performative encounters, we discover that the characters do not even have to agree on their definitions of the word "power" for that power to manifest itself. The issue, in this case, is potentially explosive: Moh and Félicie are discussing religion or, more specifically, the intersection between superstition and the sacred, between beliefs and the Book. The short story invites us to think about what it means for Félicie, a Christian woman who goes to church every Sunday, to be saved by the name of Allah that she wears around her neck on a little pendant.

The scene takes place during the Algerian war. Surrounded by a crowd of Europeans, she is suddenly threatened by a man armed with a knife, who only sees in her a "French" woman and tries to cut her throat. In this example, no dialogue seems possible. History has already written the encounter, and the two subjects are constructed as each other's enemy. But the predicted tragedy is suddenly interrupted, and the encounter becomes performative as the obvious roles are redistributed. As the man is about to use his knife, Félicie tells us, "le 'collier-cravache' que je portais jaillit de dessous mon col" [the necklace that I was wearing sprang out of my collar] (347). And just as the jewel itself is the subject of the verb (as if it had been moved by a mysterious force) the killer-to-be seems to lose his own strength: "Il me lâcha. Son couteau tomba (j'entends encore le son d'acier de sa chute sur la pierre du trottoir)" [He let go of me. His knife fell down (I can still hear the sound of steel falling on the pavement stones)] (347). The necklace springs out of the collar, and the knife falls, as if moved by a different type of energy than the one that would have allowed the man to say "I." The text does not tell us that he dropped his weapon but that it fell to the ground. He loses both the instrument and his position as a killer.

But what is exactly the force that turns the confrontation into the moment when Félicie's life is spared? How does the narrative explain both the interruption of the predictable script and the power of the necklace that has performed a different type of encounter? When she returns home, Félicie offers the following explanation: "Ton cadeau, mon chéri, ton collier et surtout ce Coran en or calligraphié au bout . . . Ce bijou m'a sauvée!" [Your gift, my love, your necklace and above all the gold Koran with a calligraphy at the end of it . . . The pendant saved me!] (340).

I suggest that the specific function of the Koran and its relationship to Félicie is worth exploring because the jewel does not represent a traditional form of identification. Félicie is not constructed as an exception to the rule: she is not a European Muslim; she did not convert to her husband's religion. The necklace does not transform her into a cultural hybrid but into an incomprehensible or undecipherable sign: "Je suis une Française et je porte cela (j'ai saisi des deux mains le Coran en or dont le dessin visible avait été une cuirasse). Je le porte par amour de Môh, mon mari." [I am a French woman and I wear this (with both hands, I had taken hold of the Koran, whose visible mark had been my armor). I wear it out of love for my husband, Moh] (348).

The "and" ("I am . . . and I wear") represents the conditions of the performative encounter and creates a moment of hesitation, of incomprehension that generates enough confusion for the violent script to be exceptionally rerouted. Djebar does not simply write about a moment of reconciliation between two religions that are traditionally portrayed as hostile to each other, nor is she tempted by a model of conversion. She insists on the power of words and on the fact that it is almost impossible to control that power.

Even the short story as a whole does not seem to have a clear interpretation of the status of the word that protects Félicie. The two lovers do not really agree on what exactly happened, and they have different interpretations of the type of power that manifested itself. On hearing the story, Moh is immediately convinced that the name of God has functioned as a sort of magic talisman and that Félicie has been saved by the power of the word itself: "Père a caressé le petit Coran. Son visage s'est détendu. Il a eu un regard tendre vers toi: 'Normal! a-t-il répondu. Il était là pour cela, pour te protéger!'" [Father touched the little Koran. His face relaxed. He looked at you tenderly and said: "Normal! That was the idea: it was there to protect you!"] (341). For Moh, the power of the word was predictable, and the divine sign produced its expected effect.

As readers, we may of course have various reactions to this. We may find the notion plausible or implausible. But it is textually even more significant to note that at least two interpretations of the encounter coexist. Nothing indicates that Félicie or the narrator believe Moh's theory. Karim-Armand, who tells the story, describes the pendant as "un objet fétiche" [a fetishized object](341). He does not seem to share the father's conviction. The text also reminds us that Félicie wears the Koran because she loves Moh and not because she worships Allah. Whose love, whose faith, is meant to be performative in this case? Or is the fact that we cannot decide even more important? We do not know if we should trust the father (the divine word has a real protective power) or assume that the aggressor was so surprised to see the French woman he was trying to kill wearing a Koran around her neck that the shock functioned as a sort of shield, an "armor," says Félicie. If that were the case, then, it is not the word itself but the linguistic and cultural context where it appears that makes it powerful.

The incomprehensible encounter between the Christian who is still a Christian and her golden Koran is powerful enough to make the knife drop to the ground just as when a divine order interrupts an imminent sacrifice. Félicie is passed over. The Islamic sign—often misread as reference to a religion, a language, and an ethnicity at the same time—becomes all the more meaningful here because it is not in its rightful place and does not belong to a predictable narrative. It is the opposite of a clear sign and, yet, its performance is extremely forceful.

In a perfectly symmetrical episode that can be described either as the same or as the opposite of the previous encounter, the short story shows that in certain cases, French words can have the same function as the gold Koran. Even if they are not understood, they can have reparative powers. The French words that Félicie uses can bring solace to the women they address, even if they only understand Arabic, their native tongue.

Once again, the passage is set during the Algerian war, and the encounter between Félicie and the women of the village successfully carves the space of a counterdiscourse, of an oppositional and dissident coalition.

ces dames-villageoises venaient autrefois au tribunal pour que tu les renseignes sur un fils arrêté, un époux disparu ou torturé, un procès en cours. Tu leur répondais en un français lent, appliqué, par courtes phrases. Elles te fixaient, le regard fiévreux, leurs mains rougies de henné relevant leurs coiffes fleuries au-dessus de leurs fronts, et elles me disaient, en arabe

—Ta mère, mon fils, Dieu la bénisse! Ce qu'elle dit, et dans son langage, je la comprends.

Toi tu leur souriais. Tu les réconfortais, les faisais asseoir, pour prendre patience, pour se consoler. (254–55)

[the villagers used to come to the court of justice to find out what had happened to a son who had been arrested, a missing or tortured husband, an ongoing trial. You answered them in a slow, meticulous French, with short sentences. They would stare at you, feverishly, pushing back the flowery scarves on their foreheads with hands that were red with henna and they would tell me in Arabic:

—Your mother, my son, God Bless her. She speaks and in her language, I understand her.

You would smile at them. You would console them, make them sit down, to help them wait, to take comfort.]

The mother's language that the women do not understand is that same one that Maghrebi writers call "langue adverse" [the adversarial language], even if their mastery of French is impeccable. In this passage, unfamiliar or otherwise incomprehensible words magically make sense.[1] Language is not transparent like the "parole engagée" [socially committed speech] that Jean-Paul Sartre advocates in *Qu'est-ce que la littérature?* [*What is Literature?*](1964). It is as opaque as Edouard Glissant's "poetics of Relation"; it celebrates "le mot comme incertitude, le mot comme chuchotis, bruit, réserve sonore contre la nuit du silence impose. [. . .] La bienheureuse opacité, par quoi l'autre m'échappe, me contraignant à la vigilance de toujours marcher vers lui" [the word as uncertainty, the word as whisper, noise, against the night imposed by silence. [. . .] The fortunate opacity, thanks to which the other escapes me, forcing me to be vigilant, to always walk towards him] (Glissant 1981: 278). Or rather, in this case, towards her, towards them. Félicie's opaque French meets the worried human beings who are looking for their missing families.

Speaking the same language does not have to be the precondition of the women's performative encounter. The text does not even state exactly what Félicie tells the women but insists on what type of French she uses, on her relationship to her own language. This passage is not about translation or about "petit nègre" or "sabir," the condescending simplification of the colonial language by the master who talks to his subordinates. Paradoxically, the native speaker's French is "slow" and "meticulous" like the language of schoolchildren who are in the process of learning a foreign tongue. She seems to have understood that she is indeed learning a language, the language of the encounter. She is learning how to speak and listen in the other's own language. Similarly, the women respond to her words with a feverish look that expresses both their fear and their extreme attention, another sort of "vibration" that cannot be translated outside of their bodies.

What the Algerian mothers say to Karim in Arabic, after listening to Félicie, is that a performative encounter has taken place. They understood, and that was unexpected. Their comment bears on the type of communication that occurred, a strange reversed echo of Glissant's formulation: "je te parle dans ta langue, et c'est dans mon langage que je te comprends" [I talk to you in your language and I understand you in mine] (1969: 52). In this performative encounter, the women understand in their own language, although Félicie speaks to them in what seems to be hers.

The felicitous manipulation of words that the characters do not necessarily understand within their own linguistic system is one of the narrative engines of the text that eventually proposes a whole theory of what can be called the performative encounter with the name, or the act of naming. The constant request for identification, which increases in times of conflict, is a test that each of the characters of the short story passes differently. Just as the narrative never proposes any sustained theory of hybridity, preferring instead to stage a series of encounters between subjects that continue to perceive themselves as different, it shows how names themselves (and what they culturally connote) are less important than the way in which the subject conceives his or her relation to private or public identity (and identification) markers.

What we think of the "proper" name is that problematic space where an illusion of absolute singularity is created, although this uniqueness is also tied to a whole community's codes and conventions. My name can sound "French" or "Muslim" to others. Even without referring to psychoanalytic theories and their emphasis on the relationship between the Law and the Name of the Father, it is relatively uncontroversial to make the claim that communities treat proper names as the locus of a subject's identity and legitimacy (or lack thereof). From the most official identification paper to the most intimate nickname, the name is evidence of a legacy transmitted by the father, or the mother, the clan, or the nation. Names often mean something, though not in every language, and Djebar's story is precisely interested in those moments when the name constitutes the place of a mediation between two languages, two religions, or two systems, that is, Islam and Christianity or French and Arabic. The text complicates these binary pairs by introducing other categories (such as nicknames) and by showing how names function in different contexts, depending on whether the mother, the father, parents, or strangers use them.

Like the passages that insist on the power of opaque words, the stories generated by the uses of different names for each character are haunted by the issues of opacity and monolingualism, incomplete bilingualisms, and constantly renegotiated contracts. No name is definitive. The relationship between the name and the person is always reevaluated, reexamined, and, sometimes, modified. No hybrid or dual identity is ever set.

The Grain of the Voice

Both Félicie and her husband are quite uncomfortable in the other's language. Karim says: "Mon père est un noble, quand il parle sa langue maternelle, et un employé de dernière classe quand il passe au français" [My father is an aristocrat when he speaks his mother tongue and a subaltern employee when he switches over to French] (269). As for the mother, her bilingualism is even more limited. She can neither speak nor understand Arabic. Yet, contrary to what happens in other short stories, the pair's linguistic difficulties are never considered as failures because they result not in a lack of "communication" but in new moments of felicitous opacity. And yet, this type of opacity is different from that which develops between Félicie and the villagers, and it is not simply the opposite of transparency or a fetishization of the other's absolute linguistic otherness. What is opaque is the word without its context, without the seemingly parasitical "noise" that accompanies the dialogue. And it is up to the narrative to make us understand the difference between felicitous opacity and pure incomprehension by helping us hear with a "third ear" or perhaps read with a "third eye."[2] The way Félicie pronounces her husband's name is lovingly detailed. As in the passage about her conversation with the villagers, the text carefully listens, with its Khatibian third ear, to what Roland Barthes would call the "grain of the voice" (1981). Here is what Karim says about his mother:

"Tu ne peux prononcer correctement le moindre mot arabe: même ton mari, tu l'appelles 'Môh,' une syllabe suspendue, vibrant de tendresse ou d'ironie, selon les jours [You cannot pronounce correctly one single word of Arabic: even your husband, you call him "Moh," a hanging syllable, vibrating sometimes with tenderness sometimes with irony.] (254)

Just as Arabic or French words acquire meaning only in the moments when Félicie meets either with other women or with a potential killer, the name itself means nothing unless one listens to the para-speech that only a careful narra- tive renders. The first name vibrates like the string of an instrument, and in order to be appreciated, this vibration requires something like a body's physi- cal proximity, a touch, a tactful attention, as if we were so physically close to the sound that we could sense the vibration, "tout contre." A third ear must appreciate the distinction between a pulsation of tenderness or of irony. The words themselves remain the same (whichever language one uses).

Only our third ear or perhaps a reader's third eye can encounter the other's language when we identify and appreciate the distinction between a tender or an ironic "vibration."[3] The word is the same, and the strange homophony between "Moh" and *mot* (or "word" in French) is itself remarkable: the given name is always meaningful in a given context but also interchangeable. Moh, "mot": an untranslatable and magical encounter.[4] Only our interpretation of the vibration gives us a clue as to the quality of the encounter.

As Khatibi puts it in *Maghreb Pluriel*, "Il faut écouter le Maghreb résonner dans sa pluralité" [We must hear the Maghreb resonate in its plurality] (1983b: 39). A name can caress or hurt: when Karim, Félicie's son, remembers that his mother used to call him Titi, he says, "J'entends tes inflexions juste dans ces deux consonnes, dans cette caresse que mon nom est pour toi" [I hear the inflexions of your voices in these two consonants, in that caress that my name is to you] (272).

And yet, talking and listening "tout contre" do not eradicate the difficulties of the original couple whose binarity is constantly reinforced by a series of linguistic, religious, and national paradigms. If the text invites us to listen to the vibrations of words, it does not pretend that the meaning of words is irrel- evant either. The ghostly couple that haunts the love story between Félicie and Moh keeps reappearing in the children's lives.

Karim-Armand aka Titi

In "Félicie's body," each of the children bears at least two names: one Muslim, given by the father, one Christian, given by the mother. It is, of course, tempting to assume that this doubling of the name is the symbol of a perfectly successful situation of hybridity where both legacies are affirmed and celebrated. A hyphen unites Karim and Armand as well as Louise and Ourdia, signifying the two pieces of the original "couple." Félicie and Moh seem to have invented a perfectly viable tactic that symbolizes their individual victory over history. For their children, identity has always been hyphenated since their documents bear, officially, two names. We could submit that they never had to choose between their parents' legacies. Instead, they have always been codified as "Franco-Algerians," "Muslim-Christians," or "European-Arabs."

However, in Djebar's story, that situation is never presented as a stable or even as a necessarily desirable solution (if "desirable" connotes the absence of friction). The narrative is not a portrait of triumphant (or even fulfilled) hybrids. Besides, for each child, the consequences of this cultural encounter are different. It is the story's originality and imaginative strength to show us that bilingualism or double identifications are not an end in themselves but the precondition of a search for new protocols. Djebar is not interested in the principle of dual belonging. Instead, each of her characters tests his or her encounter with what it means to have a split name. Double identities are not presented as a solution. Rather, they are a theoretical hypothesis that the narrative will develop. Instead of turning one hybrid protagonist into the symbol of *métissage*, the short story offers us a whole series of case studies. In other words, we are not asked to choose between hybrid and nonhybrid subjects, but to consider the different trajectories of double identities.

Although each parent's contribution is equally valued, equally respected by the father and the mother, new hierarchies keep reappearing. It is almost as if, once Félicie and Moh resolve their specific historical problems—(within the couple, Moh's culture is not treated as inferior and he does not consider Félicie as the member of a minority after 1962)—the ineluctable opposition between the same and the other always resurfaces in terms of difference and power. Strangely, however, this apparently unavoidable imbalance is desirable because it reintroduces the need for encounters and negotiations. Love and tolerance do · not lead to a perfect and stabilized fusion.

Instead, the characters' mutual respect and affection are presented as the elements that introduce some flexibility in the system of nomination and also the possibility of change. They invent forms of unique hybridity that are not the opposite of monolithic identities but unpredictable, diverse, and unexpected encounters. The original couple does not simply represent a new starting point; the second generation will continue to test the encounter, solving in their own imaginative ways the challenges of each subversive and transgressive relationship with otherness, even if that otherness is a part of each one's self. They do not let us imagine the hybrid as the third and stabilized term that transcends the original encounter between two differences. They are not the equivalent of mutants or the representatives of a new and homogeneous essence. Their relationship to what their names mean to them and to each other is always in flux.

Each reaction is unique, and each child will identify his or her own problem, find his or her own solution. There is a certain jubilatory effect to this always-unfinished series of experiments that renounces closure and promises that more stories must be told. For each name, points of friction emerge: which one is going to be the first, and who gets to decide (the father, the mother, the child)?

For example, Karim-Armand, the firstborn son who addresses his dying mother, tells the following story: "Tu m'as eu moi, ton premier garçon, en 1943 (à cette occasion, Père, m'as-tu rapporté, a tenu à m'accoler le prénom musulman en premier: 'Karim décida-t-il, et après tu choisis un second prénom' [. . .])" [You had me, your first son, in 1943 (you told me that on that occasion, Father insisted on giving me a Muslim name that would go first: "Karim, he decided, then you choose a second name [. . .])" (252).

Here, every word counts, and the silences are just as significant. I note that for the son-narrator, the story of the first name is in parenthesis, as if the text wanted to represent the fact that, for Karim, this is a self-contained and relatively marginal issue rather than an identity crisis. We will see that for the daughter, it is quite a different matter. I also note that the father's choice is not inscribed as the law but as his desire: "Father *insisted* on giving me a Muslim name that would go first." His desire is strong, more than just a preference, but it is neither presented as an order nor as a custom or time-honored protocol. The decision is not the only legitimate possibility in the face of which the mother would have no say. Furthermore, the story that Karim-Armand tells us was first narrated by the mother, who "told" him about the father's insistence. In other words, she is responsible for representing the father as an individual subject who had desires of his own rather than as a typical male Algerian whose "culture made him do it."[5] *He* insisted, *he* decided. No collective agency legitimizes this decision in the narrator's text. Her description does not mention the relevance of stereotypical gender roles either. She does not rationalize her lack of power in terms of a predictable position as a woman, even if the reader is likely to speculate about her silence.

And it is just as significant that the result produced by the force of his desire is at best ambiguously successful. The mother does not simply accept the father's choice. She does not give up on her own desire to name her son, and the text tells the story of her subterranean, but unformulated, resistance to the father's decision. She does not openly fight him, but in this particular case her way of speaking "tout contre" preserves the two sides of the word. She does not choose between the two meanings of "against"; she maintains a position where conflict and intimacy stay together. If we remember that the son is retelling the mother's story, we have to recognize that her narrative preserved the tensions that existed that day and still exist as the son speaks. And those frictions exist because she did not give up on her own desire, she did not simply ignore her own preference for another name. Here is the end of the parenthesis that I left interrupted in the quotation above: "'tu as répondu à voix basse, précipitée et basse: Armand, ce sera donc Armand!' [. . .])" ["you answered softly, with a voice both hushed and rushed: Armand, it will be Armand then! . . .")] (252).

The second name, "Armand," reaches us through a textual echo chamber that makes it indistinguishable from the mother's reluctance and from the way in which she articulates her lack of enthusiasm in a very specific context. The words are less important than the tone of the voice, the "voix basse, précipitée et basse" that is imported into the story thanks to the son's (written) narration. The tenor of the message—she is not happy with the father's choice—is present in the grain of her voice. And yet, they do not discuss the situation. This response is an original moment of nonstruggle/nonresignation whose ambiguity would be lost if the son had simply reported "My mother then chose 'Armand.'" Only the quality of the voice keeps this moment alive.

The father's strong desire (he "insisted," he "decided") manifested itself without causing any conflict between the parents. The mother did not protest overtly. Yet, her own (apparently weaker) desire is not eliminated from the text. Her voice is present and a slight level of friction remains. Her reluctance is encoded in the text in spite of the delicacy of the emotion. She is "against" the father's decision, but here is a moment when the two meanings of the word "against" are preserved. This "tout contre" neutralizes the potential violence of a confrontation without eliminating the disagreement.

> Mais tu vois, m'as-tu avoué plus tard, peut-être parce qu'Armand venait en second, alors, ce n'était plus pareil, tu es devenu pour moi "Titi." Ni Karim, ni Armand, Titi! (253)

> [But you see, she later on confessed, maybe because Armand came second, then, it was no longer the same and you became "Titi" for me. Neither Karim nor Armand, Titi!]

The trace of the performative encounter between the two parents manifests itself in the text in at least two ways. First, a new name appears so that the rational binary pair (Christian-Muslim) is replaced by a trio, a more unstable and less Cratylian system. The third space is not really a name but a tender and slightly infantilizing nickname. The excess of names is accompanied by a double negation ("Ni Armand ni Karim") reminiscent of the doubly negative identities theorized by students of migrant literatures (Laronde 1993). The allusion to a "confession" (the mother "confesses") inscribes this portion of the narrative as the story of something that the mother can be guilty of.

It is also meaningful that Karim carefully documents the timing of the elements of the story. This confession was made "later" so that, as readers, we are to place this piece of the puzzle into a temporal frame. If we think about the figure of Scheherazade, whose life-saving storytelling also depends, crucially, on the moment when the tale unfolds, the order in which the son reveals what his mother says constructs or performs quite a different identity. The mother has slowly added details to the overall picture, and only the accumulation of layers enables us to understand the types of complex choices that she made.

The two parents' tactic is not simply a perfect balance between their two cultures and their respective desires. The egalitarian addition of two names is not a stable protocol that can be agreed upon once and for all. After a time, the original binary pair is modified by the mother's unilateral decision to call her son Titi, a nickname that we cannot link directly to any of his national, religious, or cultural legacies. Just as the refusal of the binary hierarchy manifested itself through a stubborn resistance to *métissage* and a counter tactic, the emergence of a nickname individualizes the son but also infantilizes him forever.

The son does not seem to have a say, or rather, he appears to have accepted the nickname without any reluctance. The text, however, immediately points out that this situation is only one of the possible outcomes and that the parents, who have the power to name, do not necessarily have the last word. Other configurations occur, and if we listen to other narrators, other textual voices within Djebar's tale, they will immediately appear and provide us with other scripts.

The given names now participate in a sort of traditional "Nouba" to the extent that they intervene one after the other, like the different movements of the classical suite. Like the women of Mount Chenoua, they take turns. and the principle can be adopted in many different contexts of encounter besides the naming of children or the sharing of storytelling responsibilities. In Patricia William's *The Alchemy of Race and Rights*, a critique of a dance company is couched in curiously similar ways. In this case, the managers of a ballet company explained that they found it difficult to include, in their choreographies, the only black dancer they finally hired in 1987. In response to accusations of racist thinking, they argued that their decision was motivated by an aesthetic criterion. A black body would have disrupted the ballet's symmetry.

> Failure to include blacks before this was attributed not to racism but to the desire to maintain an aesthetic of uniformity and precision. As recently as five years ago, the director of the Rockettes, Violet Holmes, defended the all-white line on artistic grounds. She said that the dancers were supposed to be mirror images of one another (1991: 117).

As a cultural critic reading the manager's discursive strategy, Williams could have chosen to argue that the primacy of aesthetic criteria in this case was a misguided assignment of priorities. How could a pleasing sense of visual "symmetry" be considered more important than its consequences, that is, the exclusion of the only black dancer whose presence in the company supposedly demonstrated the managers' strong will to promote an integrated environment? Instead, here is what Williams writes:

> Mere symmetry, of course, could be achieved by hiring all black dancers. It could be achieved by hiring light-skinned dancers, in the tradition of the Cotton Club's grand heyday of condescension. It could be achieved by hiring an even number of black dancers and then placing them like little black anchors at either end or like hubcaps at the center, or by speckling them throughout the line at even intervals, for a nice checkerboard melting point effect. It could be achieved by letting all the white dancers brown themselves in the sun a bit, to match the black dancers—something they were forbidden to do for many years because the owner of the Rockettes didn't want them to look "like colored girls." (117)

The originality of Williams' intervention—what we could call her imagination—consists in going beyond the binary opposition between an all-white symmetry versus black and white asymmetry. She thus redefines the notion of symmetry to offer a whole new list of possibilities. Each "solution" is bound to attract criticism, of course. Some will object to ideological consequences, others to the aesthetic results, and others still will not appreciate the means used to reach the desired end. Thus, the allusion to what we could call a "Cotton Club" logic reminds us that racism and inclusion are not systematically incompatible. The principle of "black anchors" or of "hubcaps" forces us to think in terms of center and periphery. The creation of a "nice melting point effect" could be distasteful to multiculturalists who are weary of assimilationist universalism. In addition, the notion that a bit of sun will solve all problems will probably make the reader laugh instinctively, at least until Williams' cleverly allusive prose makes us realize that she is superimposing several colonial myths about skin color. The old Césairian cry of despair, "je ne suis pas différènt de vous; ne faites pas attention à ma peau noire: c'est le soleil qui m'a brûlé" [I am not different from you; never mind my black skin: I've been burnt by the sun] (Césaire 1995: 126, 127), as well as the old advertisement for imperial soaps capable of washing the black off black skins have their paranoid narrative equivalent among whites.

Like Williams, Djebar offers us a multiplicity of models so that her text does not encourage her reader to interpret one of the characters as the only possible archetype of hybridity and of *métissage*. Each child constructs a different type of relationship with their identity that develops as the result of the encounter with their given names. The story that describes the ongoing negotiation is carefully individualized.

In the case of the eldest son, the narrative is driven by tensions between the father and the mother rather than between the parents and the child, and the result of their *mésentente* is a third name, a nickname adopted by the mother and by Karim-Armand as well. Two of the female children invent radically different patterns of symmetry, and the text treats that difference differently too. For example, in the case of one of the daughters, a personal story of union and separation is dealt with in a few words and literally put in parenthesis. The short story mentions this only once, like an open and shut case. Marie, who lives in Paris, has adopted a radical and definitive solution to the issue of hybridity. When she is introduced to the reader, Titi, who is still the narrator at that point in the text, explains:

> Celle-ci a barré définitivement son prénom musulman et ce, depuis qu'elle a divorcé de son mari d'Oran (enrichi par les trois hammams de sa mère, le beau-frère s'était mis en tête de prendre seconde épouse: j'étais descendu là-bas—à l'époque, tu te souviens, Mman, je me faisais fort de régler les affaires de mes sœurs en quarante-huit heures!). Marie n'avait pas hésité à venir en France avec moi, suivie peu après de ses deux fils. (240)

> [She definitely crossed out her Muslim name when she divorced her husband from Oran (his mother's three hammams had made my brother-in-law a rich man, and he wanted a second wife. I had gone down—do you remember Man, it was the time when I would make a point of taking care of my sisters' business in forty-eight hours!). Marie had not hesitated to come to France with me, and a little later, her two sons followed her.]

Whereas the passages of the story devoted to Karim-Armand-Titi scrutinize the decision-making process, here, the text insists on the definitive aspect of a quick and unilateral initiative made in the absence of any dialogue or *mésentente*. Marie simply transposes the failure of her union with a man from Oran onto her own identity. She "definitively" strikes through her name, and the narrative tells us nothing about how she arrived at her decision. For us, it is a fait accompli. No allusion is ever made to the tone of the voice, nor does a metaphor introduce vibration into the passage. Only verbs describing actions are present in that paragraph: she divorced, he went down, she left, she crossed out the name. There is no "hesitation." Only "forty-eight hours" are necessary for the change to occur, and if Karim-Armand-Titi helps his sister take care of her "business" with a no-nonsense pragmatism that he seems to laugh at a few years later, he plays no part in her decision to delete one half of her identity. The story mentions her gesture solely as a practical rather than a symbolic act.

Surely one physical instance of "crossing out" could not have been enough for her new identity to be as functional as the old one, but the text is not interested in the administrative or familial obstacles that might have made Marie's choice a difficult one in the long run. The separation from her husband manifests itself as a separation from and within the given name. The hyphen disappears.

Obviously, the parents' felicitous encounter does not function as a sort of cultural capital that one inherits. The union between the French mother and the Algerian father cannot be simply repeated or reproduced by the children's generation, whose positioning is different anyway. The children are already double, and they have to link their own "I" to a double identity. And yet, Marie's trajectory creates a sort of echo between two archetypal couples: one united, one separated. Her reaction to her divorce also creates a link between her own identity and her marriage. Her decision to cross out what is Muslim in her given name means that she interprets the hyphen as the symbol of her union with a Muslim man (rather than of her own hybridity). The fact that she deletes her Muslim name is not described as an amputation of a part of herself or of her double culture. It becomes, instead, the precondition of new alliances: "Elle épousa, après une année de secrétariat, le premier amoureux qui se présenta: elle eut dans l'année un troisième garçon, Alain, maintenant âgé de sept ans" [After one year as a secretary, she married the first suitor who came along: that year, she had a third boy, Alain, who is now seven years of age] (240). In other words, the children who represent the third generation (although I am here using the expression in ways that do not correspond to current sociological definitions), reflect the return to a duality that the mother recreates as an opposition between France and Algeria. Alain, Nourredine, and Halim are half brothers. The family, as a whole, reproduces the encounter between Muslim names and Christian names that Marie refuses to welcome for herself as one individual. This neat double symmetry is altered by a trio: two Muslim names, one Christian name. When her husband was on the verge of bringing in a wife whose name, we must assume, would have added a second Islamic component to that nuclear family, Marie refused the possibility of a *ménage à trois noms*. It obviously made her own double identification intolerable. But her three children strangely allow that 2 to 1 ratio to resurface in a different context.

The most interesting case is yet to come. While the text shows in detail how Karim-Armand moves from the double to the triple, and how Marie-Khadidja moves from two to one, but also to three, it pays even more attention to the youngest daughter, Louise-Ourdia. At the beginning of the second part of the short story, the portion of the text devoted to this daughter is called, like her, "Louise-Ourdia." This character becomes the first-person narrator, and what she reveals about the dying mother and the family is much less elaborate than what Karim-Armand-Titi had to say. In fact, most of her shorter intervention has to do with the story of how she coped with her name. Like her sister, she repudiates the heritage and will end up with only one of the two given names, but she will do it for reasons that are completely different from her sister's. While Marie deletes a part of her identity, renounces her link with Algeria, and modifies her name to make it coincide with a new reality, Louise-Ourdia, by contrast, refuses the name because it fails to express her duality as she herself wants to define it. Paradoxically, she too will end up with one single name only but unlike Marie, she will not simply cross out one part of her herself, she will rewrite her name.

For her, that moment is a serious crisis and not a radical move. It takes much longer than forty-eight hours, because what she wants (and manages to get) involves someone else: she wants her mother to stop calling her Louise and to use Ourdia only. Once again, the writing of the encounter insists on the tonality of that negotiation, on the vibrations and the melodic repercussions of the interactions between mother and daughter. This is no theoretical discussion but the performance of a metamorphosis.

Like all the other children, she has two given names, but she interprets them as a betrayal rather than as evidence of her double legacy. And because she cherishes her hybridity, she refuses what she sees as an internal separation. In spite of the parents' clear intention, she reads the hyphen as a *trait de désunion*, a mark of division that separates the parents' loving couple.

> Ces deux-là, ils s'aimaient, ils ne sont pas séparés un seul jour depuis leur mariage . . . mais pour les huit enfants, ils ont eu besoin de voir leurs rejetons chacun de son côté, chacun dans sa langue, et dans chacune des deux religions [. . .] comme s'ils avaient placé leur fils et leurs filles (et cela, dès le premier jour, à notre naissance) sur une frontière, une crête, un no man's land. (292)

> [These two, they loved each other, after they married, they were never apart for more than one day . . . But their eight children? They had to see them on each side of the divide, each in his or her language, and in each of the two religions [. . .] as if they had placed their sons and their daughters (from our very first day, the day of our birth) on a border, a cusp, a no-man's-land.]

The triple image (border, cusp, no-man's-land) is not made of incompatible elements. The three spaces in question all point to the absence of center; they are typically not territories to which one belongs, and the "neither/nor" of Beur literature reappears here, complicated by the presence of a third element. This positioning is experienced not only as the result of the parents' decision (the children are passive) but also as a disadvantage from which they are likely to suffer.

And yet, it is difficult not to hear through Ourdia's tirade the echoes of other recent celebrations of liminal and interstitial positions. After all, the definition of Michel Serres' "third" tends to reappropriate minority and multiple positions (1991). The allusion to the "border" evokes Mary Louise Pratt's contact zones (1992). And for many theoreticians and writers, the spaces described by Ourdia are metaphorically linked to transgression and trespass: they represent a way of life or a way of thinking and a form of "intelligence" (Détienne and Vernant 1970); "logic" (Amselle 1990); or even, as Walter Mignolo calls it, a "border gnosis, the subaltern reason striving to bring to the foreground the force and creativity of knowledges subalternized during a long process of colonization of the planet" (2000: 13).

The act of naming is often always already linked to the desire to categorize that will then be used to exclude. To name is precisely to leave the no-man's-land, to accept the responsibilities that come with belonging, even if they are experienced as a constraint. In *Islam and Postcolonial Narrative*, John Erickson suggests that many postcolonial narratives shared this instinctive reluctance to name:

> the unfolding of their narratives is most often governed less by a desire to name the unnameable than to devise tactics to *ward off* the effort of Western critics and readers to name that ineffable space out of which postcolonial writers write—that space lying between the adversary's language and her/his other tongue/culture, that same space likened by Assia Djebar to the *rebato* of the Spanish occupiers of Algeria in earlier times— a term referring to an "isolated spot," a no-man's land lying between the aggressor and the aggressed, from which the former sallied forth to attack, and to which he withdrew in search of refuge or to replenish provisions. To name is to render accessible, to transform the other into the same, to categorize, neutralize, and assimilate. (1998: 35–36)

Within that tradition, Ourdia's position is the exception to the rule, for she refuses to inhabit the cusp or to venture into the "rebato." Her character is not necessarily presented by the text as the new and improved model, but it is not discredited either. The allusion to the "cusp" remains ambiguous. It evokes the edge, imbalance, and danger, but generally the image of a summit is positive. What is, however, more original in Ourdia's point of view is that she interprets the duality of her name not as a destabilizing factor but as an inclusive tactic that reintroduces equilibrium between two legacies.

In the text, the spatial metaphors remain ambivalent, but when Ourdia describes the dialogue that takes place between the daughter and the mother, the level of hostility conveyed by the passage is significantly higher than the reluctances expressed by Félicie when the first son's name is discussed. When

Marie rejected Khadidja, the break was sudden, brutal, and unilateral. No encounter occurred. In Ourdia's case, the discomfort generated by the unstable name leads to a performative encounter with Félicie. It is a moment of crisis that leads to the reconfiguration of the whole situation.

For Ourdia, the hyphen between the two names cannot be a symbol of their parents' love. It marks a division and a gap. It turns the family into children with "deux faces, deux visages, deux" [two faces, two sides, two] (294–95). When she remembers the conversation she had with her mother about it, the "grain of the voice" clearly indicates that this is not a casual conversation, a happy encounter: "Je lui en fis vivement le reproche" (293); "je continuais agressive"; or "je tremblais d'agacement" (294) ["I said reproachfully"; "I continued aggressively"; or "I was trembling with irritation"]. Félicie, on the other hand, seems completely indifferent to her daughter's predicament: "Maman me caressait, me cajolait, désinvolte, ajoutait: 'Des prénoms, ce ne sont que des mots, quelle importance'" [Mother would give me a hug and add, casually: "Names, they are only words, who cares?"](294). Here, the bodies' vibrations are not in sync: Ourdia trembles as the mother "caresses" her.

The mother, who had responded to the father's decision with a moment of reluctance and a subtle change in the quality of her voice, is presented as tenderly indifferent to the daughter's anger and trembling body. Her "caress" seems to compete with words that she declares powerless and useless. Whereas the son seems quite capable of listening to the vibrations as well as, or perhaps rather than, to what is said, here, the daughter seems unable to use her "third ear" to get past the mother's sentences. Does Félicie act in bad faith? After all, the text has already demonstrated that one word, in the past, had the power to save her. Ourdia's originality lies in refusing the double name, because she constructs her encounter with it not as with two camps between which she could hypothetically choose (as Marie did), but because she rejects the *type* of hybridity that her parents have chosen.

According to her, much more elegant configurations existed that would have preserved the hyphen as a sign of union between two cultures, languages, and religions within one unique name. Her solution would have been to restrict her parents' choice to a set of names that have an equivalent on each side. She proposes Louisa for herself and Yahia as a possible equivalent of Jean that is to be found in the Koran—not because she wishes to take sides, but because one way for her to refuse relegation to the border is to limit her parents' choice to that liminal category of names that resides on the linguistic and cultural border zone between the two countries. In other words, she opts for a different type of hybridity. Her knowledge of Arabic and French leads her to prefer a different type of encounter, and she presents her idea as self-evident, as the obvious and "simple" move that makes the double name unnecessary and wrong. Of her own name she asks, "Tu n'aurais pas pu, simplement choisir 'Louisa'? C'était valable pour vous deux" [Couldn't you simply have chosen "Louisa"? That would have worked for the both of you]; while about Kader-Jean, she says: "vous n'auriez pas pu mettre simplement Yahia et toi tu l'aurais appelé 'Jean'?" [Couldn't you have simply put down Yahia and you would have called him "Jean"?] (294). Her recipe for the name as encounter is hers and hers only. She wants to get rid of the hyphen and replace duality with *métissage*. The name would then become undecidable for whoever asks, "where is it from?"

She just as adamantly objects to the principle of replacing the official name with a nickname: "ni 'Titi' ni 'Kaki,' aucun de ces surnoms ridicules qui nous coupent en petits morceaux!" [neither "Titi" nor "Kaki," enough of these ridiculous nicknames that cut us up into little pieces](295). Whereas Karim heard a "caress" in the vibration produced by the repetition of one syllable in "Titi," Ourdia interprets the nickname as a sign of separation that hurts her multiple identities.

Curiously, Ourdia imagines her solution as an example of "simplicity" whereas, for the mother, her determination to take her names so seriously is evidence of her "complexity." As Ourdia recriminates and nags, she responds with a caress and a refusal to buy the myth of "simplicity": "Elle m'embrassait: 'Compliquée, la plus compliquée est la dernière?'" [She would give me a kiss: "Complicated, my youngest is the most complicated one?"] (295)

Félicie blames history and the colonial context. When Ourdia criticizes her for giving them either double names or ridiculous nicknames, she does not object to the principle of a better and more representative choice. She does not say, for example, that she would not have liked Louisa or that neither the father nor the mother would have enjoyed that solution. She does not theoretically reject Ourdia's notion of fused hybridity. (She could have argued, for example, that the search for a smaller common denominator is a reductive strategy.) After all, what Ourdia proposes is to limit the list of names among which she would have had the right or the duty to choose. The daughter is strangely prescriptive, and her idea to establish the category of names that belong to the Bible as well as to the Koran could well be experienced as bureaucratic and authoritarian. Her recommendation is reminiscent of the reluctance with which colonial civil servants greeted supposedly exotic, that is, non-Christian, names when parents declared their children's birth for official records. The conversation is not about how to define *métissage* and hybridity.

On the other hand, the mother explains that, from a historical point of view, the choice of a contact zone name was not part of the repertoire of possible tactics. "Mais mon chou, répliquait Maman placide, je ne savais pas. On ne m'avait pas dit qu'il y avait Louisa comme prénom arabe!" [But my darling, Mother would say, quietly. I did not know. I was never told that Louisa existed in Arabic!] (294). And later: "Ne t'impatiente pas, disait patiemment Maman. On ne t'explique pas cela à la mairie: du temps des Français comme maintenant du temps des Arabes. Moi avec mon certificat d'études, je n'ai jamais su ce qu'il y avait dans le Coran" [Don't be impatient, Mother would say patiently. No one tells you that at the town hall. Neither the French then nor the Arabs now. I did not have much of an education. I had no idea what was in the Koran] (294). In other words, she blames her own (colonial) education: either the republic failed to teach her enough or failed to teach her what the colonial regime did not consider relevant.

If I am presenting this exchange as a felicitous performative encounter between the mother and the daughter, it is not because they agree (their conversation is perceived as a moment of crisis), but because they will finally agree to disagree on *what* is important and on the *ways* in which one can be different and double. The conclusion of this episode is far from innocuous. The daughter does not accept the mother's patience, her quiet indifference to the issues she brings up. To Félicie's calm words, she responds with agitation and an emotional body language: "Je tremblais d'agacement" [I was trembling with irritation] (294). And in the end, she, like Marie, chooses to rename herself, in spite of the mother's insistance, in spite of the fact that her choice was sanctioned by administrative authorities.

Moi, ce sera Ourdia! Ourdia seulement!

—Mais Louise est en premier sur ta carte!

—Non, j'habite l'Algérie, et même si j'allais en France comme Titi, comme Marie, Ourdia je serai toujours. (295)[6]

[—I will be Ourdia. And only Ourdia.

—But Louise comes first on your identity card.

—No, I live in Algeria and even if I went to France, like Titi, like Marie, Ourdia I shall be, always!]

In this case, the encounter takes place between the mother and the daughter rather than between the parents. And it is a direct confrontation rather than a subtle and invisible tension. The mother has no choice but to finally ask, "Comment veux-tu donc que je t'appelle?" [Which name would you like me to use?] (295). But this is not a real question. First of all, Ourdia does not make a request. She does not plead with the mother. She renames herself and performatively attaches her name and her identity: "Ourdia je *serai* toujours" [Ourdia I *shall be*, always!] (295, my emphasis).

As for the mother, her reaction to this clear-cut refusal is strange at first. This character, who used to let names and nicknames proliferate around her children, suddenly falls completely silent. Her daughter's name disappears altogether for her: "Elle ne m'appelait plus, Maman. Ou seulement 'mon chou,' 'ma chérie.' Cela dura des années" [She did not address me by name any more, my Mother. She would call me "my dear," "my darling." It lasted for years] (295).

The tenderness of the "tout contre" has not disappeared, but it has found refuge away from words. And this is, of course, an example of an unhappy encounter that is at the same time felicitous. There is friction, tension, and probably unhappiness in this dialogue and in the mother's refusal to talk. The daughter, who would have liked to have had a truly bilingual name (Louisa, for example) becomes intransigent and, since she cannot have a name that lives on the intersection between the two cultures, she refuses the hyphen and opts for the Muslim name. Here, only the anonymous "vibration" of love remains; the name disappears. The allusion to "years" symbolizes the complexity of the problem, as well as the patience of the characters who needed all that time to solve the tremendous theoretical difficulty raised by their situation: how can one define a different difference that would suit them both? Until something happens:

Un beau jour, le matin, elle m'interpella:

—Ourdia, ma chérie.

Je l'ai regardée, Maman, ma maman! Elle avait prononcé mon prénom comme si elle parlait l'arabe: elle avait dû s'exercer longuement, toute seule avant de me le sortir ce "Ourdia"—avec le r roulé et l'accent tonique sur le i: il faisait soleil, ce matin de printemps." (295)

[One lovely day, in the morning, she called out to me:

—Ourdia, my dear.

I looked at her, my mother, my mommy. She had pronounced my name as if she spoke Arabic. She must have practiced a long time, on her own, before uttering this "Ourdia" with a rolled r and the stress on the i. It was sunny, that Spring morning.]

In retrospect, then, the long silence is revealed to be the time it took the mother to learn the daughter's language (the daughter tongue), a venture that required enormous effort, even if the achievement, in the end, is one word, the first name, correctly pronounced with all the right vibrations.

Just as Félicie knew how to speak to the women in a French that was "lent" and "appliqué" (slow and careful), she accepts learning her daughter's tongue, even if the communication seems reduced, as in this passage, to one single but well pronounced word. Whereas the husband's name remained one syllable "Moh," one "word" in French, the name of the daughter as she has reinvented herself is finally delivered, recited, as the result of a long alchemical reaction during which the dialogue is interrupted. "For years" and "on her own," Félicie learned how to pronounce one word. As in "Annie and Fatima," the mother learns the daughter's language, which happens to be the language of the father's land or fatherland. The text takes seriously the issue of time and the immense distance that separates the moment of total ignorance from the moment of rudimentary utterance. Placed by history in the situation described by Derrida in his *Monolingualism of the Other*, Félicie finally finds a performative way of giving to her daughter the gift of defining her own identity.

Conclusion

Djebar's text suggests that it is illusory to create ideal hybridities by "simply" adding two national or cultural legacies (as in the case of the two names separated or united by a hyphen), by "simply" positioning oneself in the third space, on the *frontera*, in the intersection between two cultures. That (commendable and desirable) will to encounter is only the beginning, and "Le corps de Félicie" gives us an example of the *types* of practices that cultures must constantly invent, at the macro and micro levels, in order to carve those new protocols of encounters.

At the moment, or at the place where the two names connect, relate to each other, one must expect imbalances, frictions: the desire for equality, for union, will not be able to get rid of the historical layers of hierarchies. Djebar is not suggesting, for example, that the daughters are more successful than their mother and that, as women, they have acquired a level of independence that their mother could not enjoy. What matters is that a more assertive generation of women does not adopt similar tactics: each daughter has her own way of being more assertive about her name. No matter how sincere individuals are in their quests, even a desire to reach perfect symmetry would only be a symptom of their fetishization of sameness. The revolutionary suggestion that the narrative makes, therefore, is that one could counter the abhorrent hypocrisy of apartheid slogans (equal and separate) with an extraordinarily difficult and controversial bet. The requirement now becomes "never equal but always together" (keeping in mind, of course, that the "inequality" in question is not inherited but that it is created, in daily practices, by individual desires which are always a blend of singular or collective narratives). The unfelicitous thing to do would be to use predictable narratives to account for and resolve each moment of inequality, imbalance, friction. (By predictable narratives I mean national stereotypes, religious assumptions, or worse, assumptions made about the religious because of the national, assumptions made about the national because of the ethnic, and so on.) These predictable narratives are precisely what created the original binary opposition in the first place, what

Djebar calls the "couple" France-Algérie, a couple whose elements were separated by unspeakable violence. Félicie's body, or rather Yasmina's body, on its way to its final destination, is renamed by the children after a long dialogue which can be seen both as the model for all negotiations around hybridity and as the result of the kind of teaching that Mohammed and Félicie, another type of "couple," did when they were raising the children.

The accumulation of that hybrid knowledge explains why, when forced to deal with a situation where the mother's national and religious identity contradicts a type of desire that no law takes into account (to be buried next to the person you love), the children are capable of dealing with it harmoniously, without giving in to history's dictates. During their long conversation, each facet of the problem (practical as well as ideological) is considered and dealt with, slowly, carefully, theoretically. Not only can the body be sent back to Oran, but the story also makes a point about the narrative potential of such moments of cooperation: at the end of the story, Félicie-Yasmina regains a voice. This character who had to be spoken for (or rather "tout contre") by all the others finally says "I" in a poem, as if her children had re-created her as a subject capable of "speaking" from a space that did not exist before the beginning of the story.

The children of an Algerian man and a French woman each have two names (one traditionally Muslim, one traditionally Christian), but instead of presenting this double reference as a solution (a bicultural hybridity), Djebar presents this dual identity as a starting point, as the ingredient of complex forms of encounters with the self and with others. Each child becomes the symbol of a different type relationship *with* hybridity. The loving encounter between the parents does not erase hierarchies between the man and the woman or between the colonized and the colonizer (each parent deriving power from one of the axes). Tensions are never resolved, and the text explores the different tactics adopted by each child in different contexts: one chooses between the two names, one opts for a third one, and one constantly fights the parents' decision. This text is not about *métissage*, it is about *fréquentage* or cohabitation, about the endless continuation and reinterpretation of the supposedly original encounter.

As we shall see in chapter 5, at the end of that story, Félicie's children, gathered around their mother's body in the Parisian hospital, agree to rename her, giving her a Muslim name. At the end of a long dialogue which, in itself, is a felicitous encounter (precisely because it contains so many contending ingredients as to start wars in different circumstances), they rename her Yasmina. They know that regardless of traditions, laws, and expectations about national or religious identities, her desire is to be buried right next to her beloved husband, Mohammed, in the cemetery of Béni-Rached, where only Muslim bodies are allowed to rest.[7]

3

Linguistic Encounters

Maghrebi "Langualization" in Francophone Fiction

J'ai rêvé, l'autre nuit, que mon corps était des mots.
Abdelkebir Khatibi 1971: 89

[The other night, I dreamed that my body was made of words.]

Je n'ai point quitté une langue maternelle mais une langue divine. [. . .] Je
n'écris pas en français, j'écris en "moi-même."
Mohamed Kacimi-El Hassani 1992: 119

[I did not leave a mother tongue but a divine tongue. [. . .] I do not write in
French, I write in "myself."]

This chapter is not about "arabisation" but about "langualization," which, of
course does not exist. And perhaps, it never will, unless we agree to adopt this
rather inelegant neologism to describe the performative encounter that develops when what is called arabisation both fails and succeeds; fails to accomplish
what governments intended,[1] yet succeeds in creating situations of literary dis-
sidence that deliberate attempts at linguistic transgression had not brought
about.

Langualization, which I obviously coin here on the model of "creolization,"
could be the name given to the constant linguistic performative encounter that
takes place in the Maghreb, or rather within Maghrebi speakers, wherever they
are, given that, for them, no equivalent of the Creole language exists. Langualization would be both the manifestation and the consequence of the fact that
they must think first and foremost *about* languages rather than *in* a certain
language or even two or three.

A Maghrebi langualization, comparable to the Caribbean phenomenon of
"creolization" will perhaps never emerge, at least not officially. In North Africa, the difficult search for inclusive forms of multilingualism has not been the
topic of an internationally famous manifesto.[2] Linguists and writers have had
less of an influence than governments, and the long-term objective of official

policies has been to impose Arabic as a national and official language in an effort to replace and displace the linguistic presence of the former colonial *métropole*. Clearly, in the Maghreb, the key word is not creolization but arabisation, and whether one agrees or disagrees (more or less violently) with the goal and means of implementation of such politics, it is difficult to claim that the issue is not of immediate cultural and political relevance (Kaye and Zoubir 1990; Gafaïti 2002; Berger 2002).

And yet, arabisation is a restrictive word, considering that national debates in postcolonial Tunisia, Morocco, and Algeria focus as much on the role of Arabic as on the function of French, multilingualism, spoken tongues, or the need to make room for Berber languages.[3] For the notion of arabisation to adequately represent an inextricable political, cultural, symbolic, and economic Gordian knot, it would have to refer to the Arab world as a whole rather than to Arabic (just as creolization refers to a multifaceted cultural process that goes well beyond the Creole language itself).

It may also be worth keeping in mind that the acuteness of linguistic debates in a given geopolitical area can be a symptom rather than a quantifiable problem for the people who live there. Most books and articles on the relationship between language and identity in the Maghreb agree that linguistic questions trigger intense reactions. Foued Laroussi suggests that language issues are indistinguishable from the tense relationship between citizens and an "Etat-nation-Parti qui n'est pas en mesure d'offrir un langage cohérent à ses citoyens et de leur garantir une certaine modernité" [State-nation-party that cannot offer its citizens a coherent language nor guarantee a certain level of modernity] (1997: 7). He refers to a unique "malaise diglossique" [diglossic malaise] and to "fantasmes idéologiques" [ideological fantasies] (1997: 7). Like him, Hélène Gill insists on the "contradictions of official discourse which have inflamed the language issue by creating a guilt-inducing conflict of loyalties for individual speakers" (1999: 123). Taleb Ibrahimi equates arabisation with a multiplicity of conflicts (1997). Djamila Saadi-Mokrane even talks about an "Algerian linguicide" and writes, "The issue of language arose with such violence that, in the space of half a century, the death of three different languages was predicted: of Arabic during colonization, and of Berber, and French after independence" (2002: 44).

Although it may be tempting to assume that a situation of crisis is almost inevitable in the context of complex multilingualism, scholars tend to avoid such shortcuts. The mosaic of languages present in the countries that constitute the Maghreb, the objectively large number of idioms and the numerous sacred or secular variations of the same official language, do not have to constitute an obstacle to meaningful communication between speakers. The intensity of the debate may instead be read as a specific protocol of encounter that leads to a symptomatic level of conflict.

The undisputable reality is the level of anguish, violence, or animosity that accompanies linguistic questions. Nonetheless, in his analysis of what he calls "Arabo-francophonie," Ahmed Moatassime reminds us of an obvious yet rarely mentioned point of comparison between the northern and the southern shores of the Mediterranean (2000). Europe, he argues, is a much less linguistically coherent ensemble than the countries located south of the Mediterranean: "L'unité linguistique sud-méditerranéenne est représentée par la langue arabe écrite dite classique, littérale ou même standard" [South of the Mediterranean, written, so-called classic, literal or even standard Arabic ensures linguistic unity] (2000: 53). Moatassime is quick to point out that this is not incompatible with a cultural diversity that accounts for the presence of Berber, French, Italian, Spanish, or Italian elements. But overall, he continues, the linguistic cohesion enjoyed by many of the Maghreb-Machrek countries is not matched in European countries. In other words, for him, arabisation (at least a certain type of arabisation) has always already occurred in spite of the long colonial period. And if we agree not to be deceived by the simple binary that opposes French and Arabic and to compare other territories besides North African nations, a more complex image emerges: "Le Nord-Méditerrannéen, tout d'abord, apparaît comme une tour de Babel infernale que l'absence d'une politique langagière claire et bien coordonnée rend de plus en plus inaccessible. Dans la seule Union européenne, on ne compte pas moins d'une douzaine de langues officielles et d'une quarantaine d'idiomes régionaux" [The northern shores of the Mediterranean appear like an infernal Tower of Babel made more and more inaccessible by the absence of a clear and well-coordinated language policy. In the European union alone, there are more than a dozen official languages and roughly forty regional idioms] (Moatassime 2000: 52). Yet, for European citizens, the issue of a common language has not (perhaps yet) become a source of daily cultural conflicts and passionate debates.[4] The stable and harmonious relationship between one nation and its national language (the French speak French, the Germans speak German) may well be an illusion that does not pass the test of close theoretical scrutiny, but as long as it continues to be a sustainable myth, the objective number of languages within a given geopolitical perimeter will not determine the intensity of the linguistic problem.

In France, questions about the role of French as a language will be perceived as relevant to the debate on "francophonie," that is, an international rather than a national reflection on the place of French as it exists beyond the borders of France. The issue is the global *rayonnement* [influence] of a national language outside its political boundaries. Within the hexagon, the issue of whether French should remain the only official language of the republic is never asked. When the encounter between different languages is envisaged, it is usually in the context of larger discussions of immigrant practices and diasporic cultures. Rather than being presented as a crucial issue of cultural relevance, the presence of multilingual speakers in France is analyzed as the consequence of her colonial past or as the specific problems of "minorities."[5] Internally, they will be defined by the relationship between regions and the center, between minority and majority.

When one language is clearly identified as the language shared by the community, and when historical reasons have turned most speakers into monolingual individuals,[6] the encounter takes place at the level of *what* is said. The issue of which tongue is spoken is not perceived as a choice, and it is not the precondition of misunderstandings or successful comprehension, meaningfulness, or a lack thereof. But when subjects are always aware of the possible use of several languages, when linguistic issues represent a constant layer of painful self-consciousness, then the question of what one means shifts from the units of language to the language itself. Success and failure, integration or exclusion, marginalization or belonging do not depend on what one says in one given language but on which language one chooses to conduct the encounter in. In other words, the performance of dialogue changes: the protocol (what one wants to achieve) and the decision about which language to speak are more obviously superimposed. Gill points out that strategic uses of Arabic or French are carefully thought through on a case-by-case basis. Neither language systematically stands for empowerment: what counts is the chemistry of the encounter between different subjects and different protocols and what the individual who chooses a language seeks to accomplish. Synthesizing work by other scholars, Gill writes:

> French is used with bureaucrats in order to impress, but also to ensure prompt and proper service, and to create a distance which erases all traces of familiarity (Riahi 1970: 132–134; Ounali 1970: 205). With the police, however, Bentahila noted that a Moroccan bilingual would naturally speak Arabic, in order to claim good citizenship and group loyalty, confirming the association of Arabic with national identity and authenticity—as well as compliance with official policy attempts to encourage "Arabisation." Similarly, when in doubt, i.e. with a complete stranger, Arabic would be used spontaneously, as an unmarked alternative, in case the interlocutor does not know French, or may have negative attitudes towards its use. In conversations among educated friends, on the other hand, French or French-Arabic mixture was often the norm (Bentahila 1983: 56–57). (Gill 1999: 127–28)

Note that throughout the passage, Gill makes no reference to what exactly is said in French, in Arabic, or in the mixture of French and Arabic that characterizes the last exchange. When nations have successfully imposed one national language and forgotten that it took aggressive policies to do so, such constraints and the resulting strategic decisions are muffled; speakers are not even aware that they could exist. Whereas the multiplication of instances when one has a "choice" of languages—or more exactly, the moment when having a "choice" becomes a systematic burden for the speaker—describes the type of situation when the relationship between the speaker and what is said becomes so complex as to fit the description of a constant, chronic, and often painful performative encounter.

How then, does literature account for this systematically complex decision? How do texts represent this type of cohabitation with language and the specific encounters that it produces? In the semiautobiographical novels or essays that the following pages focus on, the author, the narrator, the protagonists, and the reader are constantly reminded that a direct and conscious link exists between the language one decides to use and the result one wants to achieve, between the linguistic decision and the perceived identity that is immediately created. The choice always results in a level of comfort, discomfort, or even violence. In such situations, all occurs regardless of what is said, or, to put it differently, what constitutes the dialogue itself has already been mortgaged and can hardly be expected to change the parameters of the encounter. And as if the stakes were not high enough, the idea that subjects "choose" a language is highly problematic given the constraints that limit that so-called choice. Neither is it clear whether the result of that "choice" should be identified as "a" language. A protocol that mixes several linguistic systems is not always recognized as a system, let alone as legitimate languages by linguists or policy makers. To examine such questions, I will focus on two Moroccan authors, Abdelkebir Khatibi and Fouad Laroui, and on one of Djebar's latest essays. These texts present us with interestingly different perspectives on the encounter between and within languages as tactical "skirmishes."

Published in the 1980s, Khatibi's *Amour bilingue* [*Love in Two Languages*] both celebrates and mourns the condition of those unhappy but creative subjects whose bilingualism is the legacy of the French colonial empire. The long lyrical prose poem is the story of a doomed love affair between the narrator and a French woman. He speaks and writes in French and in Arabic, whereas his lover does not speak or understand his mother tongue. The relationship soon becomes an allegorical crucible in which the infinite tensions generated by the encounter between two languages are transformed into poetical prose. The performative encounter with the foreign-woman-as-language makes the poet understand that he can neither live with nor get rid of either side of his linguistic self. The concept of *bilingua* ["bilangue"] is his answer to the dilemma.[7] *Bilingua* is as different from bilingualism as Derrida's "monolingualism" is from the mastery of only one language. *Bilingua* is an unstable and elusive nonspace, the tension between two languages. It is another name for a performative encounter.

Khatibi's *bilingua* involves movement and dynamic tensions; it can never constitute the third phase in a dialectical system. The attempts at describing *bilingua* are never completely successful, and it is even more difficult to pinpoint moments when the narrator can actually be said to inhabit or to be that liminal vortex. "Je suis, se disait-il, un milieu entre deux langues: plus je vais au milieu, plus je m'en éloigne" (1983a: 10–11) [He told himself, I am a midground between two languages: the closer I get to the middle, the further I am from it] (1990: 4).

The unstable nature of such a relationship with *bilingua* accounts for the fact that French remains an object of repulsion and attraction but also of constant attention and fascination. "La bi-langue? Ma chance, mon gouffre individuel, et ma belle énergie d'amnésie" (1983a: 11) [*Bi-langue*? My luck, my own individual abyss, and my lovely amnesiac energy] (1990: 5). That level of involvement in what language is, how it works, how it traverses the speaking subject and transforms his or her identity is not a Lacanian perspective (although Khatibi's characters could be said to be the locus of a *ça parle* which summarizes the effects of the unconscious). What speaks through the subject is not an ultimately ahistorical and transnational unconscious. Intertextually, Jacques Lacan has already appeared when Khatibi dreams in *bilingua*, and his narrator is obviously aware that there is no simple possible adequation between agency and speech, between meaning and language. One of the principal differences, however, is that the unconscious is not only structured like *a* language (Lacan 1973: 23). In Khatibi's universe, the unconscious is caught in the web of the *French* language. What Lacan used to call *lalangue* is "dite maternelle, et pas pour rien dite ainsi" [said to be the mother tongue and not for no reason thus called] (1975: 126). In other words, in French, for Lacan, the mother tongue is not different from the mother's tongue. But for Maghrebi authors, imagining that the *ça* can be described and named in one language would already betray the detour that troubles the relationship between the words and the body.

It is not enough to remember that, for Khatibi, *ça* has an equivalent in a different alphabet. Even if we consider that an Arabic *ça* intervenes, the opposition between Arabic and French already ignores Berber languages or the presence of other European elements in spoken dialects. It also hides the deceptive simplicity of calling "Arabic" both the language of the Koran and the dialect of Algerian urban youths, or that of old women from Oujda, and the Arabic used by political leaders when they address the nation.

In her *Ces voix qui m'assiègent...en marge de ma Francophonie* [*Besieged by Voices...On the Margins of my Francophony*], Djebar proposes a different frame and a different definition of *bilingua*. At the beginning of the series of essays and intellectual biographical texts, she rereads her own *L'Amour, la fantasia* and reminds her readers that even three languages are not enough to describe the Maghreb: to Berber, Arabic, and French, it is necessary to add yet another language, "un quatrième langage: celui du corps avec ses danses, ses transes, ses suffocations" [a fourth language: that of the body, with its dances, trances, suffocations] (1999a: 14). But at the same time, the total sum of four languages is both reduced to two and further subdivided by the addition of another layer of complexity. Djebar points out that the multiplicity of idioms is also redoubled by a rarely made distinction between the spoken and the written word. Her essay insists that to be a Francophone voice is different from inhabiting the world of "Franco-graphy" (29).

The performative encounter with languages thus entails a constant awareness of their multiplicity, of what they do as well as what they say differently at the same moment. In Khatibi, the protocol leads to the emergence of *bilingua*, whereas in Djebar's *Ces voix* it is called an "entre-deux-langues" [in-between-two-languages](30).[8] What she proposes is to:

> Rester sur les marges d'une, de deux ou trois langues, frôler ainsi le hors-champ de la langue et de sa chair, c'est évidemment un terrain-frontière hasardeux, peut-être marécageux et peu sûr, plutôt une zone changeante et fertile, ou un *no man's land*, ou . . .
>
> En tout cas, c'est ce qui sépare, ce qui lie et divise à la fois, dans chaque langue, l'écrit et l'oral. (1999a: 30)
>
> [To stay on the margins of one, two or three languages, to brush against what's beyond language and flesh, that is of course a dangerous border-land, an unsafe swamp perhaps, or rather a changing and fertile land, or a *no man's land* or . . .
>
> At any rate, it is what separates, links and divides at the same time, within each language, the spoken and the written word.]

The encounter with (or rather the encounter that creates) that in-between space coincides with the emergence of what we could call the *langualized* writer/text, the Maghrebi equivalent of the Caribbean creolized author or novel. Or, to preserve the distinction that Edouard Glissant establishes between *créolité* and *créolisation* (1990: 104), we could say that such writers are in constant process of *langualization*.

What happens then, to the text itself, when writers have a "brush with," as Djebar puts it, *langualization*? Typically, the narrators and characters of these fictional or autobiographical tales are forever asking questions about the status of their language, its power or powerlessness. They are fascinated by the troubled encounter between the agent and the linguistic system. And because *langualization* tends to take place in a context that has already unleashed animosity and suspicion, it also makes a strong theoretical and political statement about the politics of language in general. The formula of what is performative about this encounter—the equivalent of the "I declare war" in the earlier models—becomes obvious after reading narratives in which a narrator comments on his or her own self-conscious relationship with words. This dynamic point of contact is always a multilayered series of confrontations between the subject and at least one language, but also between several languages and several types of languages.

In this context, Khatibi's *bilingua* and Djebar's *entre-deux-langues* constitute historical landmarks that formulate one possible script of encounter. But a third author of the diaspora will provide us with a slightly different protocol that clearly retains some of the elements of the other two systems, although I would argue that it adds new facets to the encounter between the Francophone author and his other languages of predilection. I suggest that, having internalized the possibilities and difficulties of *bilingua* or of the *in-between-two-languages*, contemporary authors are moving on and providing us with new models. Fouad Laroui, a writer and economist of Moroccan origin who currently resides in Amsterdam and writes in French, is a perfect representative of what can hardly be called a literary movement but rather a new manifestation of the encounter between the Maghrebi subject and his or her philosophy of multilingualism. Having earned university degrees in a scientific discipline that some clichés continue to view as incompatible with literary studies, Laroui publishes in the former *métropole* but works and resides in another European country where his talents as a writer and as a professional researcher are equally recognized. He is not one of the children of immigrants who grew up in the projects and is therefore expected to provide us with the insider's view of *banlieue* literature, nor is his trajectory comparable to that of his predecessors, such as Khatibi and Djebar. Laroui belongs to what literary history calls another generation. Although this seemingly evident notion deserves to be taken with a grain of salt (especially given the spatial discontinuities that affect all diasporic subjects), some of the implied consequences are worth accepting: both differences and similarities between authors have to be thought of in terms of a problematic genealogy and filiation. Like his elders, Laroui refutes the conventional definition of origin and legacy as a form of continuity, but the solutions adopted in his novels are slightly different. Both generations grapple with the issues of linguistic and cultural encounters but they do not come to the same rhetorical conclusions.

Laroui's performative encounter with language results in the articulation of alingualism rather than bi- or interlingualism. His protagonists are not so much torn between idioms as fundamentally deprived of one strong language of origin. Remarkably Laroui, who himself masters five languages, constantly writes about the seemingly improbable absence of any mother tongue.[9] Yet this is not described as a linguistic disaster: Laroui's work will most probably sound lighter and less tragic than Khatibi's or Djebar's. After all, the most perceptible and obvious difference between Laroui and the latter two authors could be summarized as a question of "tone," or perhaps of "atmosphere." That is, Khatibi's and Djebar's characters are often tortured souls, while Laroui's heroes are funny and self-mocking but self-assured. The three authors' relationship with linguistic issues has obvious if nuanced political implications, but in Laroui's writing the literary energy liberated by the other authors' lyricism is here converted into self-derision.[10]

No more than ten years have passed between the publication of Khatibi's *Love in Two Languages* and Laroui's 1999 *Méfiez-vous des parachutistes* [*Beware of Paratroopers*], and Djebar's essay came out one year after the latter. Yet, the authors' radically different treatment of the vexed linguistic issue suggests that a cultural gap has widened between two worlds. A cultural divide separates a first generation of colonized then decolonized Maghrebi intellectuals who started publishing around the time of the Algerian war and contemporary novelists who are renegotiating their conception of a globalized North African identity.

In *Beware of Paratroopers*, the first-person narrator has just accepted a position in Morocco after completing his higher education in France. He is called, or rather calls himself "Machin," which loosely translates as John Doe, although the French goes even further than the English equivalent: a "machin" is a nondescript thing, an object, and also the word used when one forgets someone's name (what's-his-name). Between "me" and "Machin," the encounter is deliberately nullified. His or her identity is not nonexistent, but it is negated by "my" forgetfulness and "my" unwillingness to make an effort to remember the name. The character who calls himself "Machin" deprives himself of both his father's and his mother's name. He is left with a simulacrum of generic identity that remains, however, quintessentially linked to the Francophone world. Our literary encounter with the narrator thus plays with the genre of the proper introduction and immediately questions the conventions of the first meeting with a stranger.

The text also begins with the story of an encounter between the hero and his country of origin whose representatives take the form of the immigration police and customs authorities. The first encounter occurs under the signs of rejection and fear. As Machin tries to cross the border to return "home," he is arrested and interrogated by frightening bureaucrats whose suspicion is aroused by his luggage full of books. The young student has brought back books by Jorge Luis Borges and Vladimir Nabokov whom the officers assume to be dangerous political leaders or terrorists. The obviously ignorant border patrol is hostile to books, and especially books written in French. By definition, literature is a threat, so when the police find a notebook on Emma Bovary in the student's suitcase, he suddenly becomes a suspect: "Le gabelou ouvrit le cahier d'un doigt méfiant. Holà! C'était plein de gribouillages et de chiffres inquiétants, il y avait même des textes, la subversion était possible" [The bureaucrat's suspicious finger flipped through the notebook. Whoa! Full of scribblings and daunting figures, there were even texts, subversion was a distinct possibility] (11).

This less than welcoming ceremony inaugurates a long and relentless series of catastrophic episodes. This is no triumphant reappropriation of a decolonized native land. Machin's adventures implicitly mock the stereotypical nostalgic immigrant dream of a return home. From the very first pages, Machin's relationship with "his" country is antagonistic, and this includes his own language or, rather, all the languages that are spoken and written in Morocco. His difficulties are due to the fact that he is constantly confronted by types of otherness and differences that make him a stranger, but within what we are tempted to call his "own" culture.

The enigmatic title alludes to one of the two main protagonists, the paratrooper, whose name is Bouazza and who represents everything that the narrator is not. He is also a sort of Moroccan alter ego that Machin does not understand but cannot eliminate either. Translating "parachutiste" by "paratrooper" underlines the potentially threatening shadows cast by the mysterious presence. In the colonial imaginary, the figure of the paratrooper brings to mind memories of horror and torture. But against that tormented historical backdrop, Laroui's "parachutiste" first appears as a harmless and silly parody of the terrifying and all-powerful colonial officer.[11] In this novel, the paratrooper is a grotesque character, an ambiguous historical or intertextual mystery. Whatever political authority he stands for seems deprived of any real power, and his role is purely decorative. When the two characters meet, the paratrooper was supposed to have landed on a soccer field during an official ceremony presented as futile and insignificant. He is apparently not even up to this purely figurative function. He has missed his mark and fallen far from the stadium, in the middle of an urban crowd, a useless and ridiculous puppet still attached to strings. This apparently meaningless chance encounter turns out to be a life-altering turning point for the narrator. As for the reader, he or she quickly realizes that the paratrooper is an allegory of sorts. He embodies a type of unavoidable fictive destiny that we could interpret as the tragic historical script. Literally fallen from the sky like an angel, he lands on Machin and moves in with him right away.

The strange couple is bilingual: Machin speaks French; Bouazza does not. Their interests are incompatible: Machin is into literature and sciences; Bouazza is mostly interested in soccer games. Machin is an atheist; Bouazza is religious. The former is individualistic, while the latter is defined by his relationship to the community. Machin is insecure and ill at ease in his new milieu; Bouazza is self-assured and authoritarian. The whole novel is the story of their difficult cohabitation, a tale about daily frictions and more or less serious conflicts. Bouazza slowly imposes or wishes to impose his opinions, which he treats as self-evident truths, as well as his own definitions of good cooking, proper hospitality, religious norms, and work ethics. His views on women and language are part of the package. The narrator never finds definitive and effective resistance tactics against Bouazza's relentless pressure, but he also refuses to betray his own values or sacrifice his own desires. The whole text is the story of a long negotiation between the two characters. Bouazza is no colonizer; he is not even the other but, instead, the narrator's mirror image of himself. The narrative revolves around the same unresolved issues of failed communication: it is a relentless accumulation of aborted dialogues. It is about fragile and dysphoric multilingualisms, precarious attempts at bridging widening gaps. Here, language is the site of misery and painful experiences. For all kinds of cultural, political, and linguistic reasons, the narrator is not at home in his own country or even house. The title sounds like a warning ("beware"), but it is not clear who is being warned.

As in *Love in Two Languages*, a fictional couple is the allegorical crucible where encounters are explored. Cultures and languages function like raw materials, the ingredients that enable subtle metamorphoses and radical transformations. But while Khatibi's lyrical and eloquent style is at the service of a sumptuous love story, Laroui's tone is on the side of parody and pastiche. The tragic bilingual and bicultural heterosexual couple is replaced by a chance encounter between two Moroccan males.

Like Khatibi, and like most postindependence Maghrebi writers, Laroui is acutely aware of belonging to at least two but often several linguistic universes. The relationship with language is impossible to consider separately from the narrator's exploration of colonial and postcolonial national identities. Like most Algerian or Moroccan writers, Laroui is fascinated by the function and definition of the so-called mother tongue, but his treatment of this potentially delicate topic is unusually witty and amusing. In *Beware of Paratroopers*, Laroui adds to the work of his prestigious literary ancestors. Since the inception of what is known as Francophone literature, rare is the author who has not always been haunted by the same fears and irritating doubts: is it desirable or even possible for a colonized subject to turn the encounter with language into a Trojan horse situation? To what extent is it realistic to hope that the colonizers' language can be dissociated from and used against their own political and cultural values? These questions are far from original, but no satisfactory or definitive answers have ever been provided. As early as 1948, in his preface to Leopold Sédar Senghor's anthology of black poets, Jean-Paul Sartre assumed that colonized writers would be forced to "destroy" the colonial language given that "l'oppresseur est présent jusque dans la langue qu'ils parlent" [the oppressors are present even in the language they speak] (1948: xx).

Negritude poets placed their hope in poetry, which remained their favorite literary tool: the words of poems, as Aimé Césaire puts it, were "miraculous weapons" (1946). Poetic language was expected to enable the writer to inhabit and bridge the "décalage léger et constant qui sépare ce qu'il dit de ce qu'il voudrait dire, dès qu'il parle de lui" [slight and constant gap opening between what he says and what he means as soon as he talks about himself] (Sartre 1948: xix). Maghrebi writers have always been more circumspect, and more than forty years later, among Francophone writers, the dream of resisting by means of literature or via a reappropriation of languages is neither confirmed nor completely abandoned. In most officially decolonized nations, the project of using European languages as a means of liberation remains haunted by doubts and fears of (self-) betrayal. In an article published in 2000, Ngugi wa Thiong'o concludes that "Europhonism" is a handicap rather than an asset in Africa.

In Khatibi's case, time seems to have brought on its share of disillusions and bitterness. In the preface to the second edition of his autobiography, *La Mémoire tatouée* [*My Tatooed Memory*], the author casts an amused glance on the unfulfilled ambitions of Francophone authors. A few years before conceptualizing his *bilingua*, Khatibi wrote, in French, that he no longer believed in the liberating potential of the French language even when authors are deliberately trying to speak or write against the grain of their colonizers' tongue:

> On soutenait avec légèreté que l'écrivain colonisé de langue française, en retournant sa rage contre le colonisateur, aurait pulvérisé—ou du moins défiguré—les lois de cette belle langue que j'aime. Rage illusoire: à citer, coup sur coup, l'apparent carnage syntaxique, la luxuriance lexicale, le redoublement du français par la langue maternelle de l'auteur. . . . Rien n'est moins sûr que ce crime imaginaire, rien n'est moins dérisoire que ce faux sacrilège. . . . La grande et magnifique loi de la toute langue est d'être indestructible. C'est bien elle qui assassine le poète et non l'inverse ainsi que le proclamait si naïvement l'écrivain maghrébin dit d'expression française. (1971: 12)

> [We used to insist, frivolously, that colonized Francophone authors could turn their rage against the colonizers and pulverize, or at least disfigure, the laws of that beautiful language that I love. Illusory rage: as they cite, back to back, the apparent syntactic carnage, the luxuriant vocabulary, the doubling of French by the author's mother tongue. . . . Nothing is less verified than that imaginary crime, nothing is less futile than that fake sacrilege. . . . The great and magnificent law of any language is that it is

indestructible. Language kills the poet and not the other way around in spite of what the so-called Maghrebi writers of French expression naively proclaimed.]

Khatibi critiques what he sees as the misguided hopes of his own adolescent years. Césaire, from a Caribbean perspective, recognized that he found it difficult—though not impossible—to express his "Martinican self" [moi Martiniquais] in French.[12] But while he attempted to "bend" [infléchir] language, Khatibi's vocabulary evokes much more violent encounters with words and linguistic laws. He talks about pulverizing and disfiguration, about rage and carnage. The virulence of the vocabulary reminds the reader that for the Maghrebi writer, the encounter between subjects and language prefigures or mirrors other types of bloody conflicts, including wars of decolonization. Even in his *Love in Two Languages*, where the metaphorical script of the encounter between two languages is a love story, *bilingua* is not a pacified or idealized third space. Although the protocol of encounter between the two lovers has nothing to do with "pulverization" or "disfiguration," the type of intermingling created by the relationship between the two languages is marred by morbidity and meaninglessness: sentences are "enlacées à mort: indéchiffrables" [intertwined to the death: undecipherable](1990: 4). The "to the death" is ambiguous or rather polysemic: Khatibi suggests, at the same time, that this type of encounter is fatal, but also that any attempt at severing the bonds thus created will be responsible for one of the parties' death.

The illusory aspect of the writer's rage is opposed, in Khatibi's text, to other less ambitious, but more tactically effective, little battles. War becomes guerilla and leads to punctual interventions that may well be pointless from a revolutionary point of view, although they do highlight the level of violence present in the inextricable situation. *La Mémoire tatouée* talks about "disfiguration" but also about "skirmishes" [escarmouches], though they are presented as the probably ineffective and chaotic tactics chosen by children who play in the streets. Here, language takes the form of graffiti, superimposed over political slogans. This relatively traditional oppositional tactic is called, by Khatibi, "l'escarmouche improvisée sur une affiche" [the improvised skirmish over a poster] (1971: 96). Even if the unique formulation treats the gesture like a work of art "improvised" by street artists, describing children involved in an "escarmouche" downplays the political significance of the statement. Khatibi clearly describes an oppositional tactic, but the choice of the word "escarmouche" allows the author to stay away from terms such as terrorism or pacification. Here, the writer does not appeal to his readers' emotions and maintains the presence of (linguistic) violence into the category of the containable, of the relatively nondangerous and short lived.

In Laroui's texts, what happens is both less than a revolutionary disfigurement and more than a skirmish. The encounter as "skirmish" does not take place in the streets but within a legitimized institutional space: the narrator's high school that he describes as "l'a-politique lycée Lyautey" [apolitical Lyautey high school] where French is presumably taught in an "apolitical" way (1999: 96). The name of the institution is a bit of an oxymoron already if we consider the strange proximity between Lyautey, whose name immediately takes us back to the time of the protectorate, and the adjective *a-politique*, which is invalidated by the historical reference.[13] The irony of the self-contradictory formula already contains the seed of the specific type of linguistic tactic that I am about to examine. The narrator's high school was not renamed after the end of the protectorate like so many streets or famous squares. After all, the renaming of public spaces after newly adopted national heroes is a commonplace official strategy. But as this whole story is about to show, the past is never erased; it is scribbled over, or, to choose another metaphor, haunted by the ghosts of dead (literary) rebels and (French) poets.

In a particularly amusing scene, Machin, then a young high school student, angers his teachers and the college's administration because he expresses, in French, something that he does not fully understand. He has written, in an essay, "J'appelle un chat un chat et Tomasini un voleur" [I call a cat a cat and Tomasini a thief] (96). He explains, in retrospect, that he was not at all trying to express any opinion, let alone a political one. He was, or so he believed, quoting a set phrase, something "très français homologué par l'Académie, la patine de l'âge, tout. . ." [a typically French [proverb], certified authentic by the Academy, by its antique patina and all that kind of thing. . .] (96). The narrator is apparently unaware that he is quoting a canonical author and making a political statement, as we are about to see.

Here, a mixture of amused skepticism and sarcastic self-criticism replaces Khatibi's lyricism and poetic virulence. Moreover, Khatibi's "illusory rage" becomes, in Laroui, self-deprecation and self-derision. The narrator is as interested in the encounter between languages as in the moments of disconnect within one language. He knows that his mastery of French, which, by any unself-conscious French native speaker's standard, would be considered flawless, contains zones of fuzziness and doubts. At times, he is no longer the subject who speaks a language; he is betrayed by a linguistic logic that he does not comprehend and that speaks through him. Like Khatibi, Laroui is very much aware of the limits of the type of necessary effort that wa Thiong'o calls "decolonizing the mind" (1986), but the difference between Laroui and Khatibi is that the former seems to succeed, at least to some extent, in troubling the encounter between subject and language, by pointing out the limits of the equation between (individual) powerfulness and (linguistic) knowledge. In Laroui's novels, characters often succeed by mistake.

The connection between the subject and the potentially adverse language is not renewed because the narrator bets on the liberating power of his words. The narrator's attitude towards the French language is not hostile, and he does not represent the process of learning as a form of collaboration with the enemy. He has no intention of waging a linguistic war or any notion that he could be using French as a weapon. And yet, in spite of an apparently peaceful protocol of encounter, incidents happen.

Generally speaking, Laroui's heroes are as disillusioned as Khatibi's narrator. They do not seem to hold much faith in their own ability to destroy the colonizer's tongue, and Machin is certainly not trying to achieve such a lofty political goal. Yet, we cannot help but notice that his studious and imitative use of language gets him into trouble. When he fails linguistically, when his sentences misfire, the standard of success against which he measures himself is not a political poster plastered on city streets but an essay, that is, an academic exercise codified from within the classroom. What the narrator triggers, however, goes well beyond the walls of the classroom, and, in a sense, affects the more powerful, not the supposedly ordinary, people in the streets; the director and the "censeur" (etymologically, "in charge of censorship") get involved. Something happens that shakes the neocolonial education system regardless of what the narrator actually tries to do. The narrator's dissident use of the French language is a miscalculation, an involuntary form of subversion.

When the narrator says: "J'appelle un chat un chat et Tomasini un voleur," the meaning of the words is obvious, but the meaningfulness of the sentence as a whole is not: the encounter between the words is explosive. Here, the misfiring consists in hitting the target by mistake, in discovering that there was a target whose existence he did not even suspect. Having learned quotations and remembered turns of phrases that he treats as bits of academic knowledge, he uses them without understanding that they have retained a strong political power of disturbance.

Like a good student, he quotes his sources—a practice that would normally guarantee his protection from any accusation of wrongdoing. He remembers finding the phrase in an old issue of *Le Canard Enchaîné*. To him, the words seem harmless, traditional, and banal. The trouble is that the narrator's peaceful and happy encounter with the quotation is based upon a double layer of ignorance. At the most basic level, he misidentifies the genre of the quoted material. He thinks it is a proverb, an unsigned tidbit of popular wisdom that draws its authority from its status as an anonymous quotation. Proverbs are repeated; their anonymous authors are not quoted. But neither is the absence of signature—a deliberate game of hide-and-seek, whereas in Laroui's text, the meaning of the words and their performative accusations will cut across the categories of author, of genre, and of national language and culture in which the sentence is embedded.

In this case, the "proverb" in question, like a set of nested Russian dolls, is constructed of embedded quotations and intertextual references. Here, the narrator makes a second mistake: he never identifies the reference to Boileau's first satire. Even if "to call a cat a cat" is (apparently) not tendentious, the end of the sentence about Tomasini becomes an act of one-upmanship. Machin, however, does not acknowledge the fact that *Le Canard Enchaîné* was already transforming Rolet, Boileau's *fripon* [crook] into Tomasini.[14] Unlike his supposedly naïve narrator, Laroui probably remembers very well that the first satire talks about the relationship between language and politics, between naming and honesty, but also between living among the powerful and the necessity to choose words carefully. In Boileau's text, the poet Damon has decided to leave Paris because he can no longer bear to "vendre au plus offrant mon encens et mes vers" [sell his verse and incense to the most generous bidder] (1966: 14). He continues, famously, and somewhat hypocritically: "Je suis rustique et fier, et j'ai l'ame grossiere. Je ne puis rien nommer, si ce n'est par son nom. J'appelle un chat un chat, et Rolet un fripon" (1966: 14) [I'm Rustic, Stout, and some may think me Rude / I can't call a Thing but by it's [sic] Name, / Or think that to Describe is to Defame: / I only speak the Truth, what wou'd you have? / A Cat's a Cat and a Rolet is a Knave](1712: 141–42). The quotation is famous enough to function as a sort of proverb, and we may even suspect that Laroui has read about Boileau's first satire in his textbooks.[15]

What is the connection, then, between Laroui's narrator and the first satire? The character claims to have found his "proverb" in *Le Canard Enchaîné*, which makes him a reader of satirical modern prose. The story is that of a poet, tired of fawning on the powerful, who explains his disgust for his position in order to stop lying to and flattering the prince. And he very specifically links the desire to leave Paris to his own conception of language: pride goes together with rusticity and with a plain (and supposedly more honest) referentiality of language.

What I find important here is that Laroui's character does not even claim to use the exact same tactic. His blissful fictional ignorance allows Laroui to continue to use a language that is far from "rustic," while invoking the possibility for the naïve writer to criticize the literary establishment and its connection to political power. Boileau's political position and frontal attack against his contemporaries haunt the relationship between the narrator and the French language, but even the ghost is changed by the encounter. Boileau's poet implicitly questions authority but, paradoxically, his belief in simple referentiality is modified when it is imported into Laroui's text through a complicated system of embedded allusions and quotes that turn the plain language imperative into much more sophisticated and postmodern literary strategies. What speaks through the narrator is the possibility to rebel against the way in which literature is institutionalized. And the ghostly encounter is both reinforced and framed by the fact that the quote is well known, but kept at a distance by

Machin's ignorance of the kind of power he is wielding. Paradoxically, a plea for honest referentiality that accepts the risk of brutal *ad hominem* accusations becomes a covert guerrilla attack whose diegetic author cannot be blamed for anything. Laroui, as the author, can be said to be the agent of this complicated and duplicitous superposition of tactical moves. He places the young student in the position of someone who defies innocently and turns him into the clumsy opponent who succeeds without even being aware of it. The labyrinthine connection between the political point and the status of the so-called "proverb" does not pacify the encounter but also does not make Boileau the unique model.

Not only is the political point of Boileau's text lost in quotation, so to speak, but the narrator demonstrates unwillingly that language is not pacified by the series of repetitions. When the narrator learns—and it is a dangerous lesson—that quotations are always already quotations of quotations, it also means that no pure (literary) origin will protect him from the potentially violent cultural scripts that lurk within the canon. Not only does he make a generic mistake when he crosses the line between proverb and authored quotation, but he also does not take into account the possibility that previous levels of mediation and manipulation—that is, previous protocols of encounter—have modified the original quotation. *Le Canard's* gesture of appropriation had a deliberately nonconciliatory purpose. The possibly obscure reference to Boileau is less significant than the polemical charge. Once again, the force of the genre eludes the narrator, and it does not dawn on him that a political and satiric paper such as *Le Canard* would make it a habit to transform literary expressions into war machines or at least moments of "skirmish."

Le Canard's ambition is to do what the young Moroccans chased by paratroopers did to colonialist posters: within the quotation, "Tomasini" is an intruder, the equivalent of graffiti on the walls. Here, linguistic guerilla warfare includes slight distortions and additions (rather than disfiguration and destruction). The narrator did not understand that literary citations can be aggressive; he assumes that quoting French literature is respectable because he is taught to respect or even sacralize literature in general. But remarkably, that type of ignorance does not prevent him from using it. It blinds him to its effectiveness.

The narrator misidentifies the border, within language and within that historic phrase, between what is set and what is not. The structure can be reused at will; it has the flexibility and plasticity that our everyday perception grants to a mother tongue. That is, we tend to assume that language will be the neutral tool that we put to use to express what we think of as our ideas and opinions. But the stubborn reemergence of a politically charged allusion in the literary quotation suggests that this confidence is at least exaggerated. The narrator thinks that he is quoting—that is, repeating without any personal intervention—words that in reality reveal a point of view.

While Khatibi presents protagonists whose grandiose and heroic dreams of "pulverizing" the colonizer's language are thwarted by the reality of colonial regimes, Laroui's child discovers that the opposite is true. Speakers who are not trying to make a political point, who make language mistakes, sometimes discover by chance the margin of latitude where ideological graffiti can be added to literary quotes that were themselves, originally, political interventions. The narrator's use of the French language can stir trouble in spite of his own supposedly apolitical intentions, because his own definition of what language is or does cannot include the element of performativity that is at work in this context: a verbal "skirmish" (escarmouche) is a political act even if no sudden change of regime is involved.[16] Khatibi's heroes fail to use language against the oppressor. In Laroui's novel, a linguistic act that perceives itself as imitative and therefore relatively submissive reaches its target.

Immediate consequences ensue: "Emoi dans l'a-politique lycée Lyautey. On me convoque, on me fait attendre dans l'antichambre du censeur" [Crisis in the apolitical Lyautey high school. I am summoned and made to wait in the principal's antechamber] (96). In response to the linguistic skirmish, the system performs a ritual ceremony that serves to criminalize an individual and mark the existence of a transgression.

But the criminal in question plays a well-known role: he follows a script written for the messenger that carries a letter without knowing what it contains. Within the economy of the text as a whole, Laroui's narrator is made to be the bearer of a cultural memory that excludes him. And just as he does not know that "to call a cat a cat" is qualitatively different from calling someone who exists "a crook," he apparently fails to identify the last name Tomasini as a reference to a contemporary politician. Another generic mistake occurs: he treats "Tomasini" as part of a set phrase.

The narrator explains to us that he did not know that he was referring to a real person: "Tomasini, aucune notion du quidam. . . . Homme de parti, semble-t-il" [Tomasini, no idea who he might be. . . . A politician apparently] (97). The minimalist development and the word "apparently" suggest that the character's historical significance is not even worth revealing or that it continues to be treated as a difference that does not make a difference. Even when the rector insists, as it were, that he should be invited to this exchange on the power of words and on the politics of language, the young Machin and his adult counterpart disregard the hint. The real Tomasini is reduced to the shadowy absence of the excluded third.

The narrator's indifference has two opposite yet compatible effects. Machin excludes Tomasini from the realm of cultural relevance in a gesture quite comparable to what happens when he gets excluded from the cultural discussion as the bearer of an incomprehensible message. Therein lies his vengeance and his moment of triumph. But the fact that the excluded victim is made to look unimportant also preserves the tone of the encounter between the speaker and language as a potential weapon. This is no war, just a relative misunderstanding or *mésentente*. Tomasini's insignificance as a real person and his significance as the place of the misunderstanding reveals the unheroic nature of Machin's original gesture and, at the same time, the potentially devastating effect of the tactic. The narrator's lack of interest in the object of satire preserves the political innocuousness of this criminalized linguistic gesture. It remains an act of unconscious rebellion, a failed nontactic.

From within the narrative, as a diegetic narrator, the encounter remains relatively peaceful. Apparently pardoned by the authorities, the student does not seem to have derived any pleasure from discovering the innocently subversive value of his disastrously inappropriate quotation. And even though he was at the origin of a performative encounter, he was not a good witness of what happened. He did not understand what was at stake.

His victory is paradoxically inscribed in the recipient's response to his use of language. The principal cannot officially sanction the student, but his reaction shows that he correctly understands the performative power and potential threat of such linguistic encounters: "Il s'éloigna. Je l'entendis marmonner: 'Où ça va, ça, où ça va. . .'" [He walked away and I heard him mutter to himself: "Where is it all going, where it is all going . . . "] (97). Just as the young hero had carefully quoted *Le Canard Enchaîné*, the narrator meticulously quotes the principal's curious and ambiguous formulation: the *ça* could include the overall situation in Morocco *and* the teenager himself (in which case, there is more than a discrete note of contempt in the principal's treating him like a generic nonentity). But the *ça* might also remind the reader of the force of the (political) unconscious that manifests itself by circumventing the subject's supposedly apolitical agency. In spite of the protagonist's supposedly submissive use of language, something rebelled. The text does not decide whether it is the teenager's riotous political unconscious that found, in language, a way of expressing itself, or if language, in spite of the speaker's lack of pugnacity, found a way to warn the colonizers that an era is about to end. Here, the performative encounter amounts to the expression of an anticolonialist warning by the colonizer, in spite of himself, as a response to the statement uttered by a colonized subject whose linguistic agency is not involved in the skirmish.

Maghrebi writers' love-hate relationship with the French language is not only due to the colonial past but also to the connection between the idealized figure of the mother and the notion of mother tongue. At the point where the history of decolonization meets childhood memories and sexual difference, powerful effects are unleashed. For Khatibi, the mother tongue is often used as the allegory of the humiliated nation, which assumes that the reader is willing to feminize the native tongue and to confuse the mother and the language of origin. Often, his lyricism hides such ideological slippages, and the mother tongue is naturalized as the mother's tongue. Laroui, on the other hand, changes the parameters of that discussion and invites us to reformulate the terms of the classic Maghrebi encounter with the mother and the tongue. Just as the student unwillingly sabotages the comfortable routine of cultural assimilation, the story that Laroui tells about strange forms of language acquisition troubles the definition of the mother tongue and the space of the maternal in the son's life and language.

Halfway through *Méfiez-vous des parachutistes*, a long digression about language and the mother tongue clarifies the author's position. The tone does not change, but the plot recedes into the background and is replaced by an almost theoretical exposé about the role of language. For the reader, the effect is one of disruption, but the type of embedded narrative that we have here is not immediately identifiable. This is not a parable or a story used as illustration or one of those highly recognizable slippages à la *One Thousand and One Nights*. Laroui effectively breaks down the implicit border between lecturing and storytelling, between linguistics and narratology. Readers who notice that this more theoretical passage appears in the middle of the novel will perhaps conclude that the author's fascination with language explains the centrality of this more academic portion of the novel.

What is original at this point is obviously not Laroui's interest in the way language works. After all, moments of self-referential analysis about how the writer relates to his or her own tools of communication and language of publication are frequent in all literatures and are almost unavoidable junctions in postcolonial texts. They have become a predictable, if not mandatory, generic ingredient of diasporic and migrant literatures so that one of the common denominators among all the authors studied in this book is their acute awareness of how language and history have conspired to make it impossible for them not to reflect on the encounter.

Not only does Laroui's *Méfiez-vous des parachutistes* resonate with Khatibi's *Love in Two Languages*, but it is also the short and humorous counterpart of such books as Dejbar's *Ces voix qui m'assiègent* and Derrida's *Monolingualism of the Other* with its anguished interrogations. Taken together, all these texts form a collective and diverse manifesto that both inaugurates and belongs to a unique transnational and postcolonial literary history and theory.

Laroui's novels and short stories document a series of unhappy episodes that expose the constant violence present in his encounter with language. The result is a sense of perpetual discomfort, but unlike Khatibi, Laroui usually converts this malaise into frictional and fictional humor. He stays away from authoritarian pronouncements, and his linguistic homelessness creates a level of uncertainty that makes dogmatism impossible. A striking formulation of his uneasiness stands out in the middle of the eleven-page manifesto, a slogan-like declaration that I propose as Laroui's critical signature, a literary logo of sorts:

"je n'ai pas de langue maternelle [. . .] Je n'ai que des secondes langues" [I do not have a mother tongue [. . .] only second languages" (1999: 90). The sentence is constructed like a typically paradoxical Derridean formula, and readers of *The Monolingualism of the Other* may hear echoes of the famous "Je n'ai qu'une langue, ce n'est pas la mienne" (1996: 13) [I only have one language; it is not mine] (1997b: 1). And like Derrida's claim, Laroui's statement is surprising because it seems to deny the obvious: how is it possible not to have a mother tongue? Is he playing on words? Is it possible that the narrator never made contact with a language he can describe as a "mother tongue" because he never had a mother? In Djebar's short story "Annie et Fatima," Fatima, the little girl, has forgotten the mother's tongue just as the narrator herself has forgotten the grandmother's tongue; but how is it possible not to have ever had a mother tongue to lose in the first place? Even if an individual were a biological and therefore linguistic orphan, would he or she not have been exposed, as a child, to at least some sort of language, be it a vernacular system or a spoken dialect not adequately recognized by the academy?

On the one hand, the idea of the mother tongue belongs to a type of discourse that privileges and naturalizes origins, and we all know how problematic such formations are. Any migrant discovers, sooner or later, that a simple return to pure origins is an elusive and illusionary dream. "On ne revient jamais chez soi, on retombe dans le cercle de son ombre" [We never go back home, we fall back into the circle of our shadow], as Khatibi puts it (1971: 157). Yet the demystification of the mother tongue has always been less important than a mourning of its loss in the writings of postcolonial (and especially Maghrebi) authors. Laroui's encounter with his own past cannot altogether bypass the force of grand narratives that tend to imagine (and idealize) the "mother tongue" as the language (or one of the languages) that the colonizer has repressed and silenced, refused to teach, refused to learn, and refused to valorize. In other words, a "return" to the mother tongue can easily be interpreted as a decolonizing gesture in and of itself, especially if the desire to learn or rediscover is accompanied by a simultaneous desire to claim ownership and idiosyncratic use of the European language to which the colonial or neocolonial regime has exposed the whole country.

Laroui parts with that tradition; he refuses the role of the pioneer. He does not seek to inaugurate a new multilingual Maghrebi literary era, and the tone of his book is in no way comparable to the triumphant opening of *Eloge de la Créolité* [*In Praise of Creoleness*] of 1989. Laroui's narrator does not construct a collective subject, a "we" that could declare "nous nous proclamons Créoles" [we proclaim ourselves Creoles] (Bernabé et al. 1993: 13/75). His ambition is not to create a hybrid language of encounter or even to celebrate a spoken language and describe the encounter between and within tongues as a form of "creolization."

When he decides to give us an example of the language that he does speak and calls "Morrocan," he is, curiously, at the same time judgmental and capable of criticizing his own negative appreciation:

> le marocain n'existe pas. Ce que ma mère, et quelques milliers d'âmes parlaient dans ma jeunesse était une ratatouille de mots arabes, berbères, français, plus quelques mots d'espagnols et des *ad hoc* pour faire nombre. Linguistes et nationalistes me mouchent: ignorantissime! C'est bien d'une langue qu'il s'agit. (91)

> [Morrocan does not exist. What my mother and a few thousand souls used to speak when I was a child was a ratatouille of Arabic, Berber, and French words, plus a few words of Spanish and ad hocs to round it all up. Linguists and nationalists scold me: Ignoramus! It is a full-blown language indeed.]

His knowledgeable comments both on his experience and on the status of the linguistic system position him at the cusp of an ongoing debate. He is the point of mediation between two radically different points of view which we can suddenly appreciate as the two sides of the same coin: the language of his youth was always already a hybrid combination rather than the pure pre- or noncolonial vernacular native tongue that would have to be rehabilitated. For this reason, it may not be useful to insist that today, and since the independence, the linguistic situation is catastrophic.

Laroui's reference to scholars who scold him is an amused and amusing exercise in self-critique. The scene prevents readers from interpreting the beginning of the comment as an ignorant and alienated neocolonial dismissal. The deliberately provocative statement is an example of performative encounter to the extent that when the narrator says "Moroccan does not exist," he carves the space of an as yet nonexistent entity by naming it. In the international dictionary of languages, "Moroccan" is not listed. In Laroui's text, the function served by that nonexistent language is implicitly recognized as necessary. Or, to be more accurate, an unanswered question lingers about the asymmetrical historical situation that results in the fact that the French speak French whereas some (decolonized) nations, such as Algeria or Morocco, do not have a national language. Laroui's statement is not dismissive and naïve. Even if he implicitly agrees that some experts will consider his position ignorant, it is not innocent that he should place the "linguists" and the "nationalists" (who celebrate Moroccan as a language) in the same camp.

Laroui's spokesperson, Machin, becomes more credible when he stages his own funny incompetence and demonstrates how impossible it is to translate, for the French reader, his pathetic attempt at Moroccan speech. After a long and funny tirade in which he complains, in French, against his roommate's linguistic intransigence, he admits that what he has just told us has no real equivalent as a dialogue because no language exists between him and Bouazza. Therefore, he can only tell us about his grievances. A strange moment of pre-terition concludes that passage and implicitly cancels out his complaint.

> Voici ce que j'aurais voulu dire au parachutiste: Mais en quelle langue? Je pense tout cela dans celle de Voltaire, mais les seuls mots de français que Bouazza comprenne sont "penalty, corner, parking et strip-tease." Alors j'essaie de m'expliquer dans son patois. Je cherche mes mots et je n'arrive qu'à baragouiner quelque chose comme:
>
> —Moi pas très content. Toi t'en aller. (77)

> [That is what I would have wanted to tell the paratrooper. But in which language? I think all this in Voltaire's tongue but the only French words that Bouazza understands are "penalty, corner, parking and strip-tease." So, I try to talk in his patois. I cannot find my words, and all I can blurt out is something like:
>
> —Me not very happy. You go.]

Suddenly, Machin's splendid mastery of Voltaire's language is perceived as a most relative art since the "translation" of what is said in Moroccan projects a pidgin effect into a language that is not French. Linguistic incompetence is now on the side of the educated Francophone speaker. The passage is interesting from a point of view of literary history, because it reverses a topos that saturates Beur literature, whether or not it is treated in a comic or tragic mode. Most immigrants' children discover, when they go to school, that their developing bilingualism is negated, interpreted as ignorance. In *Georgette!*, Farida Belghoul's heroine brings to school a notebook on which her father has written a letter in Arabic on what he considers to be the first page. But that sign remains invisible to the teacher for whom that page is the last one and who is incapable of imagining the existence of a different type of alphabet (1986).

Rare are the texts, though, that reverse such a situation and force European readers to appreciate the relativity and fragility of their privilege. Machin, who exposes the limits of his own linguistic competence in the presence of a supposedly uneducated and ignorant Bouazza, puts himself in a fictional position that denounces all forms of triumphant Francophonie as a narrow-minded superiority complex.[17]

And yet, Laroui does not create a character who will help him idealize some true and more authentic definition of a popular vernacular language. Bouazza himself is ruthlessly mocked. He is not bilingual, or rather his form of bilingualism is a parody of competence. His French is reduced to a disparate and small collection of words of English origin and the only Francophone cultural traces left in his vocabulary have nothing to do with what we imagine as a preindependence republican canon. The influence of "France" has little to do with Voltaire or Rousseau: "les seuls mots de français que Bouazza comprenne sont 'penalty, corner, parking et strip-tease'" (77).[18] The implicit denunciation of Bouazza's hobbies will sound slightly elitist, but it also functions as a satire of "pure" languages that could be opposed to impure or adulterated dialects. The implications of the distinction are all the more important as the author is obviously not keen on idealizing Bouazza's language. Unlike many linguistic observers, Laroui does not seem to put his hopes in the development of local mother tongues.

Moroccan is a corrupt and bastardized language that no one writes. It has always been what the author calls a "magma." Here, he only retains the derogatory connotations of chaotic and unproductive mixture (for it is important to keep in mind that even that seemingly self-explanatory metaphor is ambivalent). For the Créolistes, the image of the "magma" links linguistic *métissage* to vitality and revolutionary power. It is attached to the symbolic force of the Caribbean volcano and intertextually is linked to the type of volcanic poetry that Césaire called "Pelean."[19] For Laroui, it is a "ratatouille," an obviously negative version of the melting pot, but also a symptom of the author's determination to avoid pathos. The pages on the narrator's linguistic difficulties are serious and potentially depressing, but they retain the sarcastic and self-critical tone that characterizes the rest of the novel and thus contrasts with other North African writers' tendencies towards lyricism and poetry. Calling his mother's tongue a "ratatouille" refuses the tenderness and poetical delicacy with which Djebar describes it: "toute en oralité, en hardes dépenaillées" [all orality, in its tattered rags] (1995b: 245). Laroui does not idealize the spoken tongue and does not allegorize his encounter with language. His "I do not have a mother tongue" is not so much a redefinition of what a language is, but a performative encounter with the mother who is relieved of the burden of incarnating the mother tongue.

In his fiction, Laroui invents a story where the mother tongue and the mother's tongue (or tongues) are different because the language that she speaks does not precede learning. Paradoxically, here, the mother is going to learn the mother's or mother tongue, redefining the distinction between the two concepts. The mother, in this text, is capable of learning languages as well as transmitting them. Her legacy is not simply passed on like a gene or inculcated like a traditional custom. In this novel, the mother is not simply, and contingently, the subject who happens to be the child's only access to culture. In a reversal of the cliché according to which the mother is less educated than her children, Laroui paints the portrait of a character whose mother tongue is not the language that the mother teaches her children but that the children have taught the mother.

Encerclée par sept enfants qui ne parlaient que le français, ma mère n'eut
d'autre choix que d'en apprendre les rudiments. Elle finit même par lire
des romans. Plus précisément, elle lut un roman, toujours le même, en
plusieurs tomes. Il s'agissait de *Jalna*, d'un certain, d'une certaine, d'une
à vraie dire très incertaine Mazo de la Roche. Lorsqu'elle avait fini le
dernier tome (il y en avait au moins dix), elle recommençait par le tome 1.
Son français devient correct. (1999: 91)

[Surrounded by seven children who only spoke French, my mother had
no other choice but to learn its rudiments. Eventually, she even read
novels, or, to be accurate, she read one novel, always the same one, in
several volumes. She read *Jalna*, by a certain, or rather very uncertain
Mazo de la Roche. When she was done with the last volume (there were
at least ten of them), she would go back to volume one. Her French
became acceptable.]

The narrator's mother resembles the "autodidact" who systematically
moves from book to book on library shelves in Jean-Paul Sartre's *La Nausée*
(1938). Laroui's female counterpart of that strange and slightly pathetic character does not even fetishize the (Latin) alphabet, an illusory promise of ex-
haustivity and fake universality that speakers of Arabic are bound to relativize.
Instead, she limits her reading list to one single noncanonical novel, which she
reads over and over again, under her son's half-admiring, half-tenderly amused
gaze. And even if Laroui is obviously skeptical of the mother's choice (Mazo de
la Roche does not become a new mandatory reference), he does recognize that
her efforts are successful. The mother is not silent; she is not alienated and
excluded by her seven children's bilingualism. We may interpret her son's ob-
servation that her French becomes acceptable as a political statement. After all,
the mother's self-teaching practices could be a satire of traditional language
acquisition methods as well as of the administrative authorities that count on
governmental decrees and policies to impose a language on a nation. To emerge
as the mother who can speak to her sons as an equal, she must learn what
becomes a new shared tongue rather than impose upon them the language of
their origin.

I suggest that this character represents a new type in our horizon of verisimilitude. If one of the possible ways of writing literary history is to identify
plausible archetypes or at least to make lists of plausible fictional figures, we
could connect the character of the autodidact mother to the little girl of "Annie
and Fatima." In both texts, the mother tongue and the child's tongue are in-
verted and mixed, and while Laroui's vision is perhaps less ambitious (the new
language is not Berber—that continues to suffer from extreme marginalization), it is more optimistic (the mother's linguistic competence goes beyond the

unique sentence that Djebar's woman manages to recite). In Laroui's text as in Djebar's short story, what matters is the fact that love and the desire to set up a linguistic encounter come first. The choice of language does not come first; it is indistinguishable from the protocol of the encounter that will create a mother-as-equal. Implicitly, Laroui's novel thus criticizes language policies that make the decision to speak Arabic rather than French as the consequence of a constraining governmental imperative. As linguists have already lamented many times, such an authoritarian attitude does little for the language that it is supposed to promote:

> les autorités ne manifestent aucune préoccupation pédagogique, aucun souci de valoriser l'arabe en profondeur, par la recherche et la réflexion. . . . la loi sur l'arabisation ne va pas dans ce sens . . . elle impose une langue alors qu'il convient de la faire aimer. (Grandguillaume 1997)

> [Unfortunately, the authorities have no interest in pedagogy nor in a thorough revalorization of Arabic through research and critical thought. . . . the new Arabisation law does not go in that direction. . . it is forcing a language on people when the sensible thing to do is to persuade them to love it.]

Laroui's demystification of the equivalence between mother tongue and mother's tongue enables him to refuse a systematic and problematic mythologization of the maternal figure. Most of the famous Maghrebi writers who belong to the first (post)colonial generation tend to draw ambiguous and contradictory portraits that both idealize a larger-than-life allegorized mother but also trap her within the confines of a golden cage.[20] In Laroui's book, a Moroccan mother who reads the same novel over and over again owes her knowledge of French to her own determination and to her admittedly unorthodox language acquisition method. No colonial republican school can take credit for her education but, on the other hand, she will not be made to stand for the picture of archaic traditionalism or supposedly more authentic cultural norms if that norm signifies illiteracy and ignorance of the son's language.

Intertextually, this character is the negative mirror image of another Moroccan mother. In Driss Chraïbi's *La Civilisation ma mère* [*Mother Comes of Age*], French words are literally dirty, and her linguistic dogmatism is expressed through domestic cleansing rituals.

> J'allais me laver la bouche avec une pâte dentifrice de sa fabrication. Non pour tuer les microbes. Elle ignorait ce que c'était—et moi aussi, à l'époque (microbes, complexes, problèmes. . .) . Mais pour chasser les relents de la langue française que j'avais osé employer dans sa maison devant elle. (1970: 16)

[I would go and wash my mouth with a toothpaste of my mother's fabrication. Not for killing microbes. Mother did not know what such
things were all about. Neither did I at that time (microbes or complexes
or problems. . .). But I followed orders to cleanse away the remnants of
the French language which I dared to use inside of her house, and right in
front of her to boot.] (1984: 12)

Machin's mother cannot and will not fall back on original linguistic certain-
ties, but her strength comes from her autonomy, from the fact that she is not
completely disempowered by the other language. *Mother Comes of Age*, like
Beware of Paratroopers, is a comedy, but in Laroui's book, the narrator does
not make fun of the mother's antagonistic relationship to technical progress.
Chraïbi's mother is baffled by the radio and the telephone. She does not understand the concept of a telephone number, and she suspects supernatural powers
to be behind new technologies. But she is not in awe of technology: her refusal
to abide by simple instructions both defamiliarizes the objects that stand for
Western civilization and makes her appear a bit stubborn and comically naïve.

In Khatibi's work, the mother and the mother's tongue are both idealized,
which makes it almost impossible to distinguish between the mother tongue
and the mother's tongue. Both the mother and her language are presented as an
indistinguishable whole, a sacred duality. The son worships this double figure
and, tragically, he constantly betrays it. When he chooses to speak or write
another language, he takes it for granted that he cheats on both the mother and
the mother's tongue, and the reader is expected to understand the nature of his
guilt. That is, he is unfaithful to the mother to whom he prefers another
woman, a rival.

The obviously problematic consequence of Khatibi's model is that he femi-
nizes the mother's tongue and forces us to envisage the encounter between the
subject and his language as a heterosexual love affair between the man-speaker
and the woman-language. But the advantage of this metaphorical system is to
constitute a powerful evocation of a protocol based on betrayal and guilt that
can be articulated in the absence of any specific reference to what is said. No
matter how the subject uses French, no matter what he says in French, the fact
that he associates the other's language with the mother's rival leads to a permanent state of malaise.

In *La Mémoire tatouée*, he writes that French is a "belle et maléfique
étrangère" [beautiful and malevolent stranger] (1971: 13); in *Love in Two
Languages*, he imagines that the price to pay for the mother's betrayal is a sort
of madness, of panic, or more exactly, of "affolement," that is, literally, a state
of permanent movement towards madness, a becoming-madness. Like creolization, which, unlike *créolité*, is not a new identity but a constant process of
becoming and metamorphosis, "affolement" is never stable. It is a process of

horrification that leads the subject to the edge of madness. Like a mythical form of punishment, a state of Promethean disgrace, "affolement" never ends and has no cure. Both lovers suffer from this chronic pain, which brings them together and separates them at the same time:

> Chacun de nous souffrait de sa langue maternelle, au seuil de l'affolement. Et peut-être celle qui prend la place de la mère doit devenir folle. Rendre la France folle fut le rêve d'une enfance humiliée, et être séduit par une mauvaise mère fut encore plus terrible. Je fus ce témoin, et ce qui souffrait en moi témoigne pour lui, dans toutes les langues du monde. (1983a: 61)

> [Each of us suffered from our mother tongues, on the threshold of panic. And perhaps the language which takes the mother's place should go mad. To drive France mad was the dream of a humiliated childhood, and being seduced by a bad mother was even worse. I was the witness and that which suffered in me is its own witness, in every language in the world]. (1990: 52)

As Hassan Wahbi beautilly puts it, for Khatibi, "L'exercice de la langue étrangère est un amour sans retour" [The use of the foreign language is like unrequited love] (1995: 161).

Laroui's metaphorical universe, on the contrary, is not obsessed with the expression of pain and malaise, although such emotions are not excluded from the protocol of encounter with French. In his stories, the distance between the speaking subject and the mother's tongue is not defined as treason or betrayal. Consequently, the distinction between the mother's tongue and the mother tongue is preserved, which makes room for a different view of what language is and what language can do. If Khatibi searches for the third space between two languages and between two women, Laroui's narrators take language outside of the mother and lover, home and abroad dyads. Here the protocol of encounter is a sort of humorous storytelling that manages to go beyond the crippling alternative between mother's tongue and mother tongue. The third space of predilection is the margin of latitude that opens up a comic rather than poetic space of linguistic creativity and freedom.

In *Beware of Paratroopers*, for example, and other texts such as *La Fin tragique de Philomène Tralala* (2003), the mother tongue is simply nonexistent. This is never presented as a betrayal of the mother but as homage to another type of woman-mother, or to what the mother could have and could become if she were not petrified by a deleterious form of worship. In Laroui's book, the absence of a native tongue is not interpreted as a betrayal of the mother figure. It is an opportunity to critique, very gently, what can be oppressive and reactionary in that vision of the maternal: an invisible layer of reactionary and antifeminist thinking can easily hide under the ostentatious request that the mother's status remain stable. Her demand that the son not change participates in her own petrifaction. In Laroui, the mother changes, evolves. She is not paralyzed by the immense respect that the paratrooper insists on lavishing upon her. In fact, as Laroui's novel suggests, Bouazza's adoration is dangerous to the mother. The long and central theoretical tirade about language is triggered by a serious fight between Bouazza and Machin, who made the mistake of starting a conversation about Darwin. Bouazza's somewhat predictable reaction is to summarily dismiss Darwinism, or rather the popular caricature of his theories: "Si tu veux croire que ton grand-père était un singe, libre à toi" [If you want to believe that your grandfather was a monkey, that's your problem] (1999: 89). But Bouazza goes much further. After getting rid of Darwinism in one simple sentence, he declares war on language itself. It is a full-blown, frontal attack that has little to do with the type of tactical interventions that Khatibi describes. This is no "skirmish," but a hypocritical and aggressive series of accusations in which Bouazza implies the existence of a connection between the narrator's use of French and an alleged abuse of his mother.

Mais, bref, à considérer mon pédigree, le voilà qui s'étonne qu'on ne croise pas souvent ma mère en ces parages et, puisque nous en sommes aux remontrances, il pousse jusqu'à me demander à haute voix si mon obstination à parler français ne constitue pas une manière de blasphème contre cette génitrice qu'on ne voit qu'oncques. C'est là que j'interromps:

—De quoi je me mêle, sale con? (89)

[And, given my curriculum vitae, he would like to register his surprise that we hardly ever encounter my mother on the premises, and, since we are on the topic of remonstration, he goes as far as wondering out loud if my stubborn determination to speak French does not amount to a kind of blasphemy against my genitrix whose whereabouts remain mysterious. Which is when I interrupt:

—Mind your own business you moron!]

After voicing his objection under the form of a gut reaction, the narrator immediately comments on the genre of his response. He knows that he has failed to provide an adequate answer to Bouazza's (rhetorical) question. Insulting him, he acknowledges, does not constitute a reply. But the stark contrast between Bouazza's sudden literary (and perfidious) eloquence and the narrator's almost instinctive vulgarity is such a reversal of etiquette and protocol that the reader is invited to draw the obvious conclusion from the exchange. Reading for genre (instead of reading for the plot, for example) reveals that Machin is so angered by the paratrooper's insinuations that he loses his verbal skills. Or, to put it another way, the text's strategic expression of Machin's loss of power is done through a representation of his lack of control over the linguistic realm when Bouazza touches a raw nerve: the allegation that he has disrespected his mother silences him.

But the deterioration of the son's rhetorical powers when confronted with a supposedly betrayed maternal icon is neither constant nor identically expressed in Laroui, Khatibi, or other North African authors such as Chraïbi. Both Khatibi and Chraïbi, for example, dedicate their work to their mothers: *La Mémoire tatouée* and *La Civilisation ma mère* are thus addressed to women who presumably cannot read their sons' books. Laroui's strategy, on the other hand, is slightly different. He prefers to create a literary mother who could read his books and understand why he is so upset by Bouazza's accusations. The long tirade about the nonmaternal language inserted within the book is precisely not addressed to Bouazza, and thus we can imagine that it is a special dedication to the mother who is not only a possible competent reader, but the most competent and ideal recipient of the linguistic fable. The pages devoted to what it means to have no native language are framed by a warning: this, the narrator announces, constitutes a "non-dialogue," a conversation that never took place, an example of what he *could* have told Bouazza had they both been capable of meeting within the same language.

Paradoxically, the narrator's mother (within this text of fiction) has earned a "mother tongue" that her son never had. Here, French symbolizes betrayal neither of the motherland nor of the mother. The language is not feminized, nor is it projected onto the female lover, the unknown rival who will implicitly confine the mother to her inferior status of uneducated, silenced, and dominated, colonized subject. Critics can interpret both *Love in Two Languages* and *Beware of Paratroopers* as novels that construct heroes who are double, made up of at least two or three characters. In order to represent bilingualism, it is often necessary to create several protagonists who, taken together, help us imagine what, in reality, is each subject's private encounter with languages. But in Laroui's book, the symbolic couple is demystified and rewritten as a parody. It is not a grandiose or sublime search for a decolonized identity. Bouazza and Machin are inextricably joined to each other, just as the many languages they speak have become almost impossible to separate.

Bonded to each other by misunderstandings, anger, and rancor, they have become inseparable, like two tragic and clownish conjoined twins. Their monstrous fusion is the allegory of painful forms of langualization that seem worlds apart from Khatibi's dream of the *bilingua*. Laroui may be inviting us to an ironic intertextual reading of the generation of authors that preceded him

(Khatibi, Chraïbi, or Djebar). The duel between the colonizer and the colonized is not so much over as it is displaced. The narrator is among his own people, but he is lost in translation. Within his own Moroccan culture, in his own native land, the hero does not discover the secret of a poetic *bilingua* but rather a perpetual comedy of errors.

For Khatibi, the genre of the encounter with language is an interracial love story, and his books present the relationship as a long series of efforts and struggles. Loving language is like loving a woman: the energy generated by the author's love is linked to the etymological pain contained in the idea of a passion. In that scenario, the relationship with the mother has been severed, and her role is to wait in the home country, hoping that the son will not be changed by the encounter with the other (language). The metaphor is one that allies the ideas of integrity and purity. She desperately waits for the narrator to come back "intact" (1971: 127). In Laroui, the only genuine love story between a man and a woman completely bypasses the issue of the mother tongue: both lovers are perfectly mute because they do not speak the same language. The first episode of the love affair is one of the rare moments where genuine tenderness replaces derision and sarcasm. The very young teenager and the narrator fall in love in spite of the fact (or perhaps precisely because) they do not talk. He claims (and the exaggeration makes a point) that he does not even know which language she speaks. Her tongue is not only heard as music or noise, but the name of the code is a mystery. Machin tries to speak to her first in French, then in Arabic, two attempts that have the following consequence: "Elle se met à ressembler à l'allégorie de la Stupéfaction s'abattant sur l'Innocence" [She starts looking like the allegory of Amazement pouncing on Innocence] (138). In other words, his efforts at choosing a suitable protocol have the amusing but powerful effect of transforming the textual addressee into a literary trope. The woman becomes an allegory—which is perhaps no different from what happens in Khatibi except that the slippage is explicit and humorous, and the scenario avoids issues of nationhood and identity.

Machin then adopts a different protocol: he tries to communicate with gestures, at which point, "elle bredouille quelques mots qui me semblent être du danois mais qui vu la situation, pourraient bien appartenir à quelque dialecte berbère" [she mutters a few words that sound like Danish but given the circumstances might well belong to some Berber dialect] (138). The latter explanation is, of course, much more likely than the former, but Laroui's highly improbable introduction of "Danish" as one of the possibilities also bumps against, and therefore reveals, the type of assumptions that we would immediately make when faced with the other's incomprehensible language. Laroui's whimsical allusion to "Danish" puts one of the less spoken Europhone languages on the same footing as what he then describes as a "dialect," thus troubling the canonical opposition between Europhone and vernacular systems.

In Khatibi, the opposition is maintained as a duality between the narrator's lover who does not understand Arabic and the narrator who is fluent both in French and in Arabic. By contrast to that gendered asymmetry, which we may tend to implicitly allegorize, Laroui's novel proposes two equally incompetent or ignorant lovers. The woman does not represent the colonizer's language, the narrator is not helped by his bilingualism, and the third tongue is not a space between known systems where the two characters could look for a solution. The multiplicity of languages is a given, but it is neither to be celebrated nor mourned as such. As long as we do not consider how the interaction occurs, no encounter can be deemed felicitous or infelicitous. In the case of Yto and Machin, the paucity of dialogue is apparently amply compensated by a desire to be together and to care for each other. The only moments of happiness that Machin experiences are found in those pages of seemingly frustrating and minimalist exchanges. And if the love affair ends in tragedy, it is not, as frequently occurs in Albert Memmi's or Khatibi's tales, because the encounter is crushed by the allegorical pressure that pushes each individual back into their culture, their language, and their norm, but because Bouazza once kicks her out without consulting his host, the master of the house.

Invoking (his own definition of) morality, tradition, and religion, he throws her out on the street, reducing her (the story later reveals) to prostitution. Bouazza's decision deprives Machin of the only harmonious encounter he has been able to construct with another human being, precisely because she does not speak his tongue and because he does not understand hers. And once Yto's silence is removed as one of the possible scenarios, the relationship with the other (as) language is displaced and turns into a grotesque and parodic tale that reinvents the conventions of the love affair. Instead of Khatibi's passionate affair with a "belle et maléfique étrangère" (1971: 13), all that is left Machin is unbearable cohabitation with the paratrooper, an obnoxious intruder who insists on calling the narrator "my brother" and whose devouring affection is expressed with "bisous goulus" [gluttonous kisses] (77). Passionate love and its sublime misunderstandings are parodied and degraded, turned into a tragi-comic domestic comedy closer to sit-coms than to classical drama.

Throughout the book, the narrator promises himself to put an end to this ridiculous relationship; he swears to kick Bouazza out. Pushing him out of his own house would be the equivalent of protecting himself from the part of Morocco that poisons his life. Bouazza represents what, in his native land, pressures Machin into giving up his freedom to be or invent himself as a unique individual capable of choosing his language and his relationship to language. But Machin never manages to disentangle himself from his detestable guest. From the very first pages, the narrative has metaphorically united them in spite of themselves by presenting their initial contact as a fake and parodic wedding ceremony. Although the reader probably does not realize it at the time, the first chance encounter is written as a prophecy and, retrospectively, the signs of an inextricable union are already present. In the very first scene, after the paratrooper has landed, his way of following the narrator prefigures the rest of the novel: "Il s'accrocha à mon bras, prétextant une douleur au genou, et comme il halait une traîne de quatre mètres de long, nous ressemblions à deux types qui se seraient mariés par inadvertence" [he clung to my arm, supposedly because his knee hurt, and because he dragged behind him a four-yard long train, we looked like two guys who had inadvertently gotten married] (65).

Unplanned and illegitimate as it is, the strange ceremony has remarkably concrete performative results and, chapter after chapter, Machin is reduced to passive and useless resistance. He constantly rebels, desperately tries, but in vain, to preserve some independence, or at least some room for maneuver, linguistically or otherwise. The uneven struggle lasts until the very last lines of the book, at which point a strange moment of epiphany finally replaces the constant bickering. The narrator suddenly renames what could become his new felicitous encounter with Bouazza. Like a message brought to him by night spirits, the realization suddenly comes to him in a dream that misunderstanding does not have to cease for a solution to exist:

Je me réveille en sursaut, mon coeur bat la chamade, je suis en nage.

Et soudain, je sais ce qu'il me reste à faire. Comment n'y ai-je pas pensé plus tôt? C'est la seule solution. Elle crève les yeux. Il faut aimer Bouazza. (190)

[I wake up with a start, my heart is pounding, I am drenched in sweat.

And suddenly, I know what I must do. Why didn't I think of it before? It is the only solution, it has been staring me in the face. I must love Bouazza.]

The strange imperative may well disconcert Laroui's readers and divide his public. Some might read the astonishing request as evidence that the author is finally resigning himself to the victory of authoritarian policy makers. Whatever the native land has become, it must be welcome. Others will suspect that he is acknowledging the reality of a cultural struggle that has resulted in tragic forms of multilingualism. Whatever the native land has become, it must be accepted. The declaration is so unexpected and irrational, however, that it is difficult to accept it as a definitive and concrete proposal. It points nonetheless towards a very specific direction. Loving Bouazza brings us back to the idea that passion and languages belong together, even if, for once, French is not allegorized as a dangerous and foreign woman and even if the mother tongue is not portrayed as the reassuringly authentic maternal figure.

The protocol of encounters between the writer and his readers, between the writer, his motherland and mother tongue now takes place in a new context. The parent is not the excluded third, the embodiment of the ideal addressee who will never read the book, a constant lack that the Francophone text longs after. The illiterate mother (or father) of the first postindependence generation and even of Beur literature has become an unconventional reader, one who acquired French of her own volition, without the help of colonial schools that left her out of their ideal of progress and modernity.

The lover, on the other hand, is not a foreigner. She is not "malevolent," but she is mute. She has no contact with the narrator's mother; she will not be in a position to take her place or become her daughter-in-law; and she will also not be able to help the narrator construct a Khatibian *bilingua*. The "third ear" that Khatibi tried to imagine in *Love in Two Languages* (1983a: 11) is not necessary because love does not speak: a whole new relationship to the body, including one's own body, has replaced the confrontation between languages. The conversation with the other, especially the western(ized) alter ego, has been internalized as an encounter with one's internal contradictions. The other woman is not French, and the high level of discomfort is caused by the difficulties of relating to the native land. The only foreigners in Laroui's story are non-Moroccan French and Francophone readers, invited as spectators who witness a struggle to which they could pretend to be indifferent.

In his study on *Love in Two Languages*, Réda Bensmaïa suggested that Khatibi had successfully transcended the opposition between French and Arabic and that a dialectical resolution allowed the author to go beyond the alternative between two languages: "Khatibi refuse d'emblée la dualité pour essayer de penser—et de, littéralement mettre en scène—un espace qui était demeuré impensable: celui précisément où les deux langues en présence (l'arabe et le français ici) [. . .] se rencontrent sans se confondre, confrontent leur geste graphique sans osmose réconciliatrice" [Khatibi systematically refuses duality in order to think—and literally stage—a space that was unthinkable until then: the space where two languages (here Arabic and French) [. . .] meet without being fused, confront their graphic gesture without any conciliatory osmosis]. Consequently, Bensmaïa suggests, "il ne s'agit plus de savoir s'il faut écrire en français ou en arabe" [the issue is no longer whether one must write in French or in Arabic] (1985: 138).

To the reader's surprise, Laroui's narrator finally discovers a last-minute solution to his dilemma and ends his tale on a note that seems to contradict the ominous title: out of the blue, Machin, who has every reason to hate his housemate and alter ego finally declares: "*Il faut aimer Bouazza*" [*Bouazza must be loved*] (190). The strangely dictatorial pronouncement allows for a multiplicity of correct translations, a process that highlights the strange mixture of clarity and ambiguity. The impersonal "il faut" may mean "I must love

Bouazza," but it can also mean "It is necessary to love [individuals like] Bouazza," or, (although this option is less likely) "Loving Bouazza is mandatory." The source of the new determination implied by this sudden resolution is never spelled out: here, a new law is laid out, and we cannot name the law or superimpose it over a national, religious, or ethnic model. The novel does not choose between virtue and necessity, and we do not know whether loving Bouazza would be the last possible survival tactic or the discovery of a new and improved relationship with oneself and the community. Machin does not seem thrilled by his own verdict, and his solution curiously falls back on a type of constraint ("il faut") that he has always adamantly resisted. "Il faut aimer Bouazza" is an unexpected and improbable ending that reads like a new beginning rather than a denouement. At the end of the narrative, at a moment when we expect closure, the narrator warns us that everything remains "à faire" [to be done]: "Je sais *ce qu'il me reste* à faire" [I know what *remains to be done*] (190, my emphasis).

The narrator will never be able to choose between two double and contradictory imperatives. Like Machin, the reader is expected to be confused by the mixed message or rather the double constraints of the title (a warning and an order: Beware of paratroopers) and of the end of the book: "I must love Bouazza." Similarly, the impertinent wedding between two men implicity parodies the narratives of grand heterosexual passions where France and the Maghreb regularly take the place of Man and Woman. In the last pages of the novel, Laroui has successfully staged a felicitous encounter between the lyricism of Khatibi's stories and essays and a completely different type of literature, one based on tenderness and humor that also flirts with impostures, with ruses and games of hide-and-seek. At the end of Laroui's novel, we may suddenly remember, without knowing why, that Emile Ajar's book, *La Vie devant soi* ended with a recommendation that sounds quite similar to Machin's newly found conviction. Momo—the abandonned Muslim boy who had alone accompanied his beloved Jewish adoptive mother, Madame Rosa, during her last moments and had stayed with her decaying corpse for a whole week—finishes his story with a powerful and impersonal: "il faut aimer" [one must love](1975: 274).[21]

4

Encounters between Historiographies

From Binational Archives to the Art of Telling "Mixed Memories"

Just as the consciousness of having lost a native tongue slowly turns into a self-conscious encounter with language as an object of desire, the relationship between individuals and their past generates encounters that create new subject and object positions. A narrative can serve as the symptomatic site, alerting readers that new types of historians, new types of historiographies are emerging. They correspond, respectively, to the subjects generated by the conversation about the past and to the protocol that had to be invented, and "History" becomes the name of the encounter and of its performance. In this chapter, historians are not professional scholars who write history books, but skilled tacticians who are created as historians through a personal and collective quest. They are ordinary men or women who have learned that their adventures are historic and that they must articulate the relationship between their own story and history. They are aware that history is often instrumentalized, and they know the limits of nationalized (or continentalized) historical discourses. They are willing to invent their own practice of historiography.

In Europe today, it is common knowledge that the memory of the Algerian war was repressed for almost forty years, silence becoming the preferred mode of remembrance, the telltale sign of repressed history. In the Maghreb, other preferred modes of memory and other types of silence prevail, as official history enshrines national heroes and forgets unglamorous episodes of the war.[1] While some have chosen to focus on the analysis of the reasons and modalities of a long and stubborn refusal to remember (Ageron 1997; Dine 1994; Schalk 1991; Stora 1991), other studies have chosen a different path. They privilege a history of encounters between historical practices that cuts across the genres of history (Stora 1995; Chaulet-Achour 1998), autobiography, documentary (Benguigui 1996, 1997; Djebar 1995b), and fiction (Sebbar 1997).

Writers whose interest in the French-Algerian conflict has led them to explore both the past and its difficult transmission need counternarratives and multigeneric histories to account for the resistance of the present to the burial of the past. Stora's classic 1991 analysis of silence and censorship in *La*

Gangrène et l'oubli already appears in retrospect as a forerunner of Djebar's 1995 *Le Blanc de l'Algérie*. Neither text allows official discourses to dictate a sole legitimate list of heroes, nor antiheroes as the case might be. Stora alternates chapters on France and on Algeria and suggests that both countries, in different ways, imposed a reductive national myth.[2] France carefully protected what Stora calls "the dark violence of family secrets" (1991: 13–117). Meanwhile, the newly formed Algerian government refused to acknowledge that the myth of a "unanimous people" (1991: 161) rested on the erasure of secret rivalries that sometimes led to massacres within Algerian revolutionary movements. That all this should now seem obvious or at least uncontroversial and publishable is a measure of how successful (and performative) these stories were.[3] They also suggest the force of the potentially explosive encounters between history and literature as cultural practices.

Francophone historical novels written about the relationships between Algeria and France during the colonial and postcolonial periods are part and parcel of a cultural turn or historical moment that may be said to culminate with the publication of Pierre Nora's *Les Lieux de mémoire* (1984). The monumental construction of historical monuments and the resulting monumentalization of Nora as a sort of archhistorian is one of the textual symptoms of a collective attention to history as a discipline and to the multidisciplinarity of historical texts. The popularity of Nora's work has familiarized us with the notion that, at the end of the twentieth century, "Totemic history has become critical history [. . .] The old symbols no longer arouse militant conviction or passionate participation" (Nora 1996: 7). Instead, a self-reflexive relationship to one's own history, to one's own identity, becomes a mandatory practice. We have, Nora suggests, entered an age of "historicized memory" (1996: 10) where each individual feels obliged to become his or her own historian. The atomization of memory (as collective memory is transformed into private memory) imposes a duty to remember on each individual. This "law of remembrance" has great coercive force. For the individual, the discovery of roots, of "belonging" to some group, becomes the source of identity and its true and hidden meaning (Nora 1996: 11).

Franco-Maghrebi novelists have added their own perspective to this historical redefinition of history as they seek to redefine the narrative tools used by different generations in order to rewrite and manage their relationship to the past.[4]

The process entails more than the freedom from censorship, the struggle against forgetfulness, or the absence of archival material, because what must be "recovered" (that is, written, narrativized) is not analogous to some raw material that one can hope to retrieve unchanged and give (or sell) to an uncritical reader.

Recent novels are interested in differentiating between different types of silence (erasure, censorship, secrecy, shame, absence of archive, repression) rather than in establishing that silence once prevailed. Their authors take for granted that silence has become a theme and that the absence of voices has been replaced with narratives about silence. The proliferation of stories about the *absence* of stories has replaced (or displaced) a missing archive with a very specific type of performative account. They do not hesitate to write the history of how history evolves and, remarkably, they do so at the very moment when the change is occurring, renouncing traditional vantage points such as time, distance, or even objectivity.

How, then, do recent narratives experiment with the encounter between histories and the creation of new historians? The grandmother of all such tales, I would submit, is Djebar's *L'Amour, la fantasia*. Through a careful interlacing of fiction and history, individual memories and archival documents, old women's stories and autobiographical vignettes, Djebar proposes a poignantly transnational vision of what it means to write a history of violent conflicts when one is an artist. Unavoidably, telling stories of painful remembrances leads to the invention of a model of what it is to tell such stories and of what it means to choose to witness.

I would not presume to revisit a passage that is so often quoted and discussed (Nagy-Zekmi 2002; Spivak 1992; Zimra 1995) if the well-known model of the severed hand did not constitute such a perfect moment of tragic performative encounter that can be formulated in a nutshell. In this example, a (dead), orientalist, male painter, Eugène Fromentin, and a twentieth-century Algerian woman writer and historian are reinvented as contemporary allies, but also as father and fictional daughter who, literally, lend each other a hand in order to write a different type of history. Their protocol requires the use of a kind of pen that they have to borrow from Arabic: the *qalam*.

> Eugène Fromentin me tend une main inattendue, celle d'une inconnue qu'il n'a jamais pu dessiner.
>
> En juin 1853, lorsqu'il quitte le Sahel pour une descente aux portes du désert, il visite Laghouat, occupée après un terrible siège. Il évoque alors un détail sinistre: au sortir de l'oasis que le massacre, six mois après, empuantit, Fromentin ramasse, dans la poussière, une main coupée d'Algérienne anonyme. Il la jette ensuite sur son chemin.
>
> Plus tard, je me saisis de cette main vivante, main de la mutilation et du souvenir et je tente de lui faire porter le 'qalam.' (Djebar 1995a: 259)
>
> [Eugène Fromentin offers me an unexpected hand—the hand of an unknown woman he was never able to draw.

In June 1853, when he leaves the Sahel to travel down to the edge of the desert, he visits Laghouat which has been occupied after a terrible siege. He describes one sinister detail: as he is leaving the oasis which six months after the massacre is still filled with its stench, Fromentin picks up out of the dust the severed hand of an anonymous Algerian woman. He throws it down again in his path.

Later, I seize on this living hand, hand of mutilation and of memory and I attempt to bring it the "qalam."] (1993: 226)

In the very first sentence of the paragraph lies the painful paradox of all attempts to write an Algerian-French history that would not be separated into two camps by official national discourses. The passage begins with what could be a peaceful and welcoming gesture: "Eugène Fromentin me tend *une* main" (my emphasis). At first, it looks as if the painter himself is holding out his hand, and in French, the only "unexpected" element in the sentence is the indefinite article. Unexpectedly, the long dead French painter seems to reach out to the twentieth-century female author in a gesture that usually connotes affection or perhaps an invitation to join him, and most certainly connotes the willingness to greet an equal. The text never abolishes the possibility of such an interpretation even if the adjective "unexpected," which, at first could be taken to refer, adverbially, to the surprising nature of Fromentin's gesture, soon proves to be much more sinister: it signifies another (severed) hand. The presence of the dead woman's hand introduces a third space between the painter and the writer, so that unspeakable violence contaminates the apparently benevolent signal. Djebar's syntax turns the scene into a horrific mixture of imaginary historical dialogue and graphic detail. The hands of the two artists, who could be connected by a transnational and transhistorical fascination for what is around them, are suddenly separated by another protagonist, an excluded third whose tragic presence-absence is the symbol of violence and cruelty.[5] The severed hand, a hand that will no longer write, a hand that will no longer paint, comes between the hand of Fromentin the painter and that of Djebar the novelist, as if to remind us that the writing of any story will now always be complicated by this unbearable Derridean supplement. The third hand is in excess. It is no longer alive, yet it cannot be buried or put to rest until its story has been told. Djebar imagines that, across the centuries, Fromentin's gift becomes a responsibility, the duty to teach the ghost of the woman how to write her own untold story.

While Djebar's powerful image is one possible model that *L'Amour, la fantasia* proposes as its own founding gesture, the severed hand's *qalam* is not imposed as the only protocol for history nor even as the necessary image others should adopt. Here is a vision that allows literature to distinguish itself from official history while reflecting on the writing of history. The amputated hand held by a contemporary writer tells us what it means to write the history of colonial and postcolonial conflicts as literature. Such powerful icons, which combine fictional imagination with an implied theoretical model of history, are the almost unavoidable by-products of the type of writing that I analyze in this chapter. Novels written by contemporary authors of Algerian origin often seek to remember the lives of individuals either swallowed by the ideological presuppositions of the colonial archive or later dismissed by the logic of official postindependence national histories. They tend to arrive at a sometimes tragic, sometimes sarcastic, and always self-reflexive definition of what it means to remember a transnational, traumatic, ghostly past.

The novel I will now turn to suggests that looking for the past means having a theory about the past and negotiating that theory not only with yourself but also with your grandfather, with your community, with your neighbors, with the people you fall in love with, and with the strangers who become your allies. It also means (re)inventing a changing past, a new past, and, consequently, a new present, which, in turn, changes the individual who has embarked on the quest. No element of the equation is safe from metamorphosis; the present, the past, and the self are put into question. The imperative is not to fill a void but to rethink the relationship between different types of narratives, including those that we have traditionally called autobiography, history, and fiction.

In Mehdi Lallaoui's *La Colline aux oliviers* [The Olive Grove], history itself is the hero, and different characters struggle between various models they think of as incompatible. Published in 1998, it invites its reader to encounter history as a project unfolding before their eyes at the same rhythm as the writing of the story. As experimental historians, the heroes will successfully craft a meeting point between different types of archives, different uses of history, different facets of what it means to search for the truth. As a result of several amateur historians' quests, the definition of memory and history will evolve from a traditional linear and individual narrative (a search for a missing ancestor) and adopt some of the conventions of a multiracial love story that manifests itself as the complex imbrication of different types of collective archives and practices (including teaching, giving, loving, or making serendipitous discoveries).

Lallaoui, a novelist and filmmaker who describes himself as a child born in France to a family of Algerian immigrants, works on contemporary memory, continually straddling the Mediterranean. His first novel, *Les Beurs de Seine*, came out in 1986 halfway through the so-called "Beur" decade and was followed by an album of antiracist posters published under the auspices of the association "black, blanc, beur."[6] Its publication coincided with the celebration of the bicentennial of the French Revolution in 1989. Since then, Lallaoui has coauthored *Un siècle d'immigrations en France* (with David Assouline) before publishing two other novels: *La Colline aux oliviers*, the story to which I would like to devote the second part of this chapter, and *Une nuit d'octobre*, a fictional account of the tragic events of October 17, 1961.[7]

Lallaoui's *La Colline aux oliviers* is as much about the "truth" discovered by the narrator as about the ways in which this truth is reached. The end of the book allows the reader a satisfactory sense of closure, but to the literary critic, the careful delaying of the ending is just as remarkable as the glimpse it gives us into a relatively unknown portion of colonial history. Consequently, writing about *La Colline aux oliviers* is almost like explaining a magic trick, a sleight of hand: something gets lost in the process, the fascination of the performance, the pleasure of being deceived and enchanted at the same time. Yet, because the novel also talks about the necessity of coming to terms with loss and of renouncing the hope that history will magically restore the past, it may be less sacrilegious than it seems to start with the end and concentrate on how revelations are arrived at. At the end of *La Colline aux oliviers*, the search for one of the ancestors who has disappeared from his village in Kabylia is finally over, and by the time the story reaches its satisfying narrative closure, the novel has also provided us with a fictional overview of events that span more than a century. The narrative opens around 1871, the time of the Paris Commune as well as the great Kabyle insurrection, and closes in the 1990s, long after the end of the Algerian war, at a time when France and Algeria were gradually coming to terms with the legacy of the conflict and preparing the fortieth anniversary of the Evian agreements.

In *La Colline aux oliviers*, Si Larbi is the alpha and the omega of the plot, not because he is the narrator or the main character, but paradoxically because his absence structures the novel: Si Larbi has been missing from the "colline aux oliviers" for more than a century. At the very end of the book, it is finally revealed that the missing hero, who had disappeared during the 1871 insurrection, was arrested by the French and deported to New Caledonia, another French colony. He stayed there until his death. As his story gradually unfolds, we learn that he did try to alert the members of the community that he was still alive and exiled, but the kind of message that he sent out to his brothers demanded a specific type of deciphering that the first generation of readers failed to realize. This lost, or rather misinterpreted, message is a historical text that the novel as a whole reconstructs, rewrites, and makes us understand through its own apprehension of history.

At the beginning of the novel, we listen to Baba Mous, the first-person narrator, who spent all his life vainly searching for his uncle Si Larbi. Baba Mous is now an old man. He did not participate in the 1871 insurrection, but he lived through World War I; he was drafted and fought in the French army. The old man's first-person narration is tightly interwoven with a second narrative voice that intervenes as early as the second chapter and transforms the novel into a duet. The second narrator, who also says "I," is Baba Mous' grandson, Kamel, a painter who has emigrated to Paris and a transnational "Beur" who is not as physically rooted in the "colline aux oliviers" as his ancestors. For Kamel, the 1871 insurrection, World War I, World War II, and even the Algerian war belong to history, a multifaceted history that he does not really know how to discover when pieces turn out to be missing from his grandfather's stories. Olive trees have become symbols of his native land and of his culture rather than a means of subsistence. Both Kamel and his grandfather are the guardians of history, although they will be able to construct very different types of stories. Kamel's different approach to history will finally enable him to let a new image emerge out of the mosaic of more or less reliable pieces of information stored in the villagers' memories.

Two significant narrative choices distinguish Lallaoui's text from other fictional historiographies that seek to displace official discourse. First of all, the events that the novel allows us to discover (the 1871 uprising in Kabylia) are even less well known by the general public than the war of independence.[8] Then, the novel tells us that it takes two generations to finally arrive at a complete narrative about the lost member of the community. In other words, this text also tells the story of a failure, of bad history-telling. The second narrator, whom the novel places in the interesting position of being the reader's docent, himself learns about the 1871 uprising and is therefore able to share his knowledge. We are reminded (or we discover) that the famous 1871 Paris Commune has often eclipsed, in French history books, the memory of a large-scale insurrection in colonial Algeria.[9] Led by El Mokrani and Cheikh El Haddad, the insurrection was crushed by the French military. Rebels were executed or deported to New Caledonia, and countless Berber farmers lost their land. Ironically, they may have been displaced by expatriates the French government meant to punish by deporting to Algeria (Ageron 1991; Hureau 2001). The 1871 uprising is often referred to as the "Kabyle" insurrection and, according to historian Marc Ferro, the description minimizes its significance:

En fait, elle souleva 250 tribus, au total près du tiers de la population algérienne. Au vrai, la plupart des chefs djouad s'agitaient depuis que l'administration les avait dessaisis de leur pouvoir [. . .] Révolte multi-forme, réprimée durement selon la "règle algérienne," et suivie d'une expropriation massive: des chansons kabyles répétèrent désormais: 1871 fut notre ruine, 1871 fut l'année où nous devînmes mendiants. (1994: 291–92)

[In fact, 250 tribes were involved in the uprising, almost a third of the Algerian population. Most of the leaders had been restless since the administration had deprived them of their power [. . .] The multifaceted rebellion was greeted with harsh repression according to the "Algerian rule" and followed by massive expropriation: Kabyle songs started repeating, "1871 was our ruin, the year we became beggars."]

In *La Colline aux oliviers*, Baba Mous is one of the villagers who had always lived by the olive grove and whose land is taken away after the insurrection. In the story, the loss of the land is compounded (but also symbolized) by the disappearance of one of the male members of the community who joined the rebels never to be seen again.

This structuring absence of the missing anticolonial hero becomes the pivot upon which the novel builds its own definition of history, and more importantly, of the evolving role of history and memory in the life of very different characters. At the beginning of the novel, the great energy deployed to bring back Si Larbi or at least to find out what happened to him is presented as a mandatory mission. According to the elders, telling the history of the village becomes impossible if the story of one individual is missing. Si Larbi's disappearance created "un vide inexpliqué [. . .] La continuité d'une histoire commune, fondée sur l'existence de chacun, se trouvait brisée. Pour renouer avec notre passé, nous avions besoin de comprendre ce qu'il était advenu de Si Larbi" [an inexplicable void [. . .] The continuity of a common history, founded on each individual's existence, was broken. To reconnect with our past, we needed to understand what had happened to Si Larbi](Lallaoui 1998: 13).

The first striking proposal made by the novel is that the definition of history presented is based on a narrow, or at least very specific, definition of a "story." After all, we could agree that the account of Si Larbi's disappearance is already a story and that his absence can be the subject of numerous tales. The statement "and then, Si Larbi disappeared" is a perfectly acceptable part of a narrative. Instead, Si Larbi's absence, about which all the characters constantly talk, paradoxically becomes the ultimate metaphor for the absence of a tale, for the end of history.

The second idiosyncratic feature of the novel's definition of history is that the search for Si Larbi and for his story is presented as an enterprise of land reappropriation. Bringing Si Larbi back is supposed to be the equivalent of recovering the land stolen by the colonizer. If the villagers are so keen to find out what happened to him, it is not only because he is a missing link in a chain of individual stories, but because his absence is also imagined as the symbol of an original spoliation that would end with his return. This type of seemingly magic thinking is due to the fact that Si Larbi's disappearance is rationalized by the villagers as the fulfilling of an old prophesy made by an astrologer years and years before. The astrologer did not belong to the village. The villagers had rescued him after his previous employer left him for dead. To thank his hosts, the guest looked into the stars and made a prediction. As Baba Mous explains:

> Le savant prédit à Si Brahim la disparition du cinquième mâle du cinquième fils de l'un de ses descendants. Cependant, par la suite, l'un d'eux retrouverait l'homme; dès lors, la colline demeurerait éternellement nôtre. (71)

> [The scholar told Si Brahim that the fifth male of the fifth son of one of his descendants would disappear. He also predicted that later on, one of them would find the man and, from then on, the land would be ours forever.]

The imperative to discover the fate of one of the members of the community, which is, metaphorically speaking, the need for history, thus becomes linked to the hope to recover the land. The legend seems to promise that the possibility of telling the tale will somehow correspond to reappropriation of the land itself. No war of decolonization is announced, and no promise is made about the birth of a new nation. The writing of history becomes the promise of a better history for the "colline aux oliviers," a microcosm that seems completely divorced from larger national and international logic. As readers, we are left to wonder whether the prophecy can be read figuratively or literally. Ultimately, the search for Si Larbi does lead to the telling of stories that history books and national memories have regularly relegated to obscurity: stories about the 1871 insurrection; about the rebels' deportation to other far off colonized islands; about their friendships with Parisian Communards such as Louise Colet. Filling the "void" left by Si Larbi's departure means the recapturing of cultural dignity, which is, in itself, a political gesture. However, readers of the novel are never told in the end whether or not the land is indeed reappropriated by its inhabitants other than symbolically.

That issue of whether or not owning one's history is the exact equivalent of owning the land (a perspective that may seem hopelessly optimistic) is never clarified; the novel draws no clear conclusion about the power of history, and the ambivalence of that position spills over to two other issues. First, the text seems to hesitate as to which is the best method of reaching historical truth, and secondly, the choice between methods raises difficult questions about whose history is being told. For if there is a connection between telling one's history and getting one's land back, it is obviously crucial to determine which community can make a claim to which land, and it is also imperative to agree on ways to identify the rightful owners of the land in question. It is especially important when the group is small, self-contained, and not bound by a unique language, religion, nationality, or citizenship. The inhabitants of the "colline aux oliviers" are not identified by a passport or an identity card: they simply recognize each other. In other words, the establishing of one individual's identity is just as important as the telling of his story.

How is identity defined in Lallaoui's novel? At first, legitimacy is defined as belonging to the land or to the hill, as having been born there, and as being attached to a metonymic olive tree as if by some sort of imaginary umbilical cord. Identity is not encoded as race, ethnicity, political belief, or even nationality. A simple and apparently straightforward construction of belonging unites all the villagers; each man is represented by one tree, and the olive grove functions as a physical equivalent of administrative records. "Pour chaque naissance, un arbre; et pour chaque olivier planté, un nom et une année." [For each birth, a tree, and for each planted tree, a year, and a name] (10). An apparently simple definition of belonging is thus created whereby the village's history is the history of whoever has had a tree planted in the olive grove to symbolize him. Instead of "one man, one vote," the slogan could be, "one man, one tree."

I deliberately say "man," because one of the difficulties at the beginning of the novel is to know whether the bodies in question are really all male (the gendered specificity of the French language authorizes some possible negligence or unverifiable doubt). At first, we may not notice that history and memory are made up only of the story of male individuals. Si Larbi is a man, the prophecy mentions only males, and it seems as if the tradition of tattooing individuals who are about to leave the land on a long journey is also reserved to men. At the beginning of the novel, whenever a physical relationship between a tree and a human body is mentioned, the pronouns are ambiguous, and the reader must draw provisional conclusions about whether or not these legitimate bodies *must* be male.

What is not ambiguous, however, is the reciprocal bond between olive trees and human bodies. For each man, a tree is planted, and if a man travels, whenever distance threatens to loosen the tie between the tree and the man, a tattoo recalls the exact location of the original tree. Physically and symbolically, the tattoo can put the man back in his place and attach him to his roots. The inerasable and unquestionable mark guarantees his identity. Si Larbi had such a tattoo. Baba Mous remembers:

> Comme à tous ceux de la colline qui partaient pour un long et incertain voyage, on avait tatoué sur notre épaule gauche, avec une épine de caroubier, trois feuilles d'olivier, un soleil et une année de naissance. Sous chacune des trois feuilles, une série de chiffres: le sept, le neuf et le deux pour mon père; le sept, le dix-neuf et le cinq pour moi. Ces chiffres correspondaient au groupe d'arbre, à la rangée et à l'emplacement de l'olivier nous représentant sur la colline. Ainsi procédions-nous depuis

des temps immémoriaux pour marquer de façon indélébile dans notre chair, notre appartenance à cette terre, à ces pierres, au ciel qui éclairait chacun de nos foyers (49)

[As the villagers did when any man left for a long and uncertain journey, they tattooed three olive leaves, a sun, and our birth date on our left shoulders with a thorn from a carob tree. Under each of the three leaves were a series of numbers: seven, nine and two for my father; seven, nineteen, and five for me. The figures corresponded to the group of trees, the row, and the place of the olive tree that represented us on the hill. This is how we had proceeded for as long as we could remember to permanently mark, in our flesh, our belonging to this land, to these stones, to the sky that brightened each of our homes.]

Yet, this model of apparently impeccable simplicity is only one possible paradigm of identification, and the novel no sooner presents it as a possibility than it immediately questions the straightforwardness of this narrative of identity. This clear relationship between men and memory, between land and men, is a dream that does not resist the reality of historical changes. Something always intervenes that compromises the integrity of a narrative whose truth is the equation between a man and a tree. The blurring of the connection goes both ways: neither the tattoo nor the tree is a perfect guarantee. From the very first pages of the novel, memory entertains problematic relationships with the principle of substitution, with telling stories, with history; any claim to the land is therefore much more uncertain than it seems at first.

Baba Mous thus reveals that the original olive grove, the original record, no longer exists, and that the history of the village is a palimpsestic forest:

Notre colline, la colline aux oliviers, avait brûlé en partie. Un morceau de notre mémoire s'échappa avec les six cents arbres disparus. Baba Ali, mon père, mit dix ans à les remplacer. [. . .] Des arbres centenaires, disparus dans la grande tourmente dévastatrice, furent ainsi remplacés; et des ancêtres, que l'on croyait oubliés avec les arbres, rejaillirent eux aussi de la mémoire. (12)

[Our hill, the olive grove had partly burned down. A portion of our memory escaped together with the six hundred trees that disappeared. It took ten years for Baba Ali, my father, to replace them all. [. . .] Century-old trees that had been destroyed by the devastating fire were thus replaced and ancestors that we thought had vanished with the trees sprang up again in our memory.]

Strangely enough, the planting of new trees, the replacement of one symbol by another, does not seem to be perceived as a problematic substitute by the villagers. If the tree disappears, then memory dissolves (the ancestors are "forgotten"), but it is apparently enough to plant other trees to restore memory, to recapture lost narratives. The fallen tree that once represented a man can be replaced by another tree that serves exactly the same commemorative function in spite of its different age. The loss of burned trees is not irreparable: unlike archival documents, this type of oral-vegetal history can be reconstructed from scratch. The image of springing up again ("*rejaillir*") suggests that memory is interruptible and that neither forgetfulness nor memory are stable. Remembrance is willed; it is a product of the determination of a villager who plants new trees to commemorate old men. It is possible for memory to disappear and then reappear. But then, it takes ten years to reconstitute the "realm of memory," which is neither a narrative nor a monument but a practice (planting) and a desire to tell, a determination to respect and transmit what must be known.[10] One may, of course, want to ask if anything is lost, gained, or at least modified, when the equation between the original tree and the original man is thus replaced by a copy, a simulacrum, a fiction. The novel does suggest that nothing is as simple as Baba Ali makes it sound, and that even if trees are replanted, some slippage occurs, due not only to time but to errors, blurrings, miscalculations. Baba Ali may be in denial because he does not pay enough attention to the function of the substitution. After all, the story of how the missing ancestor's story is eventually recaptured suggests that the replacing of one sign with another creates enough noise in the system as to endanger the system itself.

For example, Baba Mous, the first narrator who will not succeed in spite of having sacrificed his life to find his ancestor, may have made the mistake of relying too much on the historical model based on trees or on tattoos. In France, he had met a wounded Senegalese rifleman, a World War I soldier like himself, and he noticed that the man had exactly the same tattoo as Si Larbi. When pressed about where he had met him and why he had this tattoo, the dying man had only been able to mutter something that was interpreted as "Paris." We find out, at the end of the novel, that he really meant Bouloupari, the name of the town in New Caledonia where the would-be "Senegalese" soldier had come from.

Unaware that the puzzle was incomplete, Baba Mous spent years in the French capital, looking for his uncle, wasting his time on a wrong conclusion. I would argue that by playing on the resemblance and partial homonymy between Paris and Bouloupari, the novel reminds us of the constant possibility of substitution and shows that slippage does occur between repetitions. Baba Mous' imagination, however, cannot accommodate the idea of a possible substitution. The difference between Paris and Bouloupari is like the difference between the original olive tree planted at an ancestor's birth and the second one that replaces the burned symbol. A mental leap is necessary to move from one tree to the other, and change, along with ideology and values of which Baba Mous is unaware, interpolates that distance. For example, the fact that the sound "pari" should immediately be heard as "Paris" rather than as "Boulou-pari" is a very plausible case of Eurocentrism that prevents Baba Mous from thinking of other far off colonized islands.

Later, when Kamel is asked to interpret the same story, his own historical perspective will have changed. While Baba Mous is drawn to the colonial *métropole* (as though "Paris" could be the only center, the only pole of attraction), the second narrator will be less eager to interpret "-pari" as Paris, to impose a Parisian subtext and logic. In this novel, the phonetic truncation of "Bouloupari" is due either to the exhausted soldier's inability to articulate or to the narrator's inability to hear properly. The text does not decide but hints at the far-reaching consequences of such literal misunderstandings between two different colonized subjects. Both possibilities (that the subaltern did not articulate or that his words were misheard) resemble (but also differ from) the phenomenon described by Jean-Paul Sartre in his preface to Frantz Fanon's *The Wretched of the Earth*. Sartre writes that intellectuals who went to school in the *métropole* go back home altered and alienated, producing "echoes" of Western culture repeated by colonized intellectuals. He imagines a situation where the colonized subject hears a word and repeats only its ending: "'Parthenon! Brotherhood!' And somewhere in Africa or Asia lips would open '. . . thenon! . . . therhood!'" (1963: 7).

In *La Colline aux oliviers*, a long word is mispronounced and shortened, but the context and the effect of the misunderstanding are considerably different. While "thenon" and "therhood" mean nothing, "Paris" means too much and generates rich and complicated narratives and travels. Paris is not a defective and inferior rendering of "Bouloupari"; it is a creative and productive mistake which, ironically, makes us think about the possibility that Paris is a copy, a pale and incomplete version of Bouloupari. Errors, here, are more important than the illusion of correct repetitions; writing on the body is no more reliable than the repetition of words. Moreover, different generations react differently when confronted with the fuzzy sign. The novel never explicitly suggests that the younger character's ability to better decipher truncated words is a sign of his postcolonial condition, but the reader is obviously encouraged to compare the two hermeneutic activities.[11]

Like the truncated word, the tattoo that is found on the black man's body is not a straightforward sign. In order to understand the message correctly, it is necessary to guess that the direct link between the body and the land no longer exists. The "devastating fire" that destroyed trees has a historical equivalent: Berber rebels were exiled and deported to New Caledonia. However, just as Baba Ali replanted trees, the tattoo that originally appeared on the missing ancestor's shoulder can be copied—inscribed on someone else's body. The tattoo is a reproduction, and as long as the connection between the skin and the tattoo is not correctly reinterpreted and reassigned, Si Larbi's disappearance remains a mystery. Kamel, Baba Mous' grandson, will have to give up on the original meaning of the tattoo in order to understand its presence on the dying soldier's body. He will discover much later (but only after finding out that Si Larbi had been deported to New Caledonia) that his great uncle had tattooed his own signature on the shoulders of young men recruited by the French army to fight against the Germans. For Si Larbi, tattooing the young men who were about to be drafted was the equivalent of planting a new tree. It was his way of sending a message, of circulating his signature. In order to be allowed to tattoo the young soldiers, he had lied to their families and pretended that he could protect their children from death thanks to a magic tattoo.

Normally, his mark should have been unique, like a passport or modern document of official identification. For a reader who knows the code (what the figures represent), the deciphering of the tattoo should require no interpretation. A simple act of recognition is needed. Whoever bears the mark belongs; his place is forever set. But, in the novel, the sign, which seems so easy to read, reveals its polysemy and the possibility of distortion. When the missing Si Larbi marks other bodies with the mark he wears on his shoulder, he modifies the purpose of the tattoo, turning it into a text, a message. The meaning of the message is unclear: did he want to be rescued or did he simply want to let people know he was still alive? The messenger does not know that he is carrying a message, and the message is not easily deciphered by its intended recipient.

Like archives, testimonies, or artifacts, the tattoo is undeniable (it exists), and the sheer force of its existence makes it impossible to ignore that something must be discovered. At the same time, many errors are possible; satisfaction with the presence of the archive is foolish. Baba Mous learns that the relationship between an event and a historical text is never direct. Eyewitnesses are storytellers, and we know that even photographic evidence can hide fabrication (not to mention that the camera's point of view is itself enough to radically change the meaning of a scene). The link between "what happened" and "what a text says happened" is always on the verge of infinite slippage, troubled as it is by the possibility of interpretation and false decoding.

When Baba Mous first talks to his grandson, Kamel, and tries to convince him that he must continue to search for Si Larbi, he has clearly failed in that quest himself. Not only has he not found his uncle, but his loyalty to the mission has forced him to betray the only woman he ever cared for. In France, he had fallen in love with Marinette, a French woman, but he is forced to go back to the village in Kabylia and marries there, continuing his fruitless pursuit of Si Larbi in Algeria. This apparently secondary female character, and the fact that she is left behind in the name of supposedly nobler causes, is a pivotal factor because, at that juncture, Baba Mous fails to perceive that he is making a choice between two different historical models. Unable to see that there are several definitions of history, he fetishizes the model that valorizes one paradigm at the expense of another. For him, history is about remembering the (male) ancestors who were born on the hill, about tattoos, and about reclaiming the land. Baba Mous' faith in this historical model is so deep that he is wholly unaware that an alternative narrative is available to him. And yet, at least one voice warns him that there may be no connection between finding Si Larbi and getting the land back: the voice of cheikh Iskandar, his beloved teacher and surrogate father.

In the text, Iskandar is the embodiment of another historical model. Paradoxically, Iskandar is entrusted with the task of turning the child into a "learned man" to better prepare him for a mission that, Iskander, as a teacher, does not really believe in. Iskandar is not the guardian of collective myths. He does not seem to have faith in the stories that the villagers repeat. When Baba Mous is about to be recruited into the French army, he notices that Iskandar's position is different from his: "A l'exception de cheikh Iskandar, nous pensions tous pouvoir retrouver la trace de Si Larbi et, peut-être, par la suite, récupérer la colline aux oliviers." [With the exception of cheikh Iskandar, we all thought that we could find Si Larbi's trail and perhaps, eventually, recover the olive grove](48). Iskandar has a different definition of history, identity, and memory. But who is this skeptical educated man, and why does he not agree with the dominant creed? Why does he symbolize the possibility of another historiographical mode?

Iskandar's presence in the village testifies to the existence of other possible models of "belonging," models that are not based on roots or on relationship to the land. The learned man does not come from the village. A nomad whose origin is never explained, he appears in the village, "à l'improviste et dépourvu de tout" [out of the blue and completely destitute] (33). Once granted hospitality, his role as Baba Mous' infinitely wise and knowledgeable teacher earns him a perfectly legitimate place among the villagers. The relationship the child establishes with him is obviously much more meaningful than the superficial bonds he forms with other people from the village. Yet, the master continues to represent a different form of identification. The absence of a tattoo on his shoulder symbolizes the possibility of different forms of identity that can be read as either a minus (he wasn't born there, he cannot claim the land) or as a plus (he is free from that bond, and he chose the hill). After all, because there is no escaping it, the idea of writing on the body may connote something slightly cruel, as if "belonging" were both privilege and curse.[12]

I would argue that Iskandar proposes another form of transmission of knowledge and of the past, one which will, in the end, turn out to be compatible with, preferable to, and complementary to the traditional (male) conception of collective memory. Iskandar does not wish to mark his pupil, but he still gives him a chance to preserve what will become history. His way of negotiating with memory is to make a gift that will symbolize the past and his affection and will also announce future gifts and future attachments. He does not write on the body, but rather gives a precious object, a substitute for identity and a metonymic token of his presence, a pair of gazelle-shaped earrings.

> C'est mon bien le plus précieux, elles sont pour moi ce qu'est pour vous la colline, le témoignage de notre existence [. . .] Garde-les aussi précieusement que ta propre vie et remets-les à celle qui les transmettra à tes descendants. (51)

> [This is my most cherished possession. They are for me what the olive grove is to you: the proof of our existence [. . .] Guard them as you would guard your own life and give them to the woman who will bequeath them to your children.]

Whereas olive trees keep the memory of a dynasty of men whose contingent birth attached them to the land, Iskandar's earrings preserve memory while authorizing exile and exogamous relationships. He gives Baba Mous the right to choose who will be the recipient of the story, just as the novelist gives us the right to hear the story rather than forcing us into the role of the soldier who thinks his tattoo is protecting him when his body is really being used to carry someone else's message. The gift of the earrings does not claim to protect, nor is it a talisman. In fact, when Baba Mous first gives the earrings to a woman, it is during a sad and tragic moment. Although neither Baba Mous nor Marinette know this, he is about to disappear from her life, just as Si Larbi had vanished from the village.

We should note, however, that Baba Mous does not exactly follow his teacher's advice: he was supposed to give both earrings to the woman who would be the guardian of his memory. Instead, he gives only one earring to Marinette. Disregarding his master's instruction, he splits the pair and modifies the double object's original purpose. Instead of representing the transmission of an intellectual and affective legacy, the half-gift is transformed into a promise that will not be kept.

Like the ancient symbol, the two halves of a loving couple are pulled apart by stories they do not fully understand, by their different origins. To the unquestioned weight of the all-powerful heterosexual norm, the novel adds an implicit critique of the pressure exerted by the villagers who treat endogamous unions as a given. Baba Mous is expected to marry, and he must choose a wife within the village—as if a traditional type of transaction has replaced the gift.

At first, it seems that the hill has won, that history-as-gift has proven less powerful than memory-as-belonging. The two pieces of the original master's gift cannot be reunited until another generation comes along, ready to accept Iskandar's healthy skepticism.

Kamel, Baba Mous' grandson, will not happily step into his ancestors' shoes. For him, the search for the elusive Si Larbi is "utopian" (102). He is not sure that he believes all the legends that his grandfather has told him, "Tout cela ressemble à un conte de fées, ironisai-je" [All this sounds like a fairy tale, I said, ironically] (72). Even when Baba Mous insists, he feels very reluctant to accept a mission that he considers doomed and fruitless: "Je n'allais pas passer ma vie à la façon de Baba Mous, à la remorque d'un fantôme" [I was not going to spend my life like Baba Mous, towed by a ghost] (102). Yet, in spite of his decidedly critical interpretation of the sacred legend, he will succeed where his grandfather failed. The novel manages to unite the two historical models proposed to the reader by suggesting that the ultimate discovery is due to the felicitous encounter between two paradigms: Baba Mous' faith in the original script and Iskandar's generous ideal. If Kamel, on the verge of telling his grandfather that he will not look for Si Larbi, suddenly changes his mind, it is because Baba Mous has sent him the remaining earring. Touched by the gift, Kamel explains:

> Par ce cadeau, le grand-père me confirmait sa foi. Comment interpréter autrement le fait de m'offrir ce bijou qui ne l'avait jamais quitté? Comprenant son geste, la honte m'assaillit. J'accrochai la boucle en évidence sur le kilim rouge fixé au mur, et je déchirai ma lettre. (104)

> [With this present, my grandfather was confirming his faith in me. How else was I to interpret the gift of a jewel that had never left him? Understanding his gesture, I was filled with shame. I hung the earring in full view, on the red *kilim* on the wall, and I tore up the letter.]

From then on, like his grandfather, Kamel becomes a devoted archivist, traveler, anthropologist, and interviewer—in a word, an interdisciplinary historian. He will only discover the truth because this second historiographical model, symbolized by the dangling earring, will manage to prevail. In a surprising denouement, we find that Anne, a woman with whom Kamel is slowly falling in love, is in fact Marinette's granddaughter. It is upon finding the earring in Kamel's room, and remembering that her grandmother owned a similar one, that she is able to finally reunite the two portions of Iskandar's gift and to act as the bearer of the complete story. The earrings have finally served their purpose, across time and distance.

This second model of history thus contains an element that we could read as serendipity (or implausibility), if the deliberate rejection of gender out of the realm of history had not problematized the notion of "chance" here. On the one hand, it is an incredible stroke of luck that Kamel's girlfriend should be the granddaughter of the woman who had been abandoned by Baba Mous. That Anne should find the second earring at Kamel's and should suddenly recognize her grandmother's earring at the very moment when the two lovers can fit this last piece into the almost completely assembled puzzle is a fictional *deus ex machina*. At the same time, this narrative decision makes a point about the presence of women in this picture. Both Baba Mous and his grandson make the same mistake of eliminating gender from history.[13] Baba Mous leaves the only woman he ever loved because he thinks that his quest is more important. Like him, Kamel is convinced that Anne has nothing to do with his search, with his work as a historian. At worst, she is a distraction, and at best, a pleasant distraction. And yet, Anne's discovery makes the point that her model of history, inherited from Iskandar, works perfectly. History as gift, history as transmitted by women and by people who do not necessarily belong to the "colline aux oliviers," is just as successful as Baba Mous' stubborn determination. Paradoxically, by turning his back on Marinette to devote himself to what he thinks is history, he perhaps delays a discovery he would have made earlier, had he been able to open his eyes to other texts and stories.

This does not mean that Kamel has given up on memory. Like an explorer looking for the one original spring of a large river, he admits that at a certain point his quest for a unique truth must take on an arbitrary quality. Perhaps he may find that the root he seeks is closer to a rhizome that implicitly and ironically displaces the image of the olive tree (Deleuze and Guattari 1980). This said, it is the distance introduced between the two earrings and their subsequent reunion that constitutes the solving of the riddle, as if, to paraphrase Glissant, it were not a question of "reversion" (to the roots, to the native land) but of "diversion" (1989: 14).

Memory as gift reconciled with a memory that tolerates substitutions proves more reliable than a tattooed memory.[14] At the end of the novel, the second narrator has demonstrated that a "trace" is not enough until it has been woven into a story and that "being given the land back" will not magically happen as the result of the discovery of the archive. However, through searching, something is transmitted, not only to the grandson but to the reader, who, like the pupil receiving a pair of earrings from his master, is now entrusted with the story of the "colline aux oliviers" and its inhabitants. If the "colline aux oliviers" can be said to belong to Baba Mous' grandson, it is because he has critically accepted the responsibility for the search. The "colline aux oliviers" never turns into "La colline oubliée," the "forgotten hill" made famous by Mouloud Mammeri's 1952 novel. Kamel has sat up all night listening to his grandfather's tales while others were asleep. He has spent hours in the library trying to connect memory and history, colonial wars and contemporary situations. And finally, he has accepted that his relationship with Anne, with the granddaughter of a woman whose happiness was sacrificed to another idea of history, may be directly relevant.

Although Lallaoui's couple is less exuberantly revolutionary than Fouad Laroui's strange union between the hero and the paratrooper, the emphasis on gender complicates the male genealogy represented by the olive grove. In the end, the book presents us with two models of memory, two versions of historical research, and suggests that it would be a mistake to eliminate either one of them—especially if tradition leads to the rejection of history as gift, history as transmitted by individuals who choose to belong, including women.[15]

5

Ghostly Encounters

On Forbidden Processions and on Listening to the Dead

La question mérite peut-être qu'on la retourne: peut-on *s'adresser en général* si quelque fantôme déjà ne revient pas? Si du moins il aime la justice, le "savant" de l'avenir, l'"intellectuel" devrait l'apprendre, et de lui. Il devrait apprendre à vivre en apprenant non pas à faire la conversation avec le fantôme mais à s'entretenir avec lui, avec elle, à lui laisser ou à lui rendre la parole, fût-ce en soi, en l'autre, à l'autre en soi: ils sont toujours *là*, les spectres, même s'ils n'existent pas, même s'ils ne sont plus, même s'ils ne sont pas encore.

Jacques Derrida 1993: 279

[The question deserves perhaps to be put the other way: Could one *address oneself in general* if already some ghost did not come back? If he loves justice at least, the "scholar" of the future, the "intellectual" of tomorrow should learn it and from the ghost. He should learn to live by learning not how to make conversation with the ghost but how to talk with him, with her, how to let them speak or how to give them back speech, even if it is in oneself, in the other, in the other in oneself: they are always *there*, specters, even if they do not exist, even if they are no longer, even if they are not yet.]

Jacques Derrida 1994b: 176

Au fond, l'une de mes premières et plus imposantes figures de la spectralité, la spectralité elle-même, je me demande si ce ne fut pas la France, je veux dire tout ce qui portait ce nom. . .

Jacques Derrida 1996: 73

[Deep down, I wonder whether one of my first and most imposing figures of spectrality, of spectrality itself, was not France; I mean everything that bore this name . . .]

Jacques Derrida 1997b: 42

In this chapter, I would like to listen to a song of mourning that only ghosts can sing. I propose to take a literary walk through imaginary and fictive cemeteries in the hope of catching the voices of unknown heroes whose task now consists of taking care of the graves that history refuses to recognize as legitimate sites of burial. The graves that I have in mind are located in France and in Algeria, but we cannot call them Algerian or French cemeteries, and even less Muslim,

Christian, or Jewish cemeteries, because their permanent or temporary residents are not reducible to the identitarian simplicity of such adjectives. I am tempted to suggest that these burial sites are "fabulous" because of their power to inspire so many fables and legends among French-Maghrebi authors. And if I propose to talk about the "residents" of those cemeteries, it is because I do not wish to dissociate the living who haunt them from the dead who rest there—although we need to find another word in this case. There, the dead do not rest; they inscribe our present as the legacy of their past. They are historical, literary, and mythic figures whose stories constitute the source of a formidable *poesis*, an international process of mourning that concerns the dead as well as the living.

Unique types of performative encounters occur in such places. Not only do the living come to talk to the dead (to their dead), but they also meet other people, individuals that history forbids them to befriend. These cemeteries are peopled by a not-yet-imagined nation whose unrecognized citizens are driven by the sometimes-unconscious desire to invent new forms of dialogue. They are a place where unique types of narrative encounters occur. Like the heroes of the first four chapters, they have not accepted the supposedly final and definitive fracture between France and Algeria, between the French and the Algerian people, but their refusal is difficult to interpret in terms of optimism.

Rarely do their creators present them as a political or cultural solution. Sometimes, they are even viewed as nostalgic or reactionary heroes who mourn the demise of the colonial regime. Their skepticism slightly rewrites the question that Stuart Hall once asked: *how exactly* "can Algerians living at home and in France, the French and the *pied noir* settlers all be postcolonial" (1996: 245), especially if some of the subjects are already dead?

In these narratives, the author or filmmaker treats the graveyard as a written page or an engraved monument on which old, half-effaced words and confusing stories start to make sense. The writer, in this case, is not the archetypal creator facing a blank page. The translator of what was previously undeciphered is a better model. The text, the protagonists, and the readers are confronted with an unknown alphabet; we are in the same position as the series of curious and passionate explorers who seek to understand the Berber stele that appears in the central chapters of Djebar's *Vaste est la prison* ("L'effacement sur la Pierre") (121–64) ["Erased in stone," *So Vast the Prison*] (122–67). All the scholars, archeologists, and adventurers find themselves confronted with signs that belong to an unfamiliar system, and the letters are inscribed on a support that progressively deteriorates. Similarly, the stories told in cemeteries put us in the presence of a form of writing that must first be recognized as such before any kind of encounter can begin. Or, rather, the beginning of the ghostly encounter coincides with the intuition that the nonsensical scribblings are a language. Part of the author's work is to convince us that something is there that we may try to decipher. Like the voices of slaves in Rancière's *Mésentente*, the message on the shrine is generally treated as meaningless, subhuman, or prehistoric noise in the flow of communication. What survives on the stone is so faint that only a performative reading will convince us that it is worth our attention.

The encounter with ghosts exists only if a story makes us believe or hope that someone is there to be met and that the attempt at communicating does not constitute utter madness. Taking the ghost seriously is a performative endeavor. Two types of exchange take place in and around these special cemeteries. The conversation that starts between subjects we normally consider "the dead" and "the living" will seem highly improbable, and its genre will have to be defined carefully if the authors want to avoid giving the impression that the fantastic has replaced the historical.

The encounter between the dead and the living is only one consequence of the types of narrative energy released in the texts. As implausible as they may at first appear, they are even less extraordinary than the other types of encounters they enable between heroes who are still alive, but who would otherwise remain forever alienated and estranged. The authors' attempts to communicate across the border between life and death succeed in launching an apparently impossible conversation among the living—among people who were previously separated by tragic scripts, the very same scripts that directly or indirectly caused the deaths that survivors now mourn.

Like other performative encounters, these are not necessarily moments of posthumous peaceful reconciliation. Each encounter is qualitatively different from an ethical and aesthetic point of view. For better and sometimes for worse, the narratives explored in this chapter reinvent the meaning of the cemeteries that they visit. Within the same novel, it is possible to find multiple, varied negotiations with the dead. Some characters look after a grave even if a stranger rather than one of their own relatives is buried there. They offer to become guardians of their former enemy's memory. Others, by contrast, are vandals who desecrate places that no one can protect. They shamelessly exploit the sorrow of an exiled population for their own financial profit.[1] Still others adopt somebody else's burial place because the original cemetery is too far away or inaccessible.[2]

There are times when the grave becomes the only possible hyphen between two mutually exclusive traditions and between protagonists. An encounter with ghosts rekindles apparently defunct dialogues. When people talk to one another in spite of the fact that they are dead (or dead to each other) the encounter must be performative. Only a performative encounter will make us believe in the representation of that sort of impossibility, because it modifies the original subject-positions that foreclosed the conversation. When the definitions of life and death are thus altered, new configurations and parameters appear. Death is no longer the cause (or not the only cause) of an impossibility to communicate; "death" is, rather, the name of the consequence of such impossibility. Not being able to listen is one way of saying that the protagonists are dead or dead to each other. Perhaps not listening or not hearing is a way of killing them.

The point here is not to emphasize the always-elusive presence of the ghost, or even to look for a metaphor of the always-ghostly nature of any encounter between speaking subjects.[3] The stories that we are about to read are examples of performative encounters because they constitute a collection of texts that I would like to propose as an ensemble, perhaps as a new literary and historical genre: they allow ghosts to speak through the writer and through the reader. By "ghosts" I mean a type of historical presence that cannot be accommodated by historical writing, that will, perforce, be excluded, foreclosed by stories whose logic requires the taking of sides, the ratification of treatises between political powers. They cannot replace history books, but they can help us invent the space of a site of memory that sometimes does not exist beyond the pages of a book, the lyrics of a song, or the images of a film.

Djebar's Le Blanc de L'Algérie [Algerian White]

"Ces chers disparus; ils me parlent maintenant; ils me parlent" (Djebar 1995b: 15) [Those dear disappeared: they speak to me. All three, each of the three] (Djebar 2003a: 15). That is what Djebar's first-person narrator tells her readers in Le Blanc de l'Algérie, a text published in 1995, during the dark years when so many Algerian intellectuals and artists were assassinated.[4] "J'ai voulu répondre à une exigence de mémoire immédiate [. . .] S'est installé alors en moi le désir de dérouler une procession: celle des écrivains d'Algérie, depuis au moins une génération, saisis à l'approche de leur mort—celle-ci accidentelle, par la maladie ou, pour les plus récents, par meurtre" (1995b: 11) [I wanted to respond to an immediate demand of memory [. . .] Then the desire was instilled in me to unroll a procession: that of the writers of Algeria, over at least one generation, caught at the approach of death—whether it be by accident, illness or, in the case of the most recent ones, by murder (2003a: 13)]. Le Blanc de l'Algérie is about mourning; it is addressed to the dead as if we could talk to them, but even more surprisingly, the narrator suggests that she intends to listen to the lost friends.[5] She hears what the "dear disappeared" have to say, because they "speak" to her.

Would it be naïve, then, to ask what such a sentence means if it is not simply a figure of speech? If the dead speak, which language do they use? In a context where multilingualism and translation are so important, what are we to understand by the "langue des morts" [language of the dead] that Djebar talks about (1995b: 13; 2003a: 9)? What kind of text will enable us to understand them?

It should be noted that Djebar's book does not present itself as the transcription of a speech read during a public ceremony. *Le Blanc de l'Algérie* is not similar to Derrida's *Adieu à Emmanuel Levinas* [*Adieu to Emmanuel Levinas*] published after the philosopher's death. In his *Adieu*, Derrida notes that the rhetoric of the public farewell speech authorizes the orator to directly address a person who can no longer be reached:

> Souvent, ceux qui s'avancent pour parler, pour parler publiquement . . . souvent ceux qui se font alors entendre dans un cimetière en viennent à s'adresser *directement, tout droit*, à celui dont on dit qu'il n'est plus, qu'il n'est plus vivant, qu'il n'est plus là, qu'il ne répondra plus. (1997a: 11–12)

> Often, those who come forward to speak, to speak publicly . . . those who make themselves heard in a cemetery, end up addressing directly, straight on, the one who, as we say, is no longer, is no longer living, no longer there, who will no longer respond. (1999: 1–2)

In *Le Blanc de l'Algérie*, Djebar does not adopt the position of someone who speaks to the dead. She claims instead that her role is to listen to them and to tell us what they said. Whereas the tragedy of any "adieu" is caused by the knowledge that the protagonist knows that he or she starts a dialogue that is already aborted, in this case, the narrator's point of view is slightly different. If Djebar does succeed in keeping alive the memory of the murdered intellectuals, it is not as a historian who asks us to remember their lives as they are narrated within the text. She does not talk in front of an audience, by their grave, or about them. Instead, she listens, and it is her way of listening that becomes the story. Her text relates what the "dear disappeared" told their friend, which does not really make them the "authors" of the book but certainly destabilizes the relationship between Djebar and authorship. Listening comes before writing in a way that redefines (or at least questions) the notion that death is what makes such a position impossible because, as Levinas puts it, no "answer" is to be expected. We may not know *what* death is, but when Levinas asks "Que savons-nous *de* la mort?" [What do we know *about* death?], his conclusion is that the dead cannot be expected to "express" themselves: "les mouvements biologiques perdent toute dépendance vis-à-vis de la signification, de l'expression. La mort est décomposition, elle est le sans-réponse" (Levinas 1993: 20) [the biological movements lose all dependence in relation to signification, to expression. Death is decomposition; it is the no-response] (Levinas 2000: 11).

The dead may have something to say, but the connection between the "what" and the "how" is cut off. The genre of the dialogue should be ruled out. And yet, the rhetorical context that inaugurates Djebar's text is her promise to let us hear that which cannot be expressed. Before starting a conversation with the departed, she promises to pay attention to what they will say to her, a perspective that makes her text rather unusual. Margaret Atwood, who suggests that all writing is a negotiation with the dead, points out that the presence of ghosts often depends on a decision by the living to conjure them up, or at least to acknowledge their presence as ghosts (and not as some inexplicable phenomenon that is not read as an encounter). The dead need our authorization to speak up and to appear as ghosts. "Societies have a way of devising rules and procedures—'superstitions,' they're now called—for ensuring that the dead stay in their place and the living in theirs, and that communication between the two spheres will take place only when we want it to" (Atwood 2002: 159).

Respecting Djebar's decision to relay someone else's message is not the same, however, as understanding how she proposes to do so. Her desire to throw a bridge of words over the chasm that separates life from death would be understandable if she clearly called upon the literary conventions of the gothic novel or of the ghost story. But such is not the prerogative she chooses to invoke. Consequently, some readers may find the system of address highly implausible. Isn't the intention to let the dead speak at best illusory? Are we not likely to dismiss the whole context of enunciation, even before wondering about what they say?

If we yielded to that temptation, many other texts besides *Le Blanc de l'Algérie* would be discredited. A recent host of Franco-Maghrebi publications reflect their authors' desires to redefine the parameters of an encounter between literature and mourning. A specific and historically recognizable genre has emerged that blends testimony and grief and can be described as ghostly performative encounters. As we will see in the work of Assia Djebar, Mehdi Charef, and Yamina Benguigui, these ghostly encounters fulfill a specific function within contemporary textual and visual narratives. Authors agree to be inhabited by the memory of their beloved departed and allow their texts to transgress generic codes. They empower both the dead and the living by modifying the parameters that had made their encounter impossible.

The encounter with the dead and the fact that the dead inhabit the writer and her text cannot be reductively equated with forms of either harmful or benevolent possession. The text is not dictated, and no spectral voice promises to reveal a hidden truth. Recognizing the presence of a ghostly performative encounter tells us nothing about what the dead have to say. Algerian ghosts, when conjured up by or during a performative encounter do not speak directly. They do not utter prophecies, nor do they solve mysteries, and if they have something in common with ancient oracles, it is that their message is delivered in a language that is not easily translatable. Artists who fictionalize ghostly encounters are primarily novelists and historians who know that fiction, reality, truth, and narrative techniques cannot be that easily separated.[6] Their assumption is that language is opaque rather than transparent and that translation is not a flow but a practice of interruption. Ghostly performative encounters are not simply moments when the dead are heard by the living. The voices and texts thus produced realign the opposition between life and death and reorganize the types of relationships that once existed among history, the so-called dead, and the survivors. Two sets of boundaries are transgressed, and because the text demonstrates that the same transgressive practices are needed in both cases, both types of borders are shown to be comparable, namely, the gap between the dead and the living and the difference between historical discourses promoted by two states, France and Algeria.

That said, the point of the ghostly performative encounter is not to impose a new version of the past. Often, fantastic cinema or popular literature treats the ghost as a super detective. His or her testimony accuses the murderer and helps the living discover a culprit who would never have been suspected of wrongdoing if the victim had not intervened from beyond the grave.[7] Historical discourse sometimes adopts the same revelatory tone: as we have seen, the denunciation of dark family secrets and of censorship is a common topos in Algerian literature, especially when the writers take up the position of vigilant archeologists who carefully scrutinize what is left of the past. Previous chapters have given us examples of that literary practice, but a ghostly performative encounter does not seek to unearth an archive that would be comprehensible and that we could then store in our memory as part of a new and improved set of truths.

Here, the text stages, provokes, and describes a type of encounter that does not exist elsewhere and which is not necessary to historians or to conjurers. The encounter is textual. No attempt is made to bring the dead person back through magic or esoteric practices. When the ghostly encounter is performed, what is narrated is still within the realm of stories. That dialogue sometimes takes place between the living, but it would not have been possible if death had not interrupted the flow of normal conversations. Ghostly encounters begin because graves, death, and mourning have become obstacles impossible to ignore.

In the case of Algeria, people go missing as a result of premeditated acts of violence, and writers must struggle not only against those who want to silence their victims but also against the destabilizing and traumatic presence of the victims' memory, of their ghosts. This double imperative is further complicated by the ideological pressure exerted by those who police official discourse on memory and seek to clean up the often-chaotic legacy of revolutionary events.

Emblematic of all the other texts studied in this chapter, *Le Blanc de l'Algérie* is a textual *lieu de mémoire*, the shrine around which the dead and the living, whom everything conspired to keep apart (including space and time), can gather.

The protocol of cohabitation is very specific: this is not about living in the same city even if the "city" is a necropolis. Their mode of interacting has to do with recognizing each other as legitimate participants in the same mourning ritual. They are invited to take part in the same "processions" that Djebar's texts organize.[8] All the dead who haunt her memory and her consciousness are her guests.

The guest list is composed of disappeared heroes to whom the writer wishes to listen, and the originality of the logic is that the dead are extended a mandatory invitation that they may not have wished to receive (and would have refused) had they been alive. The dead are at their own funeral, and the community of mourners is created by the text. Consequently, between the pages, the men and women who are in contact with each other are people who were not on speaking terms, who would have remained isolated on one side of the wall of violence erected by history.

If we can "listen" to dead Algerians in this book, it is also because Djebar, by choosing to let them exist as a compatible group, creates them as such, rather than as more or less "proper" Algerians.[9] They are naturalized, as dead Algerians, and united by the author's text. When she listens to the "dear disappeared," Djebar blurs the distinction between accidental deaths and murders. Frantz Fanon, who died of leukemia long before 1993, appears. The three assassinated friends to whom the book is dedicated are together with "[un] écrivain, encore jeune et célèbre" (103) [a writer, still young and famous](89), who died in a car crash on January 4, 1960. Not only was Camus a *pied-noir* whose sometimes-overt opposition to revolutionary ideals earned him much hostility during and after the war, he was also not the victim of a terrorist attack, like Mouloud Feraoun in 1962 or Tahar Dajout in 1993.

Le Blanc de l'Algérie also brings together the two sides of the same side, the victims of forms of violence that history insists on distinguishing from terrorism and war. Djebar offers her reader a long portrait of Abane Ramdane, *moudjahid* betrayed and killed by other *moudjahidine*. She also extends an invitation, no doubt controversial for some, to the gay poet Jean Sénac, who died in 1973 "au coeur de la Casbah d'Alger [. . .] assassiné probablement par un amant de rencontre"(152) [in the heart of the Algiers Casbah [. . .] probably killed by a one-night stand] (129).[10]

The refusal to allow certain kinds of difference to make a difference is not only significant from a political point of view, but it is also an implicit reassessment of the genre of the story that can be told. For example, the clear-cut watershed between detective fiction and elegiac songs of mourning is blurred.

The ghostly encounter creates subjects that are both mourners and mourned and a text that forces history to give up on its tendency to allow only epic heroes and innocent victims to participate in the national song. Collaboration and treason cohabit here. The ghostly encounter shakes up chronology (the dead did not live at the same time) and also makes us think about those unwritten rules of propriety that function like the laws of a genre: Is it proper to bury the victim and the perpetrator next to each other? Should enemies share the same cemetery?[11]

A ghostly performative encounter is also a *coup de force*, imposing the genre of a procession that history refuses because its official forms of mourning are governed by a different logic of belonging and identity. In Djebar's texts, the dead speak up not so much as ghosts who haunt the living but as actors cast by a director to play a role in the same film. Djebar does not ask for their consent. She haunts them when she imposes the encounter and the dialogue between individuals that the historical script should separate. Their deaths generate possibilities that their lives prevented. Only Djebar's writerly mourning practice creates the space of the encounter. Yesterday's enemies are reimagined as a community whose diversity was simply unthinkable while its members were alive.[12]

When the Dead Laugh: Djebar's "Le Corps de Félicie"

Djebar's authoritarian invitation thus mirrors and criticizes the type of (religious, national, or political) law that separates people who wish to be buried in the same ground. This is precisely what happens to the two protagonists of "Le Corps de Félicie" (1997b: 235–363). When Félicie dies in her Parisian hospital, one of the crucial issues that the children must discuss and agree on is the place of her inhumation. Her beloved Moh has been laid to rest in Algeria, in the cemetery of Beni-Rached.

We already know that Félicie was constantly forced to negotiate the consequences of her marriage to Moh and to find unique and singular answers every time her couple was asked to perform according to the stereotyped historical script. Accustomed to the subtle maneuvering required by such a constant process of realignment, the children must continue this cultural work when the time comes to bury their mother.

To bury Félicie in France because she is French would be a plain betrayal of that model. As the eldest son notices, "si l'on se place du point de vue de Mman" [From Ma's point of view], it seems obvious that she would want to be "enterrée auprès de son homme, naturellement! Cinquante ans de mariage, cela sert bien à ça, non?" [buried next to her man of course! Married for fifty years surely gives you that right don't you think?] (304). But because the cemetery where Moh is buried is land reserved (by the living) to Muslim dead, Félicie's "point of view" triggers a whole series of frantic negotiations, metamorphoses, and storytelling activities.

When Karim, the eldest, hopes to impose what he sees as an obvious conclusion—"Un peu de bon sens, non?" [Please, have some common sense](304)—he must first convince the other children, and soon his "vehemence" is replaced by a democratic procedure. The children vote, and the variety of their positions reflects a number of different points of view. The fact that some of the children live in France is one issue: the parents' separation mirrors their own exile. Others wish to take into account potential financial and administrative difficulties. No preestablished set of rules exists. A new protocol must be invented. But in the end, the only argument considered valid above all others is the mother's (spectral) desire.

Like all ghostly performative encounters, the process by which this desire is narrated is posthumous, as if a will had been written *after* the subject's death. As is always the case, the living are confronted with the problem that they will be suspected of speaking for the dead rather than of listening to them. In Félicie's case, the "speaking for" is all the more problematic as it entails a drastic resubjectivization. In order to have the right to bury Félicie next to her husband, they must transform her into a Muslim after her death, and they must also impose this ironically identitarian narrative upon a whole audience of potentially hostile guardians of the border between two religions. As Younes explains to his siblings, "Le problème est le suivant: il s'agit du corps de Félicie épouse Miloudi. Pour qu'il soit enseveli près de Mohammed Miloudi, il faut que ce corps soit *décrété* 'musulman.'" [Here is the problem: we are talking about the body of Félicie, Miloudi's spouse. For her to be buried next to Mohammed Miloudi, her body must be *declared* "Muslim"] (308, my emphasis).

The "declaration" (in French, literally a "decree") emphasizes the performative aspect of the children's act. The point is to avoid transgressing the law of identity thanks to tactics that rely on identification markers. The strategy is neither simple nor free of risk, including the risk of self-betrayal. Djebar's narrative describes the endless series of meetings and conversations (including one exasperating visit with the Consul), the enormous amount of administrative work required to reach the children's and the mother's goal. In a highly symbolic and ironic gesture (given the sensitivity of the issue when the children were growing up), the mother's name is changed: Félicie becomes Yasmina. The text also details the long list of decisions that must be made: which ritual will they choose to perform, which one will they skip?

Each episode forces them to rethink the answer to the same theoretical question: what margin of latitude exists between a ritual and the imitation of a ritual, between apostasy and a tactical identification, and what are the risks involved in a misapprehension of the distinction? Won't the children's dissident will inadvertently reinforce the power of the laws that they are trying to question?

Only the absolutely meticulous staging of all the debates offers the reader some limited guarantee that the reinvention of the mother as one of the Muslim dead and as Yasmina does not constitute a radical act of violence against her. After all, she can no longer decide, and in colonial and postcolonial Francophone Maghrebi texts, most literary conversions are written as stories of submission and resignation.

Memmi's *Agar* (1955), in which the French wife of the first-person narrator must convert to Judaism when it becomes obvious that her son will otherwise have no legal existence within the community, comes to mind here. The experience generates an extreme level of bitterness, and the woman's consent is viewed as a tragic defeat.

In Félicie's case, the short story celebrates the complicity between the living and the dead. For the ghost to be heard, Félicie must first be repositioned as a Muslim body, and the difficulties involved in that transformation constitute the encounter. The metamorphosis does not simply change Félicie into something else; it must first create an extremely complex network of unstable subject-positions that mirror the types of choices she made while she was alive. What she must turn into does not yet exist.

The difficulty is not *that* the children must "declare" her Muslim; it is in *how* to do so. The apparent flippantness of such a "decree" is contradicted by the slowness and tediousness of the procedure. There is nothing peremptory about this subjectivization; it is a narrative construction, the long preparation for a trip that is not just metaphorical.

At the end of the story, the author suggests that the children have indeed been successful in listening to the dead mother's voice. The proof is that she actually speaks. Instead of closing on the story of her burial, the text chooses to finish on a poem, whose rhythm suddenly interrupts the flow of the prose. Those last pages are given a title: "Le rire de l'ensevelie" [The buried woman's laugh] (359). In this last section, the mother is finally able to say "I" once again. And yet, her "I" is not individualistic at all. It has become the place where collective memory can be nurtured and preserved. Her "I" represents the encounter that unites and creates the community of all the "femmes d'ailleurs" [women from elsewhere] (362).

Tout à côté femmes d'ailleurs se rassemblent
pour espérer pour se trouver
pour chanter psalmodier
"Qu'on me porte l'on m'emporte

Moi ou toi avec le corps de Félicie!"
(362)

[Right next to her the women of elsewhere gather
to hope and to find themselves
to sing and to chant
"Take me away, carry me away
I or you with Félicie's body!"]

The mother's dead body has been successfully transformed into an encountering ghost, who says "I" after her death, who speaks the poetic language of the encounter because her unique type of identification with two lands, two religions, two legacies, and many children allows her to be heard by (and become a model for) the women who gather around her.

Mehdi Charef's *Le Harki de Meriem*

Far from being an end, a return, Félicie's resting place is a new space of destination for the women who wish to establish a connection with her life. By describing the place of burial as a beginning for Félicie and for her newly found community, the short story breaks with more traditional narrative lines where death is equated with the ultimate return to the earth of origin. The metaphorical association between death and an ultimate return to the native land did not require any explanation in the past; it used to be an obvious parallel.[13] The myth is still just as powerful, and recent stories still describe the separation between the body and the land of origin as a crisis, a tragedy.

Today, however, the assumption that there is a strong, inevitable, and desirable physical or symbolic link between the land and the human being who was born there, between that person and the bodies of his or her dead ancestors, is only one of the possibilities. In the previous chapter, we encountered the tradition by which each inhabitant of Lallaoui's "olive grove" used to live his/her life and spend eternity in the same place (under one of the olive trees symbolizing that individual's existence). If that principle were modified by someone's departure, the whole village experienced a sense of imbalance, and history could no longer be properly told. Because it was published in 1998, in a globalized context that must cope with massive and diverse migration patterns, the novel had to make the reader understand that should one villager not be buried among his peers, the land itself and the memory of the village would suffer from a devastating syndrome: the relationship between the villagers and their own narrative, their own history or conception of history would be in jeopardy.

This type of relationship between the body and the land is not a hegemonic commonplace. Recent texts acknowledge that being buried where one was born is only one of the possible scenarios. It is no longer obvious that someone's birthplace coincides with the place where that person's ancestors are buried, which suggests that the encounter with the place of burial has to be reinvented, narrated, scripted. The land where one is going to be buried has to be reconsecrated by new types of stories (the language of the encounter). Just as Franco-Maghrebi subjects must actively refuse predetermined historical attributes to construct their speaking positions, the reinvention of the place of burial will modify our expectation of how the dead speak to the living, of how the living respect the dead, of how nations and religions relate to each other.

For generations, versions of the ultimate return have characterized diasporic literatures. The return to Africa was a powerful myth for Caribbean blacks.[14] The hope of going back to their native Maghreb has sustained the first generation of Maghrebi immigrants. And "nostalgeria" has haunted many *pieds-noirs*. But now, new stories are emerging that take into account the increasing dissociation between the old script and the new realities of nonnative burials.

More than forty years after the Evian Accords, many autobio-historical texts recognize that one of the (perhaps unexpected) consequences of the Franco-Algerian war is that it is no longer possible to imagine a simple "ultimate" return to the native land. The final journey must be envisaged as a construction, a penultimate moment. The increasingly familiar emergence of some "pre-ultimate" stage—the emphasis on the just-before- or just-after-death-that-is-not-death-yet—can be imagined as the literary space of the ghost. That space opens up when death has occurred but is not yet final, when it is either not accepted or not narrated as such. Somebody still has something to do, something to say. The dead body travels, encounters obstacles that no previous tale has predicted. The friends, allies, or relatives that survive must accompany the dead on that uncharted path and create new stories, new songs of mourning; they must invent new ways of preserving the memory of their departed. The site of burial does not represent a peaceful closure but the beginning of intense negotiations and interrogations. Sometimes the grave is the theater of new forms of violence and does not provide the desired sense of peacefulness and nonpartisan ending.

Although the French-Algerian axis is not unique in this regard, it provides us with an obvious case study and a model. Migrations between the two countries intensified when Algeria became independent, but the living and the dead are sometimes separated by new geographical and political frontiers. After the war, even if long years of conflict had prepared individuals to accept the inevitable, two subjects who could claim "France" as their country of origin were suddenly able, or forced, to represent themselves as either French or Algerian.

But what of the dead? Forever immobilized, their buried ancestors were not necessarily well served by historical treatises. Both countries are equally (or rather differently) affected.

A whole community of *pieds-noirs*, harkis, and Jews who left Algeria for the métropole after 1962 abandoned not only their homes but also access to burial grounds. On the other hand, for North African migrants who settled in France even as they desperately clung to narratives of mythical return, the place of burial was no longer automatic. When film and literature narrate those separations, new encounters must be imagined. Perhaps even more significant is the ghostly dialogue that authors must invent to talk about couples whose identity cannot be reduced to each individual's religion, ethnicity, or nationality. Sometimes, it is impossible to draw a clear line between the Muslim and Christian burial sites: the concept itself is self-evident, but the boundary that separates the two plots of land risks cutting through the common memory, the unique narrative of a hybrid couple. Other bodies are left with no burial site at all and their survivors are deprived a place of mourning.

In hindsight, it was perhaps predictable that authors who migrated (or whose parents migrated), who live between two nations, and whose country of origin underwent such drastic changes, would eventually experience a collective fascination for that other type of passage: the passing away, the trespassing.[15] Yet, even the presence of this obsession is more ghostly than triumphantly self-assertive. In literary or cinematic narratives, the cemetery is not systematically central to the plot; death and burials do not function as obvious, dominant themes. Often, stories about a character's death constitute a pretext, a door that will be used to open up a passage between the dead and the living and also between France and Algeria. But clearly, the place of burial slowly becomes an obsession, a haunting, and a reminder that something or someone refuses to be forgotten. The issue of the place of burial is like the soundtrack of a film, or rather like that specific type of background noise that certain films add to the plot in order to signal that the characters are dismissing crucial historical data. In Brigitte Roüan's *Outremer* [*Overseas*], the characters' conversation is ironically echoed by the background noise of a radio broadcasting snippets of speeches by Charles de Gaulle. No one listens to them, but we cannot completely eliminate them either, and their presence forces us to decide which narrative layer should be interpreted as parasitical to reality.

Like a film's soundtrack, a novel's dedication is both central and liminal: Mehdi Charef's *Le Harki de Meriem* is dedicated to "Amaria, ma soeur, qui repose près de la rivière, et m'attend à Beni-Ouassine" [Amaria, my sister, who is buried by the river and who is waiting for me at Beni-Ouassine]. At the beginning of the story, Selim, the son of Meriem and the harki Azzedine, is killed by three racist thugs. After demanding to see his identification papers, they are infuriated to discover that he is a French national. They do not want "de basanés dans les mêmes registres que nous" [wogs in our public records] (28). They stab him to death.

Selim, who has never migrated or left Reims, his native town, takes his first trip to Algeria in a coffin. Here, in a tone remarkably more somber than his famous *Le Thé au harem d'Archi Ahmed* [*Tea in the Harem*], Charef imagines what happens to the body of a harki's son. The return to the parents' native land is impossible. National rancor has erected new borders. The assassinated son's coffin never reaches its destination. It is stopped on the national border by an officer who refuses to allow the harki's son into Algeria. According to the stubborn civil servant, national memory forbids this, "Elle a de la mémoire, l'Algérie! [. . .] Le pays ne veut pas de la progéniture des traîtres!" [Algeria remembers! [. . .] Our nation does not want its traitors' children!] (38).

The dead son's sister, who had accepted this ultimate mission to take her brother's body back to the country of origin, does not comment on the allegorization of Algeria or on the officer's assurance that he knows what "she" wants and how "she" remembers. She points out, however, that he paradoxically reempowers the body when she remarks, bitterly: "Expulser un mort!" [To kick out the dead!] (41). The "expulsion" is a type of protocol of encounter that gives back some existence to her brother. The Algerian State does not see Selim as a nonentity whose harmlessness is definitively established by his death. Rejected by both countries, the dead body is in limbo, forever in movement, forever from "elsewhere" like the women of "Félicie's body" but with no community of his own.

The fact that the body's final journey cannot be completed is the reason for a ghostly performative encounter that will also reposition Selim's sister; she will become the granddaughter that she did not know she was. The failure to bury a dead son in Algeria provides the opportunity for a brief and forbidden encounter between Sahila and the grandmother she has never met. As a stranger greets Sahila at the airport, the omniscient narrator (another sort of ghostly voice) turns the unknown woman into a dissident grandmother who has taken this opportunity to impose her own wishes. She has had to brave her own relatives' interdiction in order to meet her granddaughter, Sahila. During this unexpected encounter that gives her a new position as a member of a family she neither knew she had nor knew she had lost, Sahila discovers that the immigration officer's intransigence is not the only force determined to stop her brother's body on the national border in the name of grand principles. The grandmother reveals that her family had also quietly and unanimously rejected Sahila's father. They never wrote to him and never acknowledged the letters, gifts, and money he kept sending from France in spite of their silence. "Ils se partageaient l'argent des mandats et se battaient pour les cadeaux" [they used to distribute the money and fight over presents](50) like people fighting over the belongings of a dead man.

In a sense, Selim's father has already been made a ghost. But that ghost *did* try to speak: the daughter discovers that for years, communication between the two shores was relentlessly one-sided. Though dead to his relatives, Sahila's father insisted on trying to reach out, to talk to them, even if the only language he could rely on was one of money and material goods. The story points out that the father's moment of transformation into a ghost predates his departure to France. Selim's father is one of the harkis who accepted work in the French military because he hoped to be able to support his family. His relatives accept his contributions to their wellbeing, but refuse to share any responsibility and ostracize him. As the grandmother puts it, "Ils ont vite oublié que s'ils ont pu manger et faire manger leurs enfants avant l'indépendance, c'est que ton père, en s'engageant dans l'armée française et en se reniant, les entretenait avec sa solde" [They quickly forgot that they were able to eat and feed their children because your father had signed up as a soldier in the French military and sacrificed himself and his beliefs to support them out of his paycheck] (50).

The father had lost his voice due to his family's refusal to acknowledge his existence. The relatives did not want to listen to the man who had disappeared from their lives and as a result, the son's death cannot be properly mourned. Breaking with this pattern, the old woman establishes a clear parallel between the present and the past and what happened before and after decolonization. She allows the daughter to discover her father's ghostly past.

The son's death and his failed burial, however, do not bring about any type of reconciliation. Sahila will have to take her brother's body back to Reims: "Selim fut enterré au cimetière communal de Reims" [Selim was buried at the municipal cemetery, in Reims](61). But the coffin, arrested on the national border, allowed the daughter to listen to her father in ways that had been impossible until then. Otherwise, she would never have known she was raised by a ghost.

Yamina Benguigui's *Inch'Allah dimanche*

In *Inch'Allah dimanche*, Benguigui organizes a slightly different type of encounter between women. This is her first fiction film, although the word fiction should be qualified in this case. As the director has pointed out in various interviews, the story of this young Algerian woman who leaves her country to be reunited with a husband who had previously moved to Saint Quentin, France, is a fictional rendition of her own mother's life.[16] Once again, the story enables not only the dead but also the living to transgress subject-positions that normally prevent the encounter from taking place at all. One possible account of *Inch'Allah dimanche* is that it tells the story of an encounter between the widow of a colonel who died in Kabylia during the Algerian war and a young Algerian woman who has just migrated to the North of France. As usual, however, the encounter radically changes what, in other contexts, we could call their identities. What develops between them is a multifaceted, ghostly encounter that requires us to listen to the voices of dead men while witnessing the budding relationship between two women involved in a process of rapid and radical change.

The narrative of the ghostly encounter needs to rely on an aesthetics of proliferation, piling up layer upon layer of narrative, but ensuring that each story is incomplete even when added to the others. The film avails itself of every opportunity to introduce discrepancies between the images and the dialogue, as well as the dialogue and the soundtrack. Ghosts and ghostly narratives are thus conjured but do not altogether invade the space of the realistic story. Instead, each contaminates the other. In the slightly different published version of *Inch'Allah dimanche*, other principles of layering produce similar effects. For example, intertextuality reinforces the ghostly character of some of the encounters between characters that time and space or their politics should keep apart.

As a rather didactic inaugural screen explains, *Inch'Allah dimanche* takes place in 1974, at a time when the French government closed its borders to immigrant workers and was therefore compelled to allow family reunions. Zouina's husband, who had left his young wife behind when he found work in France, decides to take advantage of the new policy. From the woman's point of view, the trip is not an unmitigated success. Abruptly separated from her own relatives and from her aging mother, Zouina finds herself confined to a small flat that she shares with Ahmed her spouse, her two children, and also a tyrannical mother-in-law bent on making her life miserable. Not only does she keep food under lock and key, but she also polices her every gesture, reporting Zouina's tiniest transgressions to her gullible and violent son and generally breeding an atmosphere of hatred and mistrust.

Desperately lonely and depressed by her mother-in-law's malicious surveillance, Zouina discovers by chance that another Algerian family, the Bouiras, live in the neighborhood. Convinced that her husband and his mother will forbid a visit, she waits impatiently until their weekly outing. The title phrase "Inch'Allah dimanche" refers to Zouina's anxious expectations of the moment of freedom that they unknowingly grant her when they both leave the house to look for a good sheep for the imminent Aïd.

Zouina waits until they are gone and secretly sneaks out with the children. But the trouble is that she does not know where to go. She has been told that the Bouiras live on "rue des Alouettes," literally "Larks street," but symbolically reminiscent of the so-called "miroir aux alouettes" (literally a trap for birds and figuratively a tempting but illusory goal, something like a wild goose chase).

Of course, she does not find the street that she is looking for. What she does find, without looking for it, is a burial place that the spectator immediately identifies as a field where soldiers are buried. This chapter of the film is called the "escapade," but the book insists on emphasizing confinement rather than freedom:

> Devant elle, aussi loin que porte le regard, des croix se dressent vers le ciel. Des centaines et des centaines de croix blanches [. . .].
>
> Une folle angoisse saisit Zouina. Comment a-t-elle pu aboutir dans ce cimetière? Elle regarde autour d'elle, accablée, prisonnière de ce labyrinthe de mort. Elle s'est perdue, jamais elle ne retrouvera la maison. (87)
>
> [As far as the eye can see, crosses rise towards the sky. Hundreds and hundreds of white crosses [. . .].
>
> A wave of anxiety submerges Zouina. How did she end up in this cemetery? She looks around her, overwhelmed, a prisoner of this labyrinth of death. She is lost, forever, she will never find her way back to the house.]

It is not clear which mythological monster Zouina is about to confront, but the omniscient narrator suggests that Zouina has reached a point of no return: "Elle s'est perdue, jamais elle ne retrouvera la maison" [She is lost, forever, she will never find her way back to the house] (87). And yet, at that precise moment, when her bearings have disappeared, in this place where people only metaphorically "visit" their dead rather than meet the living, a performative encounter will take place. Not knowing where she is, not knowing where to go, incapable of going forward or backward, Zouina is in a no-man's land whose dream-like quality is emphasized by the strangeness of the encounter she is about to make. An etymologically utopian space, the cemetery will allow new narratives to redeploy chains of solidarity between actors: not only the roles and functions of civilians and soldiers, of Algerians and French citizens, but also of dead men and women who survived them, will be radically altered by the encounter.

Zouina is not alone with her children in this foreign graveyard. When she breaks into tears (and it is not clear if she is frightened to have lost her way or appalled by the presence of so many graves), she is suddenly found by a woman in black, barely a silhouette at first. Both in the film and in the book, the newcomer asks her not to cry because "cela fait de la peine aux défunts" [it saddens the dead] (88). The text explicitly compares this woman to a ghost: "Comme sortie de terre, une femme, tout de noir vêtue, portant des lunettes aux verres fumés, un chapeau noir et des gants noirs, se tient devant elle" [A woman in black, wearing dark glasses, a black hat and black gloves stands in front of her, as if she had emerged from the ground]; she is an "apparition" (88). The conversation that is about to start is already framed by parameters that exceed the rational. In this unreal space that is also overdetermined by national history, the dead are already part of the dialogue. The tears of the living affect them, and Madame Manant, whose garb indicates that she is in mourning, seems to forbid that type of grief.

The uncanny (or serendipitous) point of connection between the two women is indeed the French-Algerian war. When Zouina explains that she is looking for the Bouiras, who are from Algeria, Madame Manant seems to lose herself in her memories and reveals that she is the widow of an officer who left for Algeria and never came back. He went missing in the Kabylian mountains.

At this point, the encounter between the two women could take a familiar turn. After all, their presence in this place of mourning begs identitarian readings where they would become the symbol either of the opposition between the two sides, or even of the reconciliation between the two countries. In both scenarios, the two female protagonists would once again be national allegories that stand for France and Algeria. What happens is completely different. In reality, neither Madame Manant nor Zouina are at home; neither woman belongs in this cemetery. Zouina is lost, and Madame Manant is only haunting this place because her husband's body is *not* buried there. He was never brought back; he is still missing; and his wife is reduced to wandering like the ghost that he has become.

In the film, Madame Manant views the absence of the body and the lack of proper ceremony as a scandal that she violently denounces, and her anger is strangely underscored by the overabundance of graves, white crosses, and other religious monuments. So many tombstones turn the rigid grid of the cemetery into a labyrinth where the women are lost, but the only grave that would give this place some meaning is missing. The French soldier is not unknown, but his body is not here. We will see that Djebar's *La Femme sans sépulture* chooses to reinterpret the topos of the absent body, but in Benguigui's film, mourning is still pathologically delayed. Only a strange alliance between the two women will allow some sort of burial ceremony to be performed. For now, they both share a sense of disorientation. No Ariadne's thread can help them out of this incomprehensible and carceral labyrinth. As in Charef's *Le Harki de Meriem*, the absence of proper burial is the pretext for the beginning of a tentative and difficult relationship between the French widow and the Algerian wife.

In the book, another element is added to the episode. A strange intertextual and literary dialogue starts between the story of the dead French officer and Djebar's *L'Amour, la fantasia*, whose graphic images of mutilation circulate as implicit or explicit quotations in the reader's memory. When Madame Manant explains how the man that she had just married disappeared during an ambush, in the novel (and in the novel only), she adds a gruesome detail:

> "On n'a pas retrouvé son corps [. . .] Enfin si. . ., ajoute Madame Manant dont la voix se brise. On m'a rapporté une main. Une très belle main, d'ailleurs." (90)

> [They never found his body [. . .] Actually. . ., Mrs. Manant adds, her voice breaking. They did bring me back a hand. A most beautiful hand by the way.]

The alliance between Fromentin and Djebar, the orientalist painter and the twentieth-century writer, haunts Benguigui's text (Djebar 1995a: 313). In this passage, the hand of a French colonel is aestheticized, the intriguing reference to the man's beauty interrupting the violence of the story. Across centuries, a male and a female hand are picked up by somebody who wishes to witness, to make them write history. Is the (admittedly problematic and thought-provoking) parallel between the soldier and the civilian, the man and the woman, another example of Stora's "mixed memories" (2001a)? The hand is all that is left, and the survivors must be content to start the grieving process in spite of the fact that everything is incomplete, including the way in which we might articulate the encounter between the female victim of the French army and the soldier killed during the Algerian war.

The film does not contain any allusion to the severed hand. Paradoxically, what could have been a terrible and powerful visual image is only present in the text. However, a similar attempt at "mixing memories" is present in the visual narrative. In the film, the difficult encounter between the dead is organized in a scene that problematizes the opposition between Muslims, Christians, French people, Algerians, and, of course, their national allegiance. A brief shot points out that some dead bodies would not have been adequately represented by the stylized military white cross. In one of the corners of the screen, we discern a quick allusion to Islam. In a marginalized and spatially decentered position, an oblong stone bears words in Arabic that beg to be read, like the mysterious monuments that keep recurring in Djebar's untraditional travel narratives such as So Vast the Prison. It is important that the director not give us enough time to figure out how the dead are repositioned by the encounter: they cohabitate, but we do not know whether the Muslim bodies were once immigrants or harkis (in which case they would have been on the same "side" during the war). Their proximity remains unexplained; the narrative does not comment. After all, this might be Félicie's grave, the site of even more complicated resubjectivizations. At this point, the contiguity between the dead could be either absurd or overdetermined, a sign of peace or war. It resembles (or rather echoes in the visual realm) the budding relationship between the two women whose presence in the labyrinth is also due partly to chance and partly to historical destiny.

From this inaugural absence (of body, of clear meaning), the tentative and difficult encounter between Zouina and Madame Manant develops. Madame Manant asks Zouina to come to her house and during one of her secret escapades, Zouina manages to do so. The ghostly encounter takes place in Madame Manant's mysterious and intimidating mansion, as the film takes advantage of the camera, the dialogue, and the soundtrack to present us with a complex and not fully articulated series of interactions between the dead and the living.

As in the cemetery, the scene starts with an interruption where two layers of narrative clash. Zouina, who holds a cup in her hand, puts it down quickly as the sound of her children's laughter is suddenly replaced by a song that, intradiegetically, she cannot hear. Both included in and excluded from the narrative, this song is the ghostly equivalent of the commentator's voice-over in historical documentaries or of the splintered broadcasts of de Gaulle's voice in Brigitte Roüan's film *Overseas*. Like the Arabic-inscribed monument that appears in front of the camera in an earlier scene, the song in Berber adds a new dimension to the French bourgeois sitting room, creating intriguing levels of proximity between worlds we cannot really describe yet.[17]

The song that only Zouina may or may not understand but cannot hear anyway is translated in the subtitles, adding a new reading space to the already visually crowded screen. This new and distracting layer interrupts the supposedly natural flow of the narrative and forces us to take several dimensions into account at once. We are also aware of the multiplicity of language and of the need for translations. This narrative layer cannot be treated like a marginal footnote or a temporary visual hindrance. It is much more than an add-on, because it makes the conversation between the two women inaudible. We know that they are talking to each other—we see them interacting, answering each other. Because we are aware of the context, we can guess that they are plotting an escapade: Zouina is determined to meet the other Algerian family and is trying to escape her mother-in-law's dictatorial gaze. The film will later confirm that the colonel's widow took care of material details, hiring a taxi to take the whole family to the "rue des Alouettes" so that Zouina can meet the Bouiras.

Yet, in that scene, the remarkable coalition between two women is beyond the spectator's reach: we are clearly expected to be torn between several layers of interpretation, like historians confronted with multiple and contradictory archival data. We have to move between the two women, the subtitles, and other visual distractions provided by the camera that focuses on photographs or other artifacts displayed in the room.

We are supposed to be confused, to be uncomfortable, and to make decisions. Should we listen more carefully to try and make out what the women are really saying, or is the content of their conversation secondary after all? The subtitles that translate the song lyrics for a non-Berber-speaking public quickly turn out to be essential: the singer reveals his identity as a *moudjahid*; he talks about torture, imprisonment, survival.

While the song colors our aural universe, other visual cues add new layers to our understanding. The camera lingers, intently, over a large portrait on the wall. We assume that this man is Madame Manant's dead husband, the colonel killed in Kabylia, the man who may have had the opportunity to torture the singer-*moudjahid*, or vice-versa (the film never tells). The presence of the two soldiers' ghosts reminds us that for history, Madame Manant and Zouina belong to two irreconcilable sides. One camp is symbolized by a faceless voice, the other by a silent face, and both are missing.

And yet, their memory is implicitly nurtured, and their story haunts the women's present to the point that we cannot listen to their conversation. This scene is not about silence or forgetting, nor about state censorship or propaganda. Instead, we hear a sort of cacophonous collection of noises, images, and sounds. The women's silence is not due to the fact that they do not speak but to the fact that we cannot hear them. And yet the fact that, as spectators, we do not understand them does not stop them from communicating, from choosing tactics, from organizing secret meetings that will eventually free Zouina from her mother-in-law's absolute control.

Once again, this is not to say that the film celebrates the encounter between the two women and the two ghosts as a blissful moment of reconciliation. Their friendship and their alliance are fragile and fraught with misunderstandings. There are as many failures as successes between them. For example, when they meet for the first time in the cemetery—where the widow looks in vain for a place to mourn while Zouina desperately needs someone to help her—the scene ends disastrously. That day, the colonel's wife has her dog, Simca, on a leash, and she agrees to let Zouina's children walk him. But no sooner have the two newly acquainted women started talking than a calamity occurs. The children, who have taken the dog for a run, apparently get involved in an accident, and Simca is killed by a vehicle. Madame Manant is hysterical. The spectator might expect the brand new friendship to end then and there. Won't the dog's death prematurely sabotage this fragile encounter, which is developing under the aegis of ghosts and death?

Benguigui chooses to imagine another conclusion to the episode. The spectator, at this point, is probably struggling to make sense of the whole scene and finding it easier to accept the atmosphere of nightmarish surreality than to find a realistic, plausible explanation for the accident. The most significant aspect of the encounter is that it is written as if it were a bad dream.

Simca, for example, is not killed by a nondescript car racing to the next town but by a military vehicle. When the camera turns towards the children, it reveals the truck—driven by a man in uniform—as one in a long procession of armored vehicles operated by a whole contingent of soldiers. The film provides no rational explanation of their presence at this place and time. We know that the scene takes place around 1974 in Saint Quentin, so we might wonder if the presence of troops in the area is one of those bizarre autobiographical memories that makes us declare that sometimes reality is stranger than fiction. We might also wonder whether or not the film makes a concerted effort to represent the ghost of military forces at the moment when the colonel's widow loses her pet.

The ghost of a war that coincides with Simca's violent death allows the omniscient narrator to reintroduce and complicate the issue of burial and mourning. For in spite of the risk that she is taking, Zouina takes the dead dog home and buries it in her garden. She gives the pet the proper burial that the colonel never got, that Madame Manant cannot give either of them. For three long hours, she digs the ground with her bare hands, terrified of the consequences of her secret, of what would happen if her husband or mother-in-law should discover what she is doing. It is after that episode that the colonel's wife, overwhelmed with gratitude, agrees to help Zouina find the "rue des Alouettes" and the Bouira family.

Meanwhile, another element has corroborated the hypothesis that the soldiers are spectral. When the ranking officer brings Zouina, the three children, and the dead dog home in one of the jeeps, followed by the convoy of tanks, we see mother and children sneak back into their home as discreetly as they can before the husband's and mother-in-law's return. Their obstreperous, racist, and slightly ridiculous French neighbor, who is forever spying on them behind her window, sees them and calls her own husband, commenting on the fact that a "whole army" has invaded the neighborhood. But when the man looks out of the window, all the soldiers have already (and implausibly) disappeared, so that his spouse's testimony is treated as a hallucination. The film conspires with Zouina to keep the ghostly encounter a secret.

Similarly, when that same night, the neighbor wakes up and catches Zouina in the act of burying the dog, a grotesque misunderstanding develops. When interrogated the next day about what she was doing in the garden at night, Zouina, who cannot tell the truth about the dog, opts for what she believes to be a harmless little lie. She was planting wild mint, she explains, and mint must be planted at night. Surprisingly, the curious and angry neighbor is hardly placated by this attempt at defusing the situation. Imagining, completely unrealistically, that Zouina has decided to enter the contest for the most beautiful garden of the neighborhood (previous scenes have informed us that the neighbor covets the prize), she exclaims, furiously: "Mais ça va envahir mon jardin!

C'est comme du chiendent, ça" [But it will overrun my garden, mint is a weed like chiendent](100). Francophone speakers will hear the name of a fast-growing weed, but Zouina does not know the word "chiendent." All she hears is "chien," the dog in French. The word is like a ghost in their conversation, and she is terrified.

Of course, her fear is misplaced. The two women have nothing to fear from each other (the neighbor did not see the dog, and there is no risk of invasion, literal or metaphorical). But they are stuck in a paranoid scenario, on the other side of the historical coin that will eventually encourage Madame Manant to act as the fairy godmother in Zouina's tale.

As in the *Le Harki de Meriem*, two women form a new alliance based on their mutual interest in a missing grave. Selim is finally buried in Reims, against his parents' wishes. His sister, in a sense, fails to return his body to the land of origin. But what national discourse lacks in compassion is at least partly compensated by the grandmother's determination to meet her granddaughter across lines of historical violence. Similarly, the two women who meet in Benguigui's cemeteries cannot change the past: they cannot give the *moudjahid* or the colonel a decent burial. But the symbolic substitution (Simca is buried in Zouina's garden) inaugurates an unlikely and difficult friendship that rearranges predictable patterns of hate and rancor.

Assia Djebar's *La Femme sans sépulture* [*The Unburied Woman*]

This chapter began with Djebar's *Algerian White* and finishes with another of her texts, her 2002 *La Femme sans sépulture*. This last example confirms, should we need confirmation, what Zouina's story intimated. The goal of the ghostly encounter is not to complete the process of individual and national mourning and to definitively bury the past (or even the dead).

In *La Femme sans sépulture*, Djebar returns to the Algerian war and, more specifically, to the way in which the children of missing *moudjahidine* deal with loss and memory. Continuing her quest for an obscured female genealogy, Djebar listens to the voice of a dead *moudjahida*, a woman who was kidnapped by French soldiers. Her body was never found, and her daughter and relatives have never been able to find a proper place where they could honor her memory together.

Zoulikha, as Djebar's foreword tells the reader, is a historical character whose story will be told, "selon une approche documentaire" [through a documentary approach] (9). The opening remark seems to exclude the possibility that this work is going to be a ghost story or veer towards the fantastic. And yet, the reconstitution of the dead woman's life and death, the narrative of how she was tortured by the French military, of how her body was never given back to the family, is also constituted of chapters unexpectedly entitled, "Zoulikha's monologues." In these pages, the dead woman addresses the reader in the first person. Her ghost speaks directly to us.

Readers who remember that Zoulikha is one of the main protagonists of the earlier film *La Nouba des femmes du Mont Chenoua* (1978) will be aware that the beginning of the novel is already an echo of previous stories. Memory stutters, repeats itself; it rereads the previous rendition of the same episode. In *La Nouba*, the narration is already a superimposition of several layers and hypotheses. We cannot simply focus on Zoulikha herself. Dream sequences, passages starting with "maybe," and unanswered questions proliferate and interrupt the flow of the stories that the female narrator tries to collect by listening to the voices of old women who represent the living archive of the Algerian war.[18] It may well be that only literary critics approach Djebar's work as an indivisible whole. Perhaps only a small minority of readers of *La Femme sans sépulture* knows about or has seen both the film and the published version of Zoulikha's story.[19]

A juxtaposition of the film *La Nouba des femmes du Mont Chenoua* and the novel *La Femme sans sépulture* reminds us that the text is a repetition, that it is already translated, or rather (precisely because this duplication remains ghostly for the majority of readers) haunted by another narrative that informs it—speaks through it—without revealing itself as a proper source of inspiration. If we systematically compared the two versions that Djebar proposes, we would be analyzing the haunting of a story by a story: the ghost of the book is a film, a different artistic voice that refuses to be laid to rest more than twenty years after *La Nouba*. Zoulikha is a returning ghost.[20]

For readers who discover the novel without being aware of the film, the ghost of Zoulikha makes its first appearance, but the principle of the encounter is not radically changed because the author must convince us, as she did in the film, that the protagonist, who refused to speak under torture, now agrees to talk to us, allowing us to historically sever ourselves from the position of potential torturers. For the book to succeed in orchestrating a successful encounter with the ghost, it must make us believe that she is willing to say "I" when the narrator listens to her and that we are capable of hearing that voice. It is both the ghost and her public need to reinvent a protocol of compassionate curiosity that constitutes the genre of the ghostly encounter.

At the beginning of the book, the narrator comes back to Césarée, the village where she is from, to look for traces of Zoulikha's life. She first questions her own status as a writer, asking what the relationship is between historiography and autobiography and between memory and faithfulness. The story anticipates an objection and defends itself in advance. The goal is to listen to the dead's message and not to make them say just anything in order to congratulate ourselves and claim that our efforts have saved them from oblivion. In *La*

Femme sans sépulture, the careful and tactical choices made by Hania, the dead *moudjahida*'s daughter, reflect the position taken by the author. They are a *mise en abyme* of the narrative as a whole. Although she is keen to preserve her mother's memory, she rejects certain ways of conjuring her up. She categorically refuses to "tenir son rôle . . . dans ce film qu'on voulait, l'an dernier, tourner à partir de sa vie" [play her role . . . in the film that they wanted to make about her life last year] (51).

—Cela, c'est autre chose!

Hania, durcie, prend à témoin l'invitée: Croient-ils qu'ils vont se débarrasser ainsi de son souvenir? [. . .] Je pense, moi, que ma mère, pas seulement comme héroïne, comme simple femme, on la tue une seconde fois, si c'est pour l'exposer ainsi, en images de télévision . . . (elle réfléchit), une image projetée n'importe comment, au moment où les familles entament leur dîner de ramadhan. (51)

[—That is something different!

Hania, tensing up, addresses the guest, expecting her to agree: Do they think that they can get rid of her memory that easily? [. . .] I happen to think that they are killing her a second time around, and not only as a heroine but as an ordinary woman if they expose my mother, as television images, . . . (she thinks for a while), an image projected thoughtlessly, just as people start eating their Ramadan dinner.]

Two practices are interpreted here as a lack of "respect" (51). Hania does not want to take her mother's place, and she does not want her body to be "exposed" to just any gaze. The old topos of the predatory eye that is already meticulously analyzed in *Femmes d'Alger dans leur appartement* reappears in a different context, as something that betrays the dead's memory.[21] Some encounters with the ghost are disrespectful and amount to a travesty.

As soon as the story begins, the issue of whether the body appears or not, whether it is exposed or hidden, whether it is framed and controlled, is linked not only to the way in which Zoulikha's memory is honored but also to the type of resistance that she chose to engage in. When she first disappears, the family's lawyer warns the relatives: "Je sais qu'il sera impossible de vous rendre le corps" [I know that it will be impossible to recover the body] (57). As in Lallaoui's novel, the missing body is transformed into the energy necessary to pursue the interminable quest for the missing ancestor. Zoulikha's victory is both denied and demonstrated by the fact that she goes missing and is turned into a ghost. Her daughter claims: "D'ailleurs, au maquis, ensuite, on disait, paraît-il, 'C'est parce que Zoulikha n'a pas parlé, pas un mot, pas un aveu, qu'à la fin, après tant de tortures, ils l'ont jetée dans la forêt! Son corps réservé aux chacals!'" [I've been told that in the mountains, people used to say: "It is because she did not talk, not a word, no confession, that in the end, after so many tortures, they threw her into the forest! Her body handed over to the jackals"](60). For the tortured combatants, the refusal to speak was a form of heroism that history would betray by replacing it with more or less fictional representations that place words, just any words, in their mouths.

Several types of relationships with the ghost are thus proposed and ruled out: it is unacceptable to expose the past, the archive, and the body as if they were objects. The ghost is not invited to choose just any form of haunting either. Certain kinds of possession and certain types of obsessive thinking are presented as temptations that will just as surely betray Zoulikha's memory as honor it. At the beginning of the narrative, the narrator and guest explain how the daughter originally searched for the mother's body in a desperate and predictably unsuccessful search. At first, she simply could not admit that there was no grave: "je n'ai même pas une tombe où aller m'incliner le vendredi . . . Une tombe de ma mère comme tant d'autres femmes de mon âge. Nous voici plus défavorisées que de simples orphelines." [I do not even have a grave where I could pay my respects on Fridays . . . A mother's grave like so many other women my age. We are worse off than simple orphans] (86). The body's disappearance leads to an obsessive quest, and the daughter is haunted by the desire to find a specific location, a tomb:

> Que dire de cette recherche, à tâtons dans les ronces et les fourrés? Et de sa sépulture, majestueuse, apparaissant en vain dans mon rêve? Je ne cessai d'errer jusqu'au crépuscule. "Où trouver le corps de ma mère?" Je criais, je me bâillonnais la bouche de mes deux mains pour ne pas hurler ces mots aux oiseaux du ciel.
>
> Si le moindre signe m'était parvenu, oh oui, j'aurais chanté à l'infini: "J'ai trouvé, moi, à force de volonté et de foi, j'ai retrouvé le corps intact de ma mère!"
>
> Hélas! Pas la moindre trace d'elle sur la pierre, ou dans un fossé, ou sur un tronc de chêne: rien. . .
>
> Dites-moi, vous qui arrivez si longtemps après: où trouver le corps de ma mère! (60)
>
> [How can I talk about how I hunted, reaching through bushes and brambles? And of how her magnificent grave appeared in vain in my dream? Till dusk I would wander. "Where shall I find my mother's body?" I would scream, I would gag my own mouth with my own hands to stop myself from yelling those words to the birds.

Had I found the slightest sign, I would have sung, oh yes, I would never have stopped singing: "I found it, I did, through sheer will and faith, I found my mother's body, and it was intact."

Alas! I never found the faintest trace of her on the stone or in a ditch or on the trunk of an oak: nothing. . .

Tell me, you who come so long afterwards: where can I find my mother's body!]

Djebar's text shows that the desire for the body prevents the daughter from relating to others and from telling her mother's story. Her obsession for the sign, for the trace, her compulsive search for something that would be "intact," has turned the living daughter into a ghost and prevents the ghost from talking to her. The daughter's words have turned into a psychotic flow that invades the body of the orphan and takes over as the only protocol of expression. Although forgetfulness is obviously impossible, this type of remembrance does not serve the dead woman's memory, because the type of obsession that the daughter is capable of does not lead to a performative encounter where she can listen to someone in spite of (or perhaps because of) the fact that everything about her is missing. That form of haunting confirms that the dead can only "come back" as frightful spirits, and listening to them is so frightening that the community will find strategies of containment to limit the power of the encounter.

In the narrator's tradition, individuals who are possessed by voices are assumed to be the prey of "*djounoun*":

Etre habitée: d'autres femmes, autrefois, disait-on, étaient "peuplées," "habitées"—en arabe, on les surnommait les *meskounates*—, mais il s'agissait à l'époque d'un djinn, bon ou mauvais esprit avec lequel ces malheureuses devaient composer, ou se soumettre en silence, quelquefois tout au long de leur vie. (62)

[To be "inhabited": about other women, we used to say that they were "peopled," "inhabited,"—in Arabic, we used to call them *meskounates*—, but at the time, we were talking about a djinn, a good or wicked spirit with which the unfortunate women had to deal, or to silently resign themselves to, sometimes during their whole life.]

The *djounoun*'s story is not what is transmitted in history books. It is a presence with which the subject must live in silence and that no one else listens to except the *meskouna*. When the ghost's presence is a type of possession, the work of mourning does not take place and silence reigns. The haunted survivors are wrapped in their own pain, and their community treats the encounter as a superstition or as a symptom.

But how is it possible that Zoulikha, who did not believe in the existence of *djounoun*, and who had even told her daughter that those beliefs were but "sornettes" [nonsense] (62), should be explained away as a *djinn*? She is not a traditional ghost who will forever haunt her daughter and expect her silent compliance. Mina, a relative that the narrator describes as her new friend, has a much more tentative explanation that takes the dead woman's agency into account: "nos souvenirs, à propos de Zoulikha, ne peuvent que tanguer, que nous rendre soudain presque schizophrènes, comme si nous n'étions pas si sûres qu'elle, la dame sans sépulture, veuille s'exprimer à travers nous!" [our memories, about Zoulikha, can only be unsteady, can only make us suddenly almost schizophrenic, as if we were not so sure that she, the unburied woman, wishes to speak through us!] (87).

The dead mother does not simply "inhabit" the daughter's body: she comes and goes, she begins the conversation, interrupts it, and then starts again. For example, when the dead mother's ghost invades her daughter, she has "de brusques accès de fièvre" [sudden bouts of fever] (61), and when absence itself talks through the daughter's body, the encounter endangers her ability to speak. She becomes "cette parole ininterrompue qui la vide, qui, parfois, la barbouille, en dedans, comme un flux de glaire qui s'écoulerait sans perte, mais extérieur" [this uninterrupted stream of words that leaves her empty, which sometimes makes her feel nauseous inside, like a flow of mucus that would run out of her without being lost, but outside] (61).

The voice that seems to emanate from the ghost is described as a mysterious and threatening force, something that is as difficult to interpret as it is to control.

> La parole en elle coule: à partir d'elle (de ses veines et veinules, de ses entrailles obscures, parfois remontant à la tête, battant à ses tempes, bourdonnant à ses oreilles, ou brouillant sa vue, au point qu'elle voit les autres, soudain, dans un flou rosâtre ou verdâtre). Quêter sans fin sa mère, ou plutôt, se dit-elle, c'est la mère en la fille, par les pores de celle-ci, la mère, oui, qui sue et s'exhale.

> Un jour, c'est sûr, tenace comme une sourde muette, la mère en elle, entêtée, soudain murmurante, la guidera jusqu'à la forêt et à la sépulture cachée. (61)

> [Words flow inside her: from her (from her veins and veinlets, from her dark entrails, sometimes going up to her head, beating at her temples, buzzing in her ears, or blurring her eyesight to the point that she suddenly sees others in a pinkish or greenish haze). To search for her mother,

forever, or rather, she thinks, it is the mother within the daughter, through her pores, the mother, yes, the mother who sweats and exhales.

One day, for sure, tenacious like a someone who is deaf and mute, the mother in her, her stubborn mother, will suddenly whisper, will guide her towards the forest and to her hidden grave.]

But the haunted subject does not hear the message that she so desperately looks for. This is partly because she does not really listen to what the ghost has to say. In fact, like the directors whose project she rejected, the daughter does not let the encounter happen. She wants the ghost to say one thing in particular. She does not so much pay attention to her voice as wait for what she wants to hear. She hopes that the mother will deliver a clear signal, that the dead woman will finally speak up clearly, but only as a dead woman, to reveal where her body is. The daughter wants the ghost to put an end to her life as a ghost, to stop this one-sided conversation that contaminates and hurts the survivor's body.

The turning point, when the encounter really takes place and the ghost and her survivor are allowed to adopt different positions, is when the narrator intervenes to propose a radically different interpretation of the ghost's haunting strategies, when she herself starts being haunted as in *Le Blanc de l'Algérie*.

Her function is to make sense, within one single story, of two narrative strands that she wishes to reconcile. The first one has to do with what she calls, in the foreword, historical accuracy, and the second one tends to be dismissively described as a hallucination and a possession. When the ghostly encounter occurs, it is no longer necessary to look for the grave, and the "I" manages to unite, within the same text, history and dream, because she has listened to what the ghost wishes to say and has not forced her to reveal what she does not consider important.

Au coeur de la nuit, revenue dans ma chambre, pendant une insomnie longue et languide, le récit de Dame Lionne que j'avais écouté sans poser la moindre question commence à se dérouler en images successives: d'abord, la silhouette de Zoulikha soudain envahit la chambre, allant et venant, moi ne me demandant même pas la raison de cette hallucination—en vérité, dans ce demi-rêve fait autant d'actions que de couleurs nostalgiques un peu passées, il me semble—moi dans mon lit, les yeux ouverts, tandis qu'à travers les fenêtres non fermées la clarté de la nuit facilite cette irréalité—il me semble que mon corps, ainsi étendu, est devenu la ville elle-même, Césarée, avec ses ruelles du quartier ancien, d'El Qsiba, et, béantes, les portes de l'enceinte telle que celle-ci existait du vivant de Zoulikha. . . (109)

[In the heart of the night, I am back in my room, and during a long and languid insomnia, Dame Lionne's story, that I had heard without ever asking a question, starts unfolding in sequences. First, Zoulikha's silhouette is suddenly inside the room, pacing back and forth, and I do not even wonder why I am hallucinating—in fact in this semidream composed as much of actions as of nostalgic, slightly faded colors, I have the impression—I am in my bed, eyes wide open, and through the open windows the night's soft light increases the feeling of irreality— that my supine body has become the city itself, Césarée, with the streets of the old neighborhood, El Qsiba, and wide open are the doors of the walls as they existed when Zoulikha was alive. . .]

The historian's body undergoes a radical metamorphosis. She becomes a city of the past, and the ghost's entrance neutralizes her will to control the genre of the narrative. The first-person narrator does not try to rationalize what she calls a "hallucination." She describes it as a gift that she accepts without feeling threatened. This is neither dream nor reality; it is a "semidream" that she neither dismisses nor understands.

The resurgence of the city from the past, as it existed when Zoulikha was alive, coincides with a different interpretation of her fate. Whereas the daughter tries to find the body at all costs and insists on finding the burial ground, the text as a whole gives Zoulikha's story another dimension. When the narrator takes over and assumes responsibility for the story, she chooses to let the missing woman speak directly in a series of "monologues" which provide us with a new version of what happened, and, more importantly, a new interpretation of what would be Zoulikha's will regarding her own grave.

For contrary to what our myths may have taught us to expect, Zoulikha is not a new version of Antigone (whose desire would be to have her own body given a proper burial). She is also the negative mirror image of the protagonists of Tahar Djaout's *Les Chercheurs d'os* (1984) whose search for the missing body parts is ambiguous at best. If we believe that the "I" who speaks in the "monologues" is indeed the result of a performative ghostly encounter, we have to believe that from her new subject-position, the historian knows something that others have never heard. That is, Zoulikha does not want her body found; she is afraid of seeing her recovered body instrumentalized and exposed in a way that would sanitize it and kill it once more.

"Ils disent: mon 'cadavre'; l'indépendance venue, peut-être diront-ils, ma 'statue,' comme si on statufiait un corps de femme, n'importe lequel, comme si, simplement, pour le dresser dehors, contre un horizon plat, il ne fallait pas des siècles de silence bâillonné pour nous les femmes! En tout cas chez nous." (207)

["They talk about my 'body'; and when independence comes, they will perhaps say my 'statue,' as if they were turning a woman's body into a statue, any body, as if, simply, to erect it outside, against the flatness of the horizon, it had not taken centuries of gagged silence for us women!"]

The text goes even further in its unexpected and astonishing celebration of the body in the process of rotting out in the open. One of Zoulikha's monologues finally reveals something the daughter wishes to know, though it is not a response she can readily accept. Zoulikha was both buried *and* desecrated by that burial. Her body was interred, but that is why it is now missing. The text dares to transgress a taboo that is shared by so many cultures and that Djebar's readers will probably take for granted: the belief that the decomposing corpse is the epitome of horror. The vision of a body that is both dead and still alive because it is now inhabited by a different type of life, a body that is both still and animated by an unacceptable overabundance of involuntary movements, is the very image of the unbearable, of the abject: "Le plus souvent, la vision de la décomposition est source d'horreur: non pas seulement de dégoût mais de répugnance épouvantée. Dans ces conditions, il est essentiel, afin que les mythologies soient et demeurent rassurantes, d'empêcher l'émergence sauvage de la putréfaction, d'éluder sa manifestation ou même son évocation dès lors qu'elles sont dépourvues de transcendance" [The vision of decomposition is most often a source of horror, not only of disgust but of terrified revulsion. Consequently, it is crucial, for our mythologies to keep reassuring us, to prevent the uncontrolled emergence of putrefaction, to avoid its manifestation or even allusions to it unless transcendence is possible] (Urbain 1989: 27). The next logical step is to suspect that the burial rite, which may well protect the living from their own fear, is at least partly instrumentalized when we treat it as a gesture that honors the dead. The terror elicited by the crawling of maggots within a human corpse may explain why the skeleton, the dried up and mummified body, the statue, or the tombstone—in short, the hardened and finally immobile monument—may be experienced as a desirable closure. It rewrites death into something acceptable, for the living.[22]

Refusing the desire for closure, Zoulikha points out the distinction between the daughter's endless quest for the body and her own wish to preserve a type of dissident energy that no one but she is willing to accept. The ghostly encounter creates a new mythology around burial, taking the risk to propose a positively charged interpretation of the unburied body left to rot above ground. The novel is more than a historical restitution of Zoulikha's torture and death. It adds an unexpected dimension that cannot find its place within a dispassionate historical puzzle where all the pieces fit and add up to constitute one coherent picture.

At the end of the book, the narrator attributes to Zoulikha a statement that might well be perceived as extravagant or even slightly obscene: the murdered *moudjahida* claims that she was indeed buried, but that, contrary to what a certain kind of historical common sense would expect, the moment when she was put into the ground was a moment of regression, a betrayal of her revolutionary act of resistance. The woman was tortured to death and then exposed for three days, outside. Then, "La troisième nuit, c'est ce qu'on a prétendu, mon corps a disparu" [the third night, that's what people claimed, my body disappeared] (207).

At this point, Djebar's text explains why the daughter's relationship with the ghost has been presented as ceaselessly frustrating and diseased. Instead of transforming its interlocutor into a whole city, the encounter has turned the survivor's organs into a shapeless flow, and the reader may not suspect that this is because the narrative proposed by the ghost is literally unbearable to the daughter.

We do not have to believe that the ghost really says "I" for the ghostly encounter to function. What we can do, however, is witness the different types of possible desires staged as a failed dialogue between Hania, who cannot properly listen to the dear departed, and the mother, whose extraordinary perspective is finally folded into the novel as a plausible story.

In a passage that celebrates the body in decomposition and blames the young man who probably expected gratitude and praise for giving her a proper burial, the "I" states:

> Ce fut un des garçons de la grotte qui vint, en voleur héroïque, me chercher. Il me porta sur ses épaules. Lourde je suis, et je l'étais davantage, non à cause de la douleur des sévices sous la tente, plutôt à la suite des heures ensoleillées qui m'avaient rendue bourdonnante et fertile, une plante grasse. (207)

> [One of the boys from the cave, a heroic thief, came to pick me up. He carried me on his shoulders. I am heavy, I was even heavier, not because of the pain of tortures endured under the tent, but because of all the sun-flooded hours that had turned me be into a buzzing and fertile succulent.]

The *moudjahid* is "heroic" but the adjective is a concession reluctantly granted to the "thief." The body, on the other hand, is "fertile" and talkative, humming or buzzing like the daughter's entrails when the memory of the dead invades her. And although Zoulikha understands and sympathizes with the man, she maintains that his gesture did her wrong:

> Car s'il y a bien un homme qui un jour me limita, qui m'étouffa, qui me trahit, certes malgré lui, ce fut plutôt ce garçon! [. . .] Lui seul, malgré lui et malgré les autres, il réussit à m'enfermer, à me plomber. Il m'enterra.

C'était sa forme d'amour. Alors que, spontanément, l'ennemi avait trouvé ce qui convenait le mieux à mes fibres, à mes muscles: pourrir en plein air, sous des youyous de femmes me transperçant. Non, il m'enterra! Selon la tradition. . . . Il m'honora selon l'Islam.

Je te l'avoue, vingt ans après, j'en souffre encore. (210)

[For if one man did limit me, stifled me, betrayed me, of course unwillingly, that boy did! [. . .] He alone, in spite of himself and in spite of others, he managed to shut me up, weighed me down with lead. He buried me. It was his form of love. Whereas the enemy had spontaneously found out what was most suitable for my fibers and muscles: to rot in the open air, as the women's youyous went through me. No, he buried me! In accordance to tradition. . . . He honored me, in accordance with Islam.

I confess to you that, twenty years later, I still feel that pain.]

As the narrator of *L'Amour, la fantasia* (1995) has done earlier with Pélissier (the man responsible for the Dahra massacre), Zoulikha praises the "enemy" for inventing a transgressive, and thus more appropriate, rite of noninterment. In spite of their hatred and malicious intent, the French soldiers offer the dishonored corpse a margin of latitude that empowers her two decades later. She can speak up in her own name and sing a song that can afford to be poetic (as well as historical), feminist, and revolutionary. She does so from a position that is not supposed to exist, namely, her missing body: "mon corps, la deuxième journée, se met à s'ouvrir. Une sorte de rumeur, intérieure à sa chair, cherche comment se mêler aux odeurs du printemps déserté" [the second day, my body starts opening up. A sort of rumor, from within its flesh, tries to blend with the smells of the deserted spring] (205). By burying her, the young boy clumsily deprives her of a chance to let that "rumor" spread. When she refuses to return to the ground, the mother's dead body chooses the place where her memory should be honored, including by her daughter. That place is a book, a text that brazenly accepts the possibility that what the dead have to say is as unbearable as the pain that they have suffered. Hania has been looking for a still and speechless grave, and the novel offers itself up as a different kind of tombstone, a terrifying and fertile proliferation of images and narratives that continues, after the protagonist's death, to support and celebrate the short but stubbornly dissident life that she had always insisted upon leading. The desire for freedom and dignity is neither buried nor missing; it is alive, if not safe, within the novel's words.

The place where the body is laid is irrelevant after all. It is but a "clairière, ma chérie, où tu ne viendras jamais [. . .] N'importe, c'est sur la place du douar, la voix de l'inconnue chantant inlassablement, c'est là, yeux ouverts, dans tout mon corps pourrissant, que je t'attends" [clearing, my darling, where you will never come [. . .] But it does not matter. In the middle of the village, as the voice of the unknown woman forever sings, there, eyes wide open, with my whole rotting body, I wait for you] (212).

At the end of the book, the image of the rotting body has been reworked and reinterpreted through a series of monologues and thanks to the combined interventions of all the female characters that remembered Zoulikha in the presence of the visitor. Zoulikha's monologues are scattered through the book, and though her voice is fragmented, the fragmentation is not the equivalent of the violence done to a dismembered body. Zoulikha is alternately silent and talkative, and the narrator herself sometimes listens and sometimes speaks up. The elegiac text remains a monologue, that is, something that must be heard as though by an audience willing to be patient, to attend up until the end without interrupting. But the links between the testimony, the autobiography, and the novel are so intricate that we can no longer distinguish between the voice of the ghost and that of the historian (who radically changes as we read). In the end, it is no longer clear whether the ghost is speaking to, or through, the narrator or if it is the other way around: "Mon soliloque à présent, au-dessus de la ville, moi qui te cherche, qui tâtonne en bouffées de poussée insidieuse vers toi et ton sommeil, mon soliloque tant d'années après—cadavre effiloché dans l'espace au dessus des flots sans avoir jamais pué—devient un chant presque glorieux" [And now my soliloquy, above the city, as I look for you, as I feel my way insidiously pushing myself towards you and your slumber, my soliloquy, so many years later—I, a body stretched in space above the waters, a body that never stank—my soliloquy becomes an almost triumphant song] (168).

Conclusion

Like all the other texts explored in this chapter, *La Femme sans sépulture* adds its tragic note to the ensemble of voices that mourn an irreparable loss. The text no longer tries to perform historical exhumation of the victims, but it is also not prepared to bury the dead if proper burial ritual is simply another way to silence them (especially as women). A new genre is progressively replacing the typical archeological writing that Djebar carried out in her first books. That narrative strategy is tentatively replaced by an attempt to perform meaningful encounters with protagonists that historical violence has definitively placed out of reach. Recent Franco-Maghrebi literature of the kind studied in this chapter is an attempt at conjuring up ghosts that must be repositioned in order for the survivors to be able to hear what they say, rather than what they think they wish to hear. At least, this is the figure of writing that is proposed, almost allegorically, in *La Femme sans sépulture.*

When a novel is haunted, it represents the symptomatic trace of the ghost as an entity that must be translated and that moves through the borders of genres and bodies. Realism and poetry, history and fiction suddenly cohabit, albeit uneasily. The characters are depicted as porous entities capable of transformation and metamorphosis. Like the mythic mediator who helps the dead cross over to their new kingdom, the text helps the reader cross frontiers that separate the dead and living by helping us visualized them as comparable to the borders that Franco-Maghrebi subjects constantly negotiate. Ghostly encounters suggest that death does not interrupt, but rather changes the movements of migrants, exiles, or deportees. They show that there is no simple relationship between the burial ground and the country of origin or between roots and native land. If there were ever a time when literature imagined that the dead haunt only their own communities or their own villages, that myth has lost its aura of immediate truth. Even the inhabitants of Lallaoui's olive grove have to recognize, at the end of the novel, that the absence that haunts them is a form of historical energy, one which promises the possibility of encounters that have nothing to do with the ancestor's identity. New truths must be discovered, and new lands must be explored instead of recaptured. To bring a body back to the village would not put an end to the quest. The novel's strength is to tolerate—even nurture—the hypothesis that the missing body will never be returned to the land of its ancestors.

Ghostly performative encounters, when they succeed, are destabilizing and can easily be dismissed as a short-lived glimpse into the uncanny. But they also invite us to reconsider the distinction between those who speak and those who listen, those who will or will not testify. The ghost, whose disturbing presence-absence blurs the convenient distinction between history and fiction, memory and forgetfulness, mourning and haunting speaks a kind of truth that is not verifiable because it can never be guaranteed by the solid reality of the archive, the silent and decaying monument. If the ghostly encounter is performative, it makes us conscious not that we have dealt with loss once and for all but that the acute sense of an irreparable loss is what must be written with the appropriate *qalam.* It treats the encounter between France and the Maghreb as what is perhaps forever both mourned and, as Cixous puts it, "indeuillable" (unmournable).[23] Even if we successfully listen to the voice of people like Zoulikha, listening obviously does not bring them back. It does not put an end to the process of mourning; it merely makes it possible. Nothing is recovered (not even the body) except our sense that something that one cannot renounce has been irreparably lost because the memory of the dead cannot "feel its way" into the statues sacralized by official history, our sense that the dead will lose their voices if we try to bury them against their will. A ghostly encounter is a proliferating, terrifying, and decomposing *logos* rather than a monument that one visits once in a while.

Neither the ghost, nor the body, nor the survivors have found (or will find) any rest or peace. The historical, mythic, and literary dead are the raw material of an international process of collective and individual mourning. The desire to find the truth about the dead hero or heroine is not a drive towards closure. The ghost is conjured, not dismissed, by the encounter, even if he or she reappears as something that we may not identify as a traditional ghost. The encounter shares with the ghost the determination to linger on and not be silenced. Something remains to be said, to be heard. Perhaps this is why cemeteries are not resting places.

6

Encounters and Acrobats

Performative encounters do not help us articulate how subjects have moved from a dual metaphor of coupling (between France and Algeria for example) to images of a mosaic that take into account a multiplicity of religious, ethnic, and gendered specificities. Instead, the protagonists of the encounter not only construct a unique relationship with the idea of duality, hybridity, and inbetweenness but also expect their audience to recognize their constructions.

The specificity of one's relationship to hybridity does not require radical transformations of narrative techniques. Performative encounters thrive on barely perceptible shifts and changes and on accented inflections rather than on revolutionary moves announced like "new" objects (the *nouveau roman*, the New Wave). Often, a second look, an oblique gaze will be necessary before the performative encounter is noticed. The reader will then be in the position of a patient and careful observer who, after remaining still in front of a shallow pool of water where nothing seems to move, suddenly becomes aware of the surreptitious movement of a shy and furtive animal that was afraid of revealing its presence. Something is where nothing seemed to be.

A historical shift has taken place, but the trace it has left in our memory or our consciousness is almost imperceptible. Unlike revolutions, performative encounters are not well served by dates or by stories that present themselves as the definitive revision of a historical lie. A comparison of narratives written roughly at the same period about what some might call the "same" issue is more likely to guide our awareness, gradually and almost in spite of ourselves, of the traces left by an encounter.

Performative encounters start appearing on a reader's critical radar when he or she pays attention to the various kinds of *practices* that hybrid subjects choose from their own palette. Once alerted to the possibilities, a reader may start comparing the types of exchange, of language, of protocol, and of subjectivization.

N'zid: Of Jellyfish and Sea Urchins

At first sight, some narratives will seem conventionally organized around a strong set of allegorical elements that do not leave much space for nuance and complexity. If we actively read for the transparent meaning of signs, we risk being frustrated by the force of allegories and miss the tiny tears that moments of encounter open up within the fabric of the text. Fatalistic scripts will seem to foreclose the possibility of performative encounters.

Mokeddem's *N'zid* is a case in point. In the novel, the amnesiac female protagonist wakes up on an unnamed ship, somewhere in the middle of the sea. We might expect her blank memory to free her from prewritten narratives of nationality, ethnicity, and hybridity. With no past and no future, no home and no address, no name and no identity, she searches for a vision of herself and works at inventing herself through art. Indeed, she inscribes herself on a page. Her medium of choice is a *qalam* of sorts, but she chooses the pen over the ink. Within the story, she does not write; she draws. Her imagination constructs the world as a collection of animals such as jellyfish and sea urchins:

> Elle peint l'histoire d'une méduse amoureuse d'un oursin. Un sédentaire des plus barricadés qui ne la regarde même pas. Vissé à son rocher, au milieu d'une tribu hérissée, il ignore totalement la subtilité des reflets de sa peau diaphane. Il s'en est fallu de peu que son ballet de séduction, autour de lui, ne tourne en danse macabre. Elle a failli se déchiqueter sur les piques de sa communauté. Elle s'éloigne à regret. (2001: 35)

> [She draws the story of a female jellyfish in love with a male sea urchin, a most barricaded sedentary creature who does not even look at her. Screwed to his rock, surrounded by his bristling tribe, he ignores the subtlety of her diaphanous skin. Her seduction ballet around him very nearly ended in a death dance. She almost ripped herself to shreds on the spines of his community. Sadly, she drifts away.][1]

Here, the text obviously treats the visual narrative as a tentative self-portrait and autobiography, and I wonder if many readers share my initial impression that the passage's symbolism is a bit disappointingly obvious. The blank slate that the main character's amnesia offers as a fictional possibility is replaced by a reorganization of her universe, and that move entails straightforward identifications to clearly symbolic animals.

At first, the scene of failed encounter between strangers seems highly predictable. When I first read those pages, I remember thinking that they could provide a counterexample of performativity to the extent that Mokeddem sets up narrative conditions that would preclude the diegetic development of a performative encounter. In what could be described as a myth of encounter, one of the protagonists suffers from the other's sedentary nature. There is no real tension or open conflict. Instead, a fundamental incompatibility causes the nomadic jellyfish to get hurt. The sedentary and nomadic essence of each of the mythic protagonists is supposed to explain why they cannot cohabitate without one being torn to shreds. The cause of the problem is difference, or, to be more accurate, the text invites us to allegorize the representation of supposedly inherent natural characteristics as social traits and then to use that grid as the explanation for individual and community conflicts.

Not only is the picture neatly symbolic, but it is also ideologically biased in favor of the jellyfish. In a barely disguised self-promoting gesture, the first-person narrator identifies with the grammatically feminine drifter. One of the animals is vulnerable, "subtle" in its transparency; the other one is endowed with spines. It is turned inward, does not look, and does not open up; the aggressiveness of its physical appearance is reenforced by the fact that it belongs to a cohesive group.

The drawing is a manifestation of the narrator's pessimistic vision of essentialized encounters between strangers who fall into the natural(ized) categories of nomadic or sedentary beings. Her choice of emblematic animals naturalizes what she sees as individuals' unchangeable characteristics and the influence exerted by communities, viewed as groups of like-minded creatures. Some subjects and societies have rigid sedentary practices. The artist's picture is about what sea urchins *are* rather than about what they do.

At first sight, then, the narrator seems to side unambiguously with the jellyfish, emphasizing a subtlety that the text lacks. An overall ironic echo within the passage is generated by this tension between a thematic celebration of nuance and diaphanous essences in sharp contrast with the story's duality and unsubtle, straightforward symbolism. The difference between the two animals encourages a simple allegorical reading in which the figures of the sedentary and the nomadic are opposed and immobilized so that the supposedly subtle jellyfish is inscribed in a text whose transparency is not subtle. Clearly, the story prefers the nomad.

In itself, that ironical tension could suffice to make us suspect that the encounter takes place at that level: between the characters and their textual destiny rather than between the diegetic protagonists themselves. This impression is confirmed by the fact that, as in most literary texts, a few self-contradictory elements reintroduce beneficial zones of opacity. However, the little myth has trouble formulating its own theory of destiny and nature. It does not consistently explain the seemingly obvious contract of encounter between sedentary and nomadic subjects, and it constantly hesitates between agency (one chooses to be a nomad) and essentialism (one was born a sedentary creature).

For example, the vocabulary blames the sea urchin, giving us the impression that the animal has free will and chose to be egocentric and self-centered instead of just being what destiny ordered it to be. The sea urchin protects himself behind "barricades" and its gaze is deliberately averted (it does not look at her). Even his relationship to the soil is painted in derogatory terms; it is not "attached" to the native land like Aimé Césaire's "laminaria" (1982), it is "vissé," literally "screwed" or metaphorically "glued" to the rock like a teenager to a television. If attachment connotes figurative faithfulness, being "glued" implies stubbornness and mindlessness instead. Besides, the guilty party is not alone and is surrounded with equally aggressive accomplices. His community displays a sort of "tribal" (perhaps archaic? primitive?) loyalty that the text describes as inhospitable and violent to strangers: the tribe is "hérissée," bristling with spines.

Curiously then, a fracture opens up between the drawing and the text that is supposed to describe it faithfully and in fact, translates it, opaquely. The mediated written account offers us a glimmer of hope by paradoxically troubling the neat duality between the incompatible animals. The tensions of any performative encounters have to be discovered in this denied margin of contestation where the drawing and its legend contradict each other.[2]

If the drawing believes that the jellyfish can be beautiful because it is both subtle and transparent, the text seems to be resigned to the impossibility of being both. The "legend" that proposes a reading protocol adds opacity and ambiguity, forcing us to doubt that either essentialism or agency can be isolated. Moments of performative encounters disturb such categories just as this passage shows that no legend can be trusted to either justify incompatibility or find magical ways of bypassing it through active and generous gestures of rapprochement.

The narrator, whose half-explicit intention is self-representational, is aware of the limits of her own art. She knows that her own portrait hides in her fable (she is reinventing herself and literally trying to "re-member" what her body means), but she also suggests that it is not up to her to provide an interpretive grid: "Tu es comme tes dessins. Des traits. Des formes. Des vibrations sans *légende*" [You are like your drawings. Lines. Shapes. Vibrations with no explanation] (43, my emphasis).

While the text supplies explanations in abundance, it also describes the relationship between the self and the drawing as an encounter that will remain opaque. The narrator suggests that no guideline is attached to the visual narrative. In spite of the seemingly obvious connection between the "I" and the jellyfish, the narrative voice warns us that she does not so much identify with *what* is drawn (she is not *like* a jelly fish) but with the art itself. She is like *her drawing*; she does not come with instructions; she cannot be read. Like Félicie's tenderness for "Moh," she can only be perceived at the level of vibrations.

The performative encounter occurs both within and beyond the narrator's attempts at allegorizing the encounter within the narrative. Within the quasi-impossibility of stabilizing the image resides the seed of a hopeful disruption of the pessimistic and fatalistic vision. As soon as the essential positions are drawn, they lose their sharpness and neat contours. The borders between the two types are immediately redrawn and made fuzzy by any attempt to narrate the encounter. Metaphors, like people and relationships, evolve as if they had a will of their own. Here, textual images do not so much articulate each animal's essential nomadic or sedentary nature as the slowly changing perception that each subject entertains when confronted with markers of his or her identity.

The complicated textual theatre of performative encounters is a dance between words and images, and the dance can be a flirtatious ballet ("ballet de seduction") or a dance of death ("danse macabre") that resembles the relationship between the woman who came from the South and the man who came from the North. Apparently unaware that her description of her parents' relationship resembles the encounter between the jellyfish and the sea urchin, the narrator remembers their love as a form of violent and amorous intertwining:

Il venait des brumes et des pluies du Nord, de la langue gaélique. Elle arrivait du Sud, du soleil et de l'arabe. Ils fracassaient ensemble le français. Il était grand et roux, elle, fluette et brune. Ils se sont jetés l'un sur l'autre comme des affamés. Enfant, je les ai toujours vus l'un contre l'autre. Ils s'aimaient et se déchiraient avec la même violence. (111)

[He came from the North, its rains and fog, its Gaelic language. She came from the South, from the sun and Arabic. Together they used to fracture the French language. He was tall and redheaded. She was slim and dark. They pounced on each other as if they were starving. As a child, I always saw them going at each other. They loved and tore each other apart with the same violence.]

Ironically, the picture, that pretends not to have captions and to draw its force from its mere self-evident presence, does not exist at all. The pencil makes a point that we cannot see, and the scene must be mediated by what is, in effect, a story. The reader must trust the author's words to capture the meaningfulness of the encounter between the two animals. Adjectives and verbs (not extratextual lines and forms) endow the animals with anthropomorphic characteristics that amount to the creation of a social environment and the description of practices of cohabitation.

The picture has no referent. It is an extratextual absence mediated, or even created, by words whose power it denies. Its only form of existence, of essence, is that it is described by words, words that not only constitute a legend but whose lesson discredits the implied message of the supposedly clear pictures. As language and images meet, subtlety and transparency lose their immediate compatibility, just as agency and essentialism, drifting and attachment get rearranged along a complex continuum. Prescribed modes of inhabiting give way to supposedly implausible practices: the stranger becomes an adroit dancer who must perform seduction then retreat, who must risk its life to challenge a hostile environment.

Plantu's Acrobat

Performative encounters often require the subject to acquire exceptional flexibility and to become a gymnast, a dancer, or an acrobat. In 1987, Gérard Fuchs published a study of Maghrebi immigration in France. The title he chose was already a thesis, or at least, a prediction. *Ils resteront: le défi de l'immigration* [They Will Stay: the Challenge of Immigration]. The reference to migrants imagined as a whole category is relegated to the subtitle as if it were more important to emphasize what they will do than who they are. The fact that they "will" stay sounds like a promise, or a warning, and, at any rate, a fact that can be predicted.

The cover of the book is illustrated by one of Jean Plantu's drawings and we can expect that most French readers will recognize his style (his work appears every day on the front page of *Le Monde*). In this characteristically evocative picture, an Arab-looking man is stretched between two chairs, one representing France and the other one Africa. His feet barely reach each continent and his position looks painfully uncomfortable. Once again, the contrast between the title and the visual narrative opens up a tension between the words and the image. While "They will stay" suggests integration, presumably into one unique country of arrival, the artist represents, in his own way, a method of "staying" (put) that involves being in between two spaces. To the title's suggestion that the migrants will be in France forever, the picture replies with a vision of a character who straddles France and Africa.[3]

Like any allusion to inbetweenness, Plantu's drawing tells a story and suggests a model of what one does, or what one says, in such a position. It also reveals what language does when the category of "inbetweenness" intervenes. For example, to suggest that the character is torn or split between two spaces, it is necessary to visualize the poles between which someone will be stretched. It is also important, in this case, that the author limits the number of spatial anchors to two—France and Africa—and that he should opt to reduce them to chairs, which the migrant cannot use normally. The fact that his hero cannot sit down is Plantu's description of the encounter with immigration, and he makes us visualize the specific protocol as an acrobatic position.

The migrant's discomfort has become a form of extreme physical flexibility. He stays in a position that few of us could endure for long or even assume at all. Such positions are typically reserved to gymnasts or dancers, perhaps even to female dancers, to whom our statistical imagination would attribute more natural elasticity. Performing "the splits" is not required in our daily activities; it is a professional attitude, part of a choreographed routine or ballet or perhaps part of an intense stretching session (something we would call exercising). The goal is to turn the body into a beautiful and exceptional spectacle. The split is a rare and admirable posture, not a commonplace attitude. For the artist, then, the protocol of encounter between the immigrant and the space(s) he inhabits is a form of gymnastics that his character performs with nonchalant agility.

And yet, something is missing from this performance, namely the admiring public and the conventions of the show. Circus drums or the crowd of supporters drawn by first-class competitions are missing from this scene, and the poor character is left to a disenchanted solitude. His prowess is not appreciated. Plantu suggests that migrants engage in tough protocols of encounter and that even when they master the difficulty, their success is not applauded. Their being-in-the-world is a type of performance that is ignored as such. Cumbersome symbolic objects that only add to the difficulty of the exercise comically replace the artist's shimmering costume or glamorous accessories.

But like Mokeddem's pictures, this scene is engaged in a dialogue with language. As visual as it is, the drawing is also implicitly linked to a sort of legend. It is made possible by the existence of a set phrase that smuggles collateral meaning. In French, the idea of sitting on the fence is typically rendered by the expression "to have one's ass between two chairs," which functions as the implicit decoder of a whole series of cultural associations. It explains why each country of residence is visualized as a seat. At the same time, the picture rewrites the expression and exposes its limits. Plantu suggests that when the two chairs are too far away from each other, no normal derriere can accommodate the distance. Sitting is impossible, and the hybrid must become an acrobat.

The force of the demonstration is impeccable, and I would like to suggest that such representations constitute performative descriptions of what it means to act inbetweenness rather than to be in between. Understanding the image is the equivalent of accepting Plantu's proposal without being aware that the conciseness and effectiveness of the story makes a theoretical point, defends a thesis that we can then compare to other similar proposals, such as Mokeddem's encounters between jellyfish and sea urchins.

The position assumed by Plantu's immigrant is not, I would suggest, a representation of his identity, let alone an essential characteristic. His flexibility is not natural: it is a skill demanded by his situation; it constitutes the protocol of the encounter in which the body is the alphabet of a specific language. As other texts will demonstrate, this protocol of bending and flexing is a common denominator that various stories of encounter decline.

The Woman as "Chetaha" in Benmalek's *Les Amants désunis*

In Anouar Benmalek's *Les Amants désunis* (1998) [*The Lovers of Algeria* (2001)], the "disunited lovers" announced by the title are Anna and Nassreddine. The former is originally from Switzerland; the latter is a Berber. In this book the European woman, rather than the Maghrebi man, is the acrobat. The plot, which mirrors historical events and makes history look like a hostile conspiracy, keeps separating the two lovers, who will only be reunited at the very end of the novel after a relentless series of tragic encounters with anti-Semitic, xenophobic, and racist forces. The supposedly "abnormal" couple is persecuted by the agents of colonial violence, by the representatives of the Vichy government in Algeria, and finally by combatants on both sides of the French-Algerian war. At first, Nassreddine is arrested and accused of having murdered and eaten two tax collectors who have gone missing not very far from his native village in Kabylia. Next, Rina, Anna's Jewish adoptive mother, is the victim of anti-Semitic violence. She is incarcerated in Algiers and dies from a bad case of typhus during her captivity. At the same moment, Nassreddine, who has become Anna's lover, is quasi-kidnapped by the military and "mobilisé d'office dans le 7e régiment des tirailleurs algériens en partance vers la grande boucherie européenne" [dragged out and formally inducted into the 7th Algerian Regiment, which is about to take ship for the great butchery in Europe] (1998: 251; 2001: 198). When he comes back, he discovers that Anna has vanished. His own father, shot during the 1945 Setif riots, is left for dead under a heap of corpses and dies after two days of abominable suffering. In spite of Nassreddine's determination and unconditional love for Anna (he is able find her trace and follow her all the way to Madagascar where she ended up with the circus that hired her), neither destiny nor the author gives the lovers a break. Each chapter of their life is tragically impacted by contemporary historical events. Page after page, the script gives them more reasons to despair, as if their couple is nothing but the expression of what is always, historically, impossible, unthinkable—an always already failed encounter. When they come back to Algeria with their two children, they decide to get married. However, the war of liberation has already started, and their loving encounter has become an unbearable provocation on both sides. In the Aurès, in 1955, the administrator who reluctantly marries them can barely conceal his disgust (1998: 16; 2001: 6). One of the soldiers who checks their passports and opens the brand new "livret de famille" (the French equivalent of a marriage license), "crache par terre de dégoût: 'Madame, vous trahissez votre race!'" (17) [spits to the ground in disgust: "Madame, you are a traitor to your race"] (6). This last identity check will prove fatal: arrested by soldiers and tortured, Nassreddine is branded a traitor by the NLF, which kills his children in reprisal. As for Anna, the soldiers take her away. A whole generation will be necessary, this time, for the two lovers to be reunited, on a territory that is, once again, in the throes of unspeakable violence. The couple's fate is ineluctably tied to Algeria's tragic destiny: terrorism, this time, separates the lovers.

This long enumeration of what happens to the lovers is not meant as a plot summary. Instead, the point is to highlight the deliberately repetitive quality of the book's structure. The historical script is presented as a relentless list of catastrophes, and this poses a narrative challenge to the author of the text. When a linear narrative of historical events can only consist of a succession of disasters, what type of story will make it possible to break the pattern of hopeless predictability? Like Mokeddem's drawings, won't this tragedy be a counterexample of performative encounters? But here, too, the performative fictionalization of a principle of hope is to be found in the author's narrative technique, namely in his delaying of the reunion and in his successful representation of the heroes' infinite patience. The narrative takes its time; the characters (and the readers) are made to wait as long as it takes, not passively but stubbornly, actively. No matter how many historically plausible obstacles the author uses as tests, the couple that he has invented resists the pressure of the prewritten script of disunion.

From a purely technical point of view, we could read the story as a constant fighting of the almost irresistible pressure exerted by referentiality. If history encodes an encounter between Algeria and its others as a prewritten fiasco, it becomes a force capable of paralyzing the narrative because it imposes its own law of the genre.

Won't the narrative voice find itself in the position of Yasmina Khadra's Inspector Llob in *Morituri*? This qualified and experienced hero and cop describes his daily confrontation with violence as a form of slowing down that leads to immobilization or regression:

Il y a, de mon immeuble au garage où je range ma voiture, deux cent mètres. Avant je les parcourais d'une seule enjambée. Aujourd'hui, c'est tout une expédition. Tout me paraît suspect. Chaque pas est un péril. Des fois, j'ai tellement les jetons que j'envisage de rebrousser chemin. (1997: 16)

[A few blocks separate my building from the garage where I park my car. It used to be a quick and straightforward walk. Today, it has become an expedition. Everything looks suspicious. Each step is perilous. Sometimes, I am so scared that I want to walk back.]

The genre of the detective story requires that the character, the investigation, and the narrative progress, move forward towards closure and revelation. When the hero is paralyzed by fear, when he wants to move backwards, the story stalls with him: the space that he used to cross absentmindedly has become a thick and impenetrable layer of reality. When everything is suspicious, suspicion becomes unmanageable. No distinction can be made within the real. Every detail is a potential threat; no choice can be made among what is meaningful, important, and negligible. If telling a story is the art of sorting out what need not be told, it is easy to see how, when the elements of the real can no longer be sorted out, narrative organization fails. Any sign may announce the hero's death; he is one of the "Morituri," one of the gladiators who are about to die in the arena. The narrative, the investigation, and the inspector stop on a non-threshold that cannot be crossed.[4]

Just as the text cannot describe the least undesirable individual trajectory, the hero cannot pick his route and he is stuck. He makes no distinction between suspicious or harmless elements of the real; he cannot tell us whether crossing here or there is more or less dangerous, preferable or even possible. Benmalek's characters occupy similar positions. How, then, does the realist novel, whose laws are slightly different from the detective story, tell the impossible tale of two characters whose encounter stretches the limits of our definition of the plausible, requiring acrobatic negotiations and mental leaps of faith. Humor would be one of the ways of bending the inflexible data imposed by language, culture, or historical events. But Benmalek does not turn to smiles and laughter as (textual) survival tactics.

Anne and Nassreddine's encounter is radically unhappy (and yet felicitous) because the novel helps them cross this catastrophic threshold where nothing makes sense. The narrative tool used by Benmalek, the relay that enables him to bypass, and therefore to change, the historical script is a new variation on the image of the migrant split between two chairs. Anna is a circus performer, an acrobat, and her physical skills are emblematic of the mental and creative agility required in order to sustain moments of performative encounters. From a narrative point of view, the tactic may well go unnoticed. At first, the heroine's unique flexibility appears to be relegated to the status of an anecdotal detail, unrelated to her quest, her travels, her nationality, or her ethnicity. In one interview, Benmalek suggests that the model for this character is his own grandmother, an autobiographical indication whose seemingly commonsensical power of explanation far from exhausts the narrative energy of that fictional choice.[5]

When Anna meets Zehra, her Kabyle mother-in-law, for the first time, the reader learns that she is not exactly welcome. Zehra has found a nickname for her: "la *Chetaha*, la Danseuse, expression peu flatteuse dans sa bouche" (1998: 14) [the Chetaha, the Dancer, a far from flattering term in her vocabulary] (2001: 4). Her hostility is understandable given the context: her son, who has been away for many years, comes back accompanied with a woman who is not his legitimate spouse although their two children are already a few years old. And yet, Zehra soon falls under the strange woman's spell. This is not because she wishes to please her son or respects his feelings for Anna, nor is Anna capable of pleading her own cause since the two women cannot talk to each other. Anna does not speak Zhera's "chaouï" language. The protocol and language of the encounter are not made of words. Instead, we have a performance that involves Anna's whole body. She juggles, literally and figuratively.

Anna defies the force of gravity; she makes objects fly. She first juggles with "trois, quatre, cinq, six pommes de terre" (1998: 15) [three, four, five, six potatoes] (2001; 4), then she performs a "véritable numéro de sauts en avant, roulades, déplacements sur les mains" (15) [a veritable performance, leaping, whirling, turning cartwheels] (4). Her body language is a form of art that physically transforms her audience: the "moue dédaigneuse de celle qui en a vu d'autres" [the bored expression of somebody who has seen it all before] (4) turns to childlike appreciation: "Zehra s'est animée, les yeux plissés d'incrédulité. Nassreddine a vu l'étonnement, puis l'émerveillement rajeunir les traits fatigués de celle qui l'avait mis au monde" (15) [Zehra came to life, screwing up her eyes in disbelief. Nassreddine saw astonishment, then wonder, rejuvenate the worn features of this woman who had given him life] (4). The French words for "came to life" ("s'est animée") imply that some "soul" or "spirit" (animus) has been blown into the exchange and the body of Nassreddine's mother.

A physical performance transforms the onlooker, whose primary identity, at that point, is that of hostile family member. She is reinvented as mesmerized member of the audience and even her body and face are changed. Anna's performance also metamorphoses the old woman into a child, who recaptures a sense of wonder that tragic historical events have almost completely eliminated.

The narrator is careful to point out that Zehra does not understand what a circus is. In other words, this is not a moment of cultural exchange and of aesthetic appreciation for the stranger's art forms. Zehra misunderstands, or rather confuses, her daughter-in-law's presentation with her own traditions. She likens the circus act to a traditional Berber practice: storytelling. She imagines that what Anna does is similar to what traditional storytellers do when they "vont de marché en marché raconter entre fruits et légumes les histoires et les légendes du temps jadis. . . . Dans les deux cas, des gens se mettent en rond pour les admirer; par terre ou sur des chaises, ça n'est pas suffisant pour les distinguer" (15) [journey from market to market recounting, amid the fruit and vegetables, the stories and legends of olden times. . . . Both were applauded by people sitting in a circle; whether on the ground or on chairs, what difference did it make?] (4). Zehra's conscious decision not to make a distinction between traditional storytellers and Anna's art gives her daughter-in-law a place within her community. Her counterintuitive reading of the similarity between the two types of performance is a political gesture that emphasizes reception and communication with the public. What unites the two practices is the fact that they generate an audience (people sit down around them). What could be interpreted, at first, as linguistic incompatibility is mediated by Anna's nimbleness and agility. Her body is so flexible that it becomes like a poem or a story, the source of wonder and pleasure capable of transcending the old Berber woman's prejudices against the stranger.

The thematic detail and autobiographical memory is now a structural element of the encounter that breaks down other identification patterns. Anna's gift is recurrently mentioned whenever her identity as a stranger is both emphasized and dismissed as what could prevent successful encounters. First greeted by a "disdainful" look and suspicion, she then lets her performance generate other reactions.

At the beginning of the novel, Anna has just come back from Europe after years of exile, and she tries to orient herself in this familiar yet strange Algeria of the 1990s. She intends to find her children's grave and to be reunited with Nassreddine now that her second husband has died. She meets a young Algerian, a street boy who seems to have nothing in common with her. Every collective category sets them apart: ethnicity, gender, age, language, and even his prejudices against the woman he calls "the Swiss." Yet, unexpected moments of performative encounters replace the strangers with "two old friends" who speak a unique language when Anna evokes her previous life as a circus performer.

. . . la vieille Suissesse et le gamin des rues d'Alger devisent comme de vieux amis, mêlant allégrement l'arabe et le français, s'aidant des mains et des mimiques quand les mots font défaut. Anna apprend à Jallal qu'elle a été acrobate dans un cirque. L'enfant ne la croit qu'à moitié:

—Toi acrobate? Mais tu es trop vieille!

—Je ne suis pas née avec des rides et des cheveux blancs. Ça ne se voit peut-être plus, mais moi aussi j'ai été jeune. Et il me reste encore des muscles de ce temps-là. S'il n'y avait pas eu autant de gens autour de nous, je t'aurais montré que je peux encore grimper à un arbre plus vite que toi, sagouin! (1998: 112)

[the Swiss woman and the Algiers street urchin are chatting like old friends, happily mixing Arabic and Frech and resorting to mime when at a loss for words. Anna tells Jallal that she used to be an acrobat in a circus. The boy only half believes her:

—You, an acrobat? But you're too old!

—I wasn't born with white hair and wrinkles. It may not look like it now, but I too was young once. And I still have the muscles from that time. If there weren't so many people, I would show you that I can climb a tree quicker than you, lazybones!] (2001:85)

All the elements of the other performance are present here: two foreigners are re-created as friends by their conversation; hands and faces are a form of language; and by-standers could become a public. Here, however, the presence of a potentially hostile audience prevents the actual performance, which makes this passage the reverse mirror image of what happens in Nassreddine's family. Anna does not want to perform for fear that others will only see a slightly ridiculous spectacle. Such a public would not compare her art to traditional Berber storytelling. She continues however to refute the simple identitarian category that onlookers impose on her: the "vieille Suissesse" [old woman from Switzerland] challenges the boy in a category of activities that transports them both into the universe of youth and play. She repositions herself as a careless little boy, a position that even Jallal can no longer occupy. And once again, language becomes hybrid: made of gestures and words; of several tongues; the mixing described as "allègre," which connotes joy but also impertinence and a certain disregard for possible consequences. Hands and faces relay missing dictionaries.

It is prudent, however, to refrain from idealizing Anna's flexibility; the model may lead to productive encounters, but in no way does it make the individual fulfilled and happy. Besides, it is not presented as a natural gift, that is, as an essential characteristic that her body happens to have been endowed with. The acrobat is an artist who treats her limbs as raw material; she subjects her muscles and sinews to a discipline that the text presents as painful and implacable.

Nassreddine est fasciné de découvrir à quel point cet entraînement peut être rude. La frêle jeune fille est capable, des heures durant, d'exécuter les mêmes mouvements, de tordre son corps sans pitié comme un torchon, de sauter en l'air, et de retomber au sol en un grand écart si brutal que Nassreddine, n'en pouvant plus, se lève et va fumer une cigarette dehors. Elle le taquine sur sa sensiblerie. (1998: 241)

[Nassreddine is fascinated to discover how arduous such training can be. The girl thinks nothing of repeating the same movements for hours on end, contorting her body like a rag doll, leaping into the air and crashing to the earth in splits so brutal that, unable to bear it, Nassreddine has to go outside for a cigarette. She teases him for his squeamishness.] (2001: 190)

Anna is all expenditure when it comes to her training sessions. She performs the same movement over and over again, she does not count, and, from the outside, the endless and relentless repetitions of the routine appear like self-imposed torture, a discipline that belies stereotypes about the delicate constitution of female bodies.

The "brutality" of the exercises, the absence of "mercy" that characterizes the training session, is more likely to evoke images of a military boot camp than the grace and elegance associated with dancing or gymnastics. When put together, the two passages from the novel help us remember that Anna pays a terrible price for being able to turn her body into a wonderful spectacle.

In other texts, the relationship between pain and flexibility is mediated through humor and inventiveness. The body does not have to stretch as much as our imagination when we are asked to envisage that certain accessories play the role of an elastic band between cultures. Like language, certain objects can be acquired: with time and effort, as well as with money. In a novel published three years before Plantu's drawing and more than ten years before Benmalek's *Les Amants désunis*, the humorist's chairs are replaced by another interpretation of the "sitting on the fence" (or rather "sitting between two chairs") concept. Other cards are added to the deck of performative encounters.

A Deck Chair on the Mediterranean Sea

Les A.N.I. du "Tassili" was Akli Tadjer's first novel, and it is still part of a certain canonical body of Beur literature.[6] The main protagonist is Omar, a young Algerian immigrant, who, as the title indicates, is an "A.N.I." ("Arabe non identifié" or Unidentified Arab, a coinage not inadvertently constructed on the model of U.F.O.). The Tassili is the name of the ship that crosses the Mediterranean and delineates the hero's fictional space. Neither departure nor arrival is as important as the moment of the crossing. As in *N'zid*, the sea (rather than France or Algeria) is adopted as the dwelling space of predilection. Neither the French nor the African "chair" is privileged, although the point of the story is not that we should simply prefer the sea over the land. As usual, the Mediterranean functions in many ways simultaneously: it is what separates or what unites the northern and southern shores; it is also a third space that one can try to adopt without taking sides;[7] and finally it is the symbol of what Balibar calls the "fractal border," which helps us conceive of both territories as the thick and dense layer never to be crossed, much like the space that no longer separates Inspector Llob's building from his garage.

In this novel, the hesitation to model "inbetweenness" as either a self-contained third space that exists between two poles or as a radical questioning of duality itself is expressed via a new metaphor of flexibility. The main protagonist consciously refuses to adopt the position assumed by Plantu's character. When Nelly, Omar's friend, asks: "Culturellement, est-ce que tu as le cul entre deux chaises?" [Culturally, do you find yourself falling between two chairs?] (174), Omar's answer rearticulates the terms of the encounter between the self and culture. There are no chairs unless we build one (and not two). And the type of custom-made "chair" that he imagines has very specific characteristics and uses:

> Tu sais ma chère, avoir le cul entre la France et l'Algérie, c'est avoir le cul mouillé, et je ne supporte pas d'avoir les fesses mouillées. Il y a longtemps que j'ai pigé que pour être bien dans sa peau et à l'aise dans ses babouches, il ne fallait surtout pas choisir entre la France et l'Algérie . . . D'ailleurs pourquoi choisir puisque j'ai les deux . . . Je ne veux pas être hémiplégique. Mais pour éviter la paralysie d'une partie de mon cerveau, il a fallu que j'investisse énormément d'argent . . . Toutes mes économies . . . Je me suis acheté un immense transat qui, une fois déplié, s'étale de Tamanrasset à Dunkerque. Mais tu peux me croire, ça n'a pas été une partie de plaisir pour déplier un grand machin comme ça . . . Maintenant j'ai le privilège de vivre allongé toute l'année la tête face aux soleils . . . Des vacances à vie si tu préfères. (174)

> [My dear, being in between France and Algeria means that your ass is wet and I cannot stand to have wet buttocks. So, long ago, I got it into my head that if I want to be comfortable and comfortably ensconced in my *babouches*, I had to refrain from choosing between France and Algeria . . . And why should I choose anyway since I can have both . . . I am not interested in hemiplegia. But to avoid a paralysis of a part of my brain, I had to invest an enormous amount of money . . . All my savings . . . I purchased a gigantic deck chair that, once unfolded, stretches from Tamanrasset to Dunkerque. But believe me, it was no fun to set up such a big contraption . . . Now, I can enjoy the privilege of lying down all year, basking in both suns . . . A perpetual holiday if you like.]

Plantu's two wooden chairs have disappeared, replaced by a special type of seat that evokes cruises and vacations, and transnationalism, at least in French ("transat," although the body of water that gave its name to the "transat" chair is the Atlantic rather than the Mediterranean). Humor gives the author the right to select which elements of the metaphor he takes into account and develops: the chair is very precisely visualized. Plantu's ordinary but nationalized (or rather continentalized) chairs are replaced by a kind of chair only used in certain situations, on the deck of a ship rather than in an office, under a circus tent, or in a performing hall.

On the other hand, the passage is not specific about what exactly constitutes, in practice, the purchase of a deck chair, nor about how such a symbolic object of mediation and encounter can be acquired. That aspect of the protocol is left to our imagination, and it does not immediately evoke practices of integration (going to school, finding a job, or renting an apartment). Acquiring is involved; we know that something was exchanged, that currency was involved, but we are told neither who sells such commodities nor why they are so expensive. The risk of "hemiplegia" is averted as inbetweenness is reconfigured. However, all difficulties do not disappear even after the deck chair has been acquired. Once again, images of stretching are proposed, but the chair, rather than the migrant's body, stretches out. The subject must deploy the contraption to its full length, in a ritual that is required of the migrant but not even expected of other dominant subjects whose encounter with something called culture is taken for granted.

In addition, we do not find out what type of difficulty the hero encountered when he says that "it was no fun" to set the deck chair up. While Benmalek talks about the brutality of Anna's training sessions, Tadjer is much more discrete about whatever pain is involved (although a few clues are abandoned here and there throughout the novel for the curious reader's benefit). In a passage that functions as an almost inaudible echo of the scene of the deck chair, the hero mentions that he has suffered from racism in France, but he refuses to be explicit about it. The few examples that he alludes to suggest that the constant risk of being humiliated and ostracized must be sublimated and transformed into humor and constructions as imaginative and surrealistic as the deck chair. In the text, the formalist equivalent of the repetitive gesture of deployment is a series of preteritions: "I will not tell you that. . ."[8]

Just as Plantu's character assumes a position that he is expected to sustain ("They will stay" in that uncomfortable position, the title of Fuchs' study claims), the presence of the deck chair is finally presented as a practice, a moment, and an identity (that is, an encounter) that is not temporary yet is highly unstable. In Tadjer's novel, the protocol creates a fake new social identity, presented as a privilege. The character claims that he now has access to two suns and that he is on vacation forever. But the imaginary configuration of this new equilibrium and therefore the metaphorical protocol of encounter is, once again, a strictly individual venture. Omar acknowledges that the model cannot be generalized. No new community is founded (even as a pedagogical horizon). No "people of the deck chair" is imagined. "And a good thing too," adds the narrator, whose level of irony becomes difficult to assess at this point: "T'imagines tous les transats qu'il faudrait si toute la planète était peuplée de gens comme moi? . . . L'angoisse! J'aurais même plus de place pour profiter des soleils . . . Remarque, rien ne t'empêche de rêver que tu es un ANI, non, rien ne t'empêche" [Can you imagine how many deck chairs we would need if the whole planet were populated with people like me? . . . Horrible! There would be no room left for me to enjoy my suns . . . Mind you, you can always dream that you are an unidentified Arab. Nothing is stopping you after all, nothing really] (174).

Conclusion

Like Plantu's drawing, Tadjer's text leaves a number of issues up in the air. The proposed solution belongs to the realm of imagination and dream. The protocol of the encounter begins and ends within the image, itself presented performatively, as an example of success. If you do not want your buttocks to get wet, then the hemiplegia of choice must be avoided, and a deck chair must be unfolded between the two shores of the Mediterranean. It is, we are warned, an expensive and tiring protocol. And while Mokeddem's bestiary contains some allusions to recognizable social practices, the image of the deck chair can hardly be translated into practical, cultural, and political suggestions.

But as was the case in Benmalek's and Mokeddem's novels, the textual ingredients of Tadjer's imaginary construction constitute a form of historical intervention to the extent that the author both encounters and reconfigures the French-Algerian nonborder as a type of rewriting or graffiti. Language is stretched as well, as if on a deck chair and exposed to two linguistic suns. Set expressions are slightly modified and the new concatenation of words creates new set phrases that can now be memorized and repeated, quoted as if they were old and traditional sayings. Using the new and unique combination of words as if it were old rather than original (perhaps even poetic), is literarily counterintuitive in our contemporary world, which valorizes a writer's individual talent and sometimes treats style as a commodity. In Tadjer's novel, what is important is not that French and Arabic words meet within a normally self-contained and impenetrable textual unit (the so-called "set" phrase that functions like a country surrounded by borders) but the type of encounter that the author manages to orchestrate.

When the protagonist stretches the deck chair between Tamanrasset and Dunkerque, an obviously parodic reappropriation of Charles de Gaulle's vision of a greater France, he both preserves the memory of the colonial past and critiques the phrase's original imperialist intent. This reappropriation does not, however, renationalize the southern post of the imaginary line.[9] As for the popular expression of "à l'aise dans les baskets" [literally "wearing comfortable sneakers," figuratively, "feeling good, well adjusted"], it is adapted and orientalized in a way that both uses and makes fun of exoticism. The normally mandatory word "baskets" [sneakers] is replaced with what could appear as a synonym (another shoe), but that object adds excess to the system and makes the phrase a more fluid and ludic, less purely French, unit. Replacing "baskets" with "babouches" not only deprives the expression of its comfortable familiarity, it also substitutes the globalized, vaguely Americanized universal comfort shoe with the clearly Maghrebi *babouches* and the homely connotations attached to a slipper. Whatever strangeness survives in that word in particular, and in the object to which it refers, does not connote danger or mystery; a pair of *babouches* is an exotic, harmless, domesticated, and comfortably reassuring attribute of the oriental. The association between well-being and *babouches* reinforces the image of a peaceful and happy perpetual vacationer, not a tortured and uncomfortable migrant.

For, just as "being" a hybrid in no way guarantees the gift to invent richer and more effective protocols of encounter with non- (self-identified) hybrids, the bilingual sentence is not necessarily either peaceful or confrontational. The insertion of an Arabic word into a French text produces as many possible effects as the encounter between two individuals. It is not enough to simply import the metaphor of the border (between languages) to discover exactly what happens to words and speakers or listeners when one unit "crosses" over a linguistic barrier. Like humans, words can be refugees or travelers, illegal immigrants or expatriates. Conversely, if we identify the protocol of their encounters within and between languages, their behavior or their linguistic fate will teach us something about how subjects encounter themselves, others, themselves as others, and the other in themselves.[10]

Conclusion

Words in Passing: From Abd-el-Kebir's *Smala* to the Reading of *Atlal*

All the performative encounters explored in the preceding chapters have at least two obvious common denominators. First, they invite us to move to a level of analysis that must take inbetweenness for granted. Second, they do not envisage conflict resolution as the ultimate goal, which is not to say that the subjects created by performative encounters are resigned to violence, or that hybridity somehow predates them in terms of historical anteriority.

Our heroes can be assumed to have read or internalized those theories of *métissage* and hybridity that had to be carefully argued and demonstrated when they first appeared on the critical and academic scene. Specifically, at the beginning of the twenty-first century, in France, in the Maghreb, or in the countries of their current residence, these social agents do not feel compelled to argue the point. They assume, some would say mythically, that cultural hybridity among diasporic Maghrebi is so commonplace that it is not oppositional or even original.[1]

Let me finish, then, with two recapitulative examples, two sets of metaphorical representations of how a performative encounter can generate at the same moment the reader and the text, the message and its recipient. Ultimately, a performative encounter makes something happen where nothing was: the desire manifests itself to decode something that, until then, was only perceived as a meaningless part of the environment, a nothing that was there as noise, as background to our stories. I would like to end this book on two final vibrations, two final words: "Smala" and "atlal."

In a passage from *Les Nuits de Strasbourg*, Djebar invites us to reflect on the ironical valence of certain linguistic transfers between languages. Like many Algerian authors, she is acutely aware of what happens when words are imported or cross over linguistic frontiers, and she also knows that it is not irrelevant to decide whether we envisage linguistic units as exportable commodities, traveling migrants, or even racialized bodies. Something happens when we start imagining that words can "pass" from one system to another.

Time, and therefore history, also play a decisive role: the protocol of exchange that governs the "borrowing" of words between languages often disappears as such from our cultural memory after a few years. After a while, the origin of words is forgotten, and the time during which they were forced, like migrant bodies, to execute the splits between phonetic or grammatical systems is lost. They are, to adopt another ambiguous image, "naturalized," which does not mean the same thing to the immigration officer checking someone's passport and to a literary theoretician weary of the power vested in things natural.

Whether their flexibility was spectacular or painful, encouraged or cursed, their movements belong to the history of encounters (between languages) or the history of languages (as encounters). Each crossing is part of a certain context, and when we forget the entry point we also deny that the encounter was sometimes pacific and sometimes violent, sometimes playful and admiring, and sometimes amorously conflictual. The point of remembering the details of the transfer and of the power relationships that it contested or reinforced is not to reveal some primeval truth, as if nothing had changed in the meantime, or as if the origin had to be treated as the only possible meaning of the encounter. Still, it allows the subject who inherits the ghosts of the encounter to become aware that even commonly used words have been marked (and sometimes scarred) by their histories, their previous contacts and travels.

In Djebar's story, the female protagonist and narrator, Thelja, meets a group of young Beur comedians who live in Alsace. They are putting together a modern version of *Antigone*. Djamila, the lead actress, is going to play this "banlieue Antigone" or "Djamila-Antigone" (1997a: 213). In a typically performative moment, the community of actors is in the process of choosing a name for their company, a name that will make them exist as the collective author of the new take on the myth. But, as usual, the naming process is, in itself, an encounter with culture and language that develops over time and triggers important debates. When one of the young men makes a first suggestion, he starts a long digression about the meaning of words whose Arabic origin has been gradually forgotten. The lost memory of their passage is resurrected and the narrative detects a resemblance between their destiny and the encounter between France and Algeria. For the comedians, the search for a public and collective identity ends up reproducing the complex work that is entailed in their carving of a unique cultural, national, and regional positioning.

—Nous pourrions nous appeler: "le théâtre de la Smala"!

—La Smala?

—C'est un des mots arabes qui est passé dans le français . . . Comme le "souk," comme . . .

—Comme l'algèbre, comme le zéro, comme . . . la chimie! dit doucement Thelja. Comptez-les tous dans un dictionnaire étymologique: vous en trouverez aisément plus de deux milles; des mots courants, en outre! (216)

[—We could be "the Smala theater"!

—The Smala?

—It is one of those Arabic words that crossed over to the French language . . . like "souk," like . . .

—Like algebra, like zero, like . . . chemistry! says Thelja gently. Count them all in a dictionary of etymology, you will find more than two thousand of them; and they are quite common too.]

For a Francophone resident of France in the 1980s, the word "Smala" was indeed common, but the cultural references it conjured up would not have been the same as Thelja's. In the absence of a specific context, the first intertext to come to mind may well have been Jean-Louis Hubert's popular film, *La Smala*, a 1984 comedy starring Josiane Balasko, Thierry Lhermitte, and Victor Lanoux. In that context, "smala" refers to a numerous tribe, a more or less chaotic family, a happy-go-lucky (and usually lower-class) community. It is thus possible to understand and use the word without having any memory of another type of historical and linguistic crossing that took place around the 1840s and that Thelja does not bring up immediately. Her first intervention only reinserts the linguistic unit into its original context and family, as if placing it back into a list of all the forgotten travelers. From that point of view, her gesture is not unlike the sustained and repetitive efforts that teachers must make, year after year, to remind or teach their audience that great "French" writers (or directors or singers) sometimes happen to be Swiss or Belgian. This is a significant "rendering unto Caesar" moment, because by deterritorializing then reterritorializing the word, Thelja points out that we have forgotten that language is not homogeneous but homogenized by our forgetfulness. Anyone tempted to take pride in the purity of his or her language would have to take Thelja's argument into account.

But even if the text were content with this reterritorialization, I still would not suggest that in this instance Thelja provides us with the elements of a performative encounter with words and history. The rest of her remarks do, because she focuses on what happens when the history of a word is remembered.

Thelja does not simply rejoice that, within French, words of Latin and of Arabic origin cohabit peacefully. She also reminds or teaches her readers and diegetic audience that the encounter between French, the French, and the word "smala" did not take place during a learned conversation between scholars and historians. When "smala" refers to Abd-el-Kebir's impressive itinerant camp, it rhymes with war and defeat.[2] It is also a reminder that the perfect Emir, as historians would subsequently call him, was eventually imprisoned and deported after being promised freedom if he surrendered. The "Smala theater" would replace a military battle with another type of struggle, the cultural work involved in the reinterpretation of myths. The immense nomadic city made up of men, women, animals, tents, schools, and libraries becomes a small troupe of Beur comedians, and the fact that they plan on using the name Smala without even knowing exactly what they are borrowing emphasizes the chaotic aspect of filiations, of the practices of conservation and memory-keeping. Thelja "se retint pour leur proposer d'aller jusqu'à Versailles, juste pour contempler le tableau fameux d'Horace Vernet" [refrained from suggesting a trip to Versailles to look at Horace Vernet's famous painting] (216). In other words, within the story, she keeps her knowledge about orientalist painters to herself, but the novel as a whole invites us to take advantage of the free history lesson. The other imported trace of the battle is not shared with the young Beur comedians; it is apparently reserved to the readers of Les Nuits de Strasbourg. As is often the case, a complicity that is not possible with the characters of the novel is built with the larger extradiegetic audience.

Paying attention to what happens when the word smala crosses a border forces us to reenact a violent episode. The pacified story of a fiercely brutal encounter can be told within "our" language, as if the words of the tribe, as Mallarmé called them, now included or defined a completely different "we."

Just as Tadjer's deck chair and references to Tamanrasset force us to pay attention to the historical script hidden within set phrases, certain traveling words act like revelators, making us see bits of writing that would normally remain invisible because time has reduced them to ruins and destroyed their support. Sometimes, a text's responsibility is to tell us the story of that erasure, of the incomplete and gradual destruction of writing on monuments erected to preserve them. The second part of Djebar's So Vast the Prison is the history of a buried alphabet, a story of "L'effacement sur la pierre" (1995c: 120)[Erased in stone] (1999b: 122). The main protagonist of that series of chapters is not a human subject, but a monument or, rather, the encounter between our memory and a ruined stele on which a bilingual text eludes one reader after another and whose deciphering will last, literally, for centuries. Discovered by Thomas d'Arcos in 1631, the inscription will remain incomprehensible for generations. Copied down carefully but as mysterious signs, the message is almost like an image that cannot be understood. Djebar meticulously records the series of failed attempts. In 1815, she writes, the signs are reproduced once more as Count Borgia takes notes in Italian and makes "de multiples esquisses au crayon" (1995c: 131) [numerous pencil sketches] (1999b: 133). Several times, the story remains unfinished, the bilingual inscription travels without being properly read, and for a while, the encounter between the text and the reader is almost extinguished, like a volcano biding its time to explode. The inscription, "va dormir, non publiée . . . jusqu'en 1959"(1995c: 132) [will remain dormant, unpublished . . . until 1959] (1999b: 134). Intellectual dormancy on the one side is matched by a frenzy of negative activity around the stone itself. In 1842, the Consul General of England in Tunis starts a very different type of relationship with the stone. His interest is predatory and destructive. He wants to commodify the text and its support. He is not interested in what the message says to him and others; he wants to sell it to the British Museum and hires "une équipe d'ouvriers pour mettre à bas le monument et revenir avec la stèle" (1995c: 142) [a team of workers to pull down the monument and bring back the stele] (1999b: 144).

This time, the inscription is negated and relegated to nothingness. Only the physical proof that some memory was kept is treated with greedy interest. The passage from one world to the other generates no translation, no creolization, only destruction and internal mutilation: "sciée en deux pour être plus facilement transportable [. . .] la stèle bilingue emportée à Tunis laisse derrière elle un champ de ruines" (1995c: 142) [the stele is sawed in two to make it easier to transport [. . .] the bilingual stele carried off to Tunis leaves a field full of ruins behind it] (1999b: 144). The text has not been deciphered yet, but it is split into two parts, it is kidnapped and damaged, it loses its context and its potential readers' fascinated respect. The real text, then—the original words—have become a sad parody of themselves; the inscription is incomplete and incomprehensible, in ruins.

And yet, the long-awaited encounter that will allow the text to come alive as text, as a voice addressed to readers, will paradoxically occur in the absence of the monument, in spite of the destruction of the support that meant to keep the writing alive. In 1857, as the result of a collaborative effort between Captain Boissonnet and a native informant, the mystery of the bilingual alphabet is finally solved by a perceptive reader. Although the consul's "barbarous crime" (1999b: 152) is irreparable, an encounter takes place that creates text, reader, and meaning where only dormancy and ruins existed. Djebar describes the moment as the end of the "dormancy." The alphabet "palpitates," and what is important is not what it has to say but the fact that it is treated as a language and not as an object to be had, destroyed, sold, or even admired as other. The presence of a reader coincides with the (re)birth of the language: "à ce moment, c'est le sens même—et la musique, et l'oralité palpitante—de cet alphabet qui se ranime et réussit à ne plus être étouffé" (1995c: 149–50) [in this same moment the meaning itself—and the music and the throbbing orality—of this alphabet comes back to life, no longer stifled] (1999b: 152).

In the chapters devoted to the stele, *So Vast the Prison* manages to tell a tale of forgetfulness and erasure that performs the remembrance of how forms of linguistic knowledge and bilingualism come and go, appear and disappear, like ghosts and travelers.

In *Les Nuits de Strasbourg*, the word smala meets us as if it were a stone, covered with letters that we will either be capable or incapable of deciphering depending on which encounter we perform with the text or with the context. As a result, we readers will be encountered, that is, invented and recognized by the text, as historians or archeologists, students or scholars, subjects who know or subjects who ignore, who learn or dismiss the chance to discover and recover meaning. Sometimes, the reader and the young comedians can only hope to adopt the position of Lyyli Belle, the main protagonist of Mohamed Dib's *L'Infante maure*, a young female child who does not know how to read the traces but becomes aware of their existence and function.

In the novel, the little girl, whose father is an Arab from the desert and whose mother comes from a Scandinavian country, meets her imaginary grandfather. During her conversations with him, he teaches her what she needs to know about stories buried in the sand. He also gives a name to what she cannot interpret or read: the traces left in the sand are "atlal," which many European readers will not know much or anything about. For now, let us put ourselves in the lay person's shoes and follow the little girl's discovery of the existence of atlal. In one strikingly poetic scene, the old man gives her something to hold, a strange animal that he tells her to put down in the sand. The child is slightly frightened and repelled by the reptile, but she follows the grandfather's recommendation. As the animal escapes, she discovers that it has left a trace in the sand, something that looks like letters, a text that she cannot make sense of. The animal, she says:

> s'est enfoncée, a fondu dans le sable, n'oubliant que les marques inscrites par ses griffes, des marques aussi nettement gravées que sur du marbre. Ainsi ce désert avec tout son sable était sa page blanche et elle y a déposé son écriture. Est-ce là sa manière de parler?
>
> Mais alors qu'a-t-elle écrit? Je contemple attentivement ces gribouillis, je les étudie. Je n'en tire qu'un mal de tête. Pas la moindre indication, ils ne parlent pas. Têtue comme je suis, je demeure encore un moment à vouloir les déchiffrer.
>
> Rien de rien, je n'en suis pas plus avancée. (1994: 158)

[burrowed into the sand, melting into it, forgetting only the marks left by its claws, traces etched as neatly as on a marble slab. The desert and all its sand was its white page and it has left its script there. Was that its way of talking?

But what had it written? I scrutinize the scribblings, I study them. I get nothing but a headache. No clue, they do not speak. Stubborn as I am, I stay there a while, trying to decipher them.

Absolutely nothing. I am back to square one.]

When she goes back to her grandfather and confesses that she cannot read the marks left by the legendary basilisk, he does not help her translate, he does not explain what the traces might mean. What he does, however, is reveal the extraordinary significance of this type of writing. He names this type of text for her; he tells her that these tracings are "atlal" and then sends the girl back to her task of deciphering: "Retourne là où tu as déposé la bête et lis ce qu'elle a écrit. Des atlals, à n'en pas douter. Va, fillette" [Go back where you put the animal down and read what it wrote. These are atlal no doubt. Go child, go] (159). By naming this type of writing in Arabic, by using, within the French text, a word that has not traveled yet, that is neither commonplace nor naturalized for the majority of Francophone speakers, the grandfather (and the novel as a whole) put us in the same position as the little girl. This time, the extradiegetic reader is not privileged. We learn not only that a language is out of our reach, but also that its existence as a meaningful system probably would have eluded us in any case. Where signs were present, we would have recognized nothing; instead, we would have treated this message as noise. Our ignorance, as well as Lyyli Belle's, are both staged and corrected by the intervention of the grandfather's description. What we did not know existed has a name, a meaning. This form of writing is called atlal. Only by looking up the word in a dictionary (an Arabic dictionary this time, not a French dictionary, even if some reveal the etymology of words) can we hope to find out that the plural word refers to "traces left by the campfire" after the clan has departed. Scholars familiar with classical Arabic literature and pre-Islamic poetry will also recognize the conventions used in the ode, or qasida, in which the poet mourns the departure of his beloved and cries over the ruins left behind in the desert, where her tribe's abandoned campsite remains (Meisami 2003; Sperl and Shackle 1996).

Direct references to the literary and poetic definitions of altal, however, are absent from the novel. As readers and companions to the little girl, we need to travel, to make a detour via the other language in order to encounter the word within its context. Like the traces left in the desert by the Smala, the atlal mean something. They signal the presence of someone's passage, of an event. But, they are not legible, and it is even debatable whether they can be accommodated by strict definitions of what it means to write. What the grandfather teaches the child and the reader is that atlal can be read even if the heroine of the novel ends up being incapable of doing what he recommends. Like the young Beur comedians of Djebar's text, she encounters the existence of a layer of scripting whose richness (its historical, polyphonic, ironic, and violent depth) eludes her for now.

As always, the performative encounter cannot be equated with the discovery of a brand new language. Instead, it is that moment that enables us to become aware that a language was already being spoken where we heard only noise or misunderstood vibrations. Where we saw only mysterious and incoherent traces, a text existed whose historical depth was already changing the meaning of our present-day conversations.

Notes

Introduction:

1. The famous hiatus that separates the first historical and political novels—*Les Enfants du nouveau monde* (1962), *Les Alouettes naïves* (1967), *Poèmes pour l'Algérie heureuse* (1969)—and *Femmes d'Alger* (1980) is not so much a "silence" (Zimra 1995: 933, n. 4) as the emergence of new types of narratives. Djebar starts generating performative encounters between historiography and autobiography when she makes films about topics that will later be addressed in her novels and that continue to resonate in her most recent texts. For example, *La Nouba des femmes du Mont Chenoua* (1977) and *La Femme sans sépulture* (2002) are two accounts of the same woman's story.

2. Thinking of subjects as "in-between" may force us to choose between two equally binary principles: the neither/nor or an and-and model. French children of Algerian immigrants may be perceived as neither French nor Algerian (Laronde 1993). Arab-Americans are Arabs and Americans at the same time. Although the second solution appears to be more inclusive and reconciliatory, both models tend to preserve the integrity of original identities as if they were monolithic and pure. Geographically, the thinking of the in-between space often generates images of "contact zones" (Pratt 1992) or visions of subjects "torn" between different identifications (Glissant 1990: 137). Theories of the third space (Serres 1991) or of the interstitial (Bhabha 1994) brilliantly describe the culture that might lead to performative encounters, and such models are precious when we need to analyze the conditions that might encourage the emergence of the performative encounters that often develop on the border, when the reality of cross-cultural exchange and transnationalism cannot be denied.

3. The semantic field of touching is not irrelevant, however, given the rapidly changing apprehension of what it means to be "in touch" in different parts of the world. For those readers of Djebar who have regular access to technology, her focus on physical proximity may at first sound dated and out of sync with our ever-increasing fascination with virtual communications and disembodied connections. But I would suggest that it is just as common for scripts about embodiment to govern the imaginary substratum of our virtual games as for our electronic metaphors to influence our love stories.

4. If only because the injurious parts of the statements under scrutiny are bound to infect the legal discourse that pretends to contain them and condemn them. As Butler puts it, "Such a redoubling of injurious speech takes place not only in rap music and in various forms of political parody and satire, but in the political and social critique of such speech, where 'mentioning' those very terms is crucial to the arguments at hand, and even in the legal arguments that make the call for censorship, in which the rhetoric that is deplored is invariably proliferated within the context of legal speech" (1997a: 14).

5. See especially the beginning of the preface in which Austin explains how he came to collect the material that he subsequently analyzed.

6. "De l'amitié," *Essais* I: 197.

7. The extreme violence of such an intervention raises ethical issues, such as the definition of responsibility (to oneself and to others, including otherness in oneself) when the need to graft an organ leads to a loss of bodily integrity. Descriptions of the surgical intervention that transforms the initial subject into an undecidable entity often encounter, performatively, stories about the migrant's "intrusion" into the social body. In "L'Intimité à l'épreuve de *L'Intrus* et de *L'Interdite*: la greffe comme (dés)saisie de soi," Alexandre Dauge-Roth (2004) cross-pollinates Jean-Luc Nancy's autobiographical account of the consequence of a heart transplant (*L'Intrus* 2000) and Malika Mokeddem's fictional representation of a male French character whose kidney used to belong to an Algerian woman in *L'Interdite* [*The Forbidden Woman*] (1993/1998).

Chapter 1

1. There is no reason to assume that this is a problem per se as long as we remember that any departure, like any point of view, entails consequences. In 1996, during an interview with Bernard Ravenel for the journal *Confluences*, Pierre Vidal-Naquet was asked to assess his involvement in the Algerian war and his political position "as a French historian" (145). His first reaction was to underscore the importance of what his interviewer had just said: "Vous faites bien de dire 'historien français' car c'est moins pour l'Algérie que pour la France que j'ai eu mon premier réflexe: on faisait des choses honteuses pour l'honneur de mon pays; je devais les combattre" [You are right to say "French historian" because my first reflex had to do with France rather than with Algeria: some shameful things were being done in the name of my country; I had to oppose them] (145). In other words, a strong pro-independence position is not at all incompatible with a French point of view, but it cannot be confused with an Algerian perspective either. (Unless otherwise indicated, all translations are mine.)

2. In a chapter entitled "L'Algérie Française: An Imagined Country," Jonathan Gosnell reminds us that colonial historians had a vested interest in constructing the Mediterranean as a natural body that would accommodate their own myths and political agenda. For a greater France to include Algeria, the sea had to be imagined as a hyphen rather than as a natural frontier: "Benevolently lying between North Africa and metropolitan France, the Mediterranean Sea for such supporters [of "Algérie Française"], did not separate but rather connected the various components of 'integral France'" (2002: 18).

3. Alice Cherki proposes to place a crossed-out hyphen [trait barré] rather than a regular hyphen [trait d'union] between Alger and Paris (2003: 107).

4. Throughout this chapter, I use "football" to refer to the game of European football or soccer. (The specific rules of the game are much less important than the place of sports events in popular culture.)

5. Keeping in mind that this type of unstable frontier is the symptom of latent insecurity and constant danger for the inhabitants of a country. Contemporary Algerian literature and cinema treats the roadblock as a recognizable topos that recreates, even in the absence of an official border, the type of relationship that we normally expect on state lines, in airports, between the immigrant and the immigration officer. See, for

example, Merzak Allouache's 2000 film *L'autre monde*, as well as Mellal 2002, Djaout 1999, and Balibar 2001.

6. See Fanon 1959. Jeanne-Marie Clerc (1997) and Rita Faulkner (1996) point out the radical differences between Djebar, Fanon, and Kateb's treatment of the comparison between woman and the nation. It is also important to note that other types of "couples" exist in the Franco-Algerian imaginary. Djebar tends to stay away from the image of fighting brothers that reappears almost obsessively in the work of other authors: see Jules Roy's *Les Chevaux du soleil* (1967–1972) or *Etranger pour mes frères* (1982), for example.

7. Although it is understandable that the Algerian war should constitute an obvious landmark for many French and Algerian subjects, whose lives were irrevocably marked by traumatic events, there is no reason to start the history of the relationship between France and Algeria either in 1954 or in 1962. The history of the relationship between France and Algeria predates not only the war of liberation but also the colonial period that started in 1830. Long before the nineteenth century, other encounters existed between what are today France and Algeria. Other conflicts and other exchanges took place between Mediterranean powers whose configurations had little to do with modern nation states. See, for example, María Garcés' study not only of Cervantes' captivity in Algiers but also of the troubled relationship between "Barbary" and its Christian neighbors until the eighteenth century (2002).

8. The tactic that Stora calls the keeping of "secrets de famille" [family secrets] (1991: 103–117) is obviously not a valid option anymore. The word "war," which used to be systematically replaced by euphemisms, was finally approved by the National Assembly in June 1999. The fact that an elected body deemed it necessary to address the issue is a highly symbolic aspect of the debate. The use of torture and political assassination is now regularly discussed in public conversations, and at the time when Aussaresses published his confession, another famous general, Jacques Massu, (famously portrayed as Colonel Mathieu by Jean Martin in *The Battle of Algiers*) chose to publicly express his regrets (see Beaugé 2000).

9. For, if recently published texts are helping their readers acquire a more nuanced and complex vision of the past, it is to be noticed that this does not constitute a radically new trend in literature. In *Algerian White*, Assia Djebar unfolds a long procession of dead Algerian heroes (and antiheroes), and she does not hesitate to expose the internecine wars that led to betrayal and murder among the ranks of those who fought for (different types of) independence (1995b/2003a). But more than ten years earlier, in his 1984 *Les Chercheurs d'os* [*The Bone Seekers*], Tahar Djaout was already poking fun at his country's tendency to instrumentalize the memory of the war of liberation. And in his posthumously published *Journal*, Mouloud Feraoun, assassinated in 1962, was already critiquing some of the political decisions made by the historic leaders of the National Liberation Front (NLF) (1990).

10. Stora writes: "Sur cette tragédie, il existe déjà des documents, des matériaux, des témoignages qui serviront d'archives aux historiens. Depuis une dizaine d'années en effet, près de 200 livres en langue française ont été publiés sur le sujet et une dizaine de films de fiction a en outre été consacrée à cet événement fort de l'histoire mondiale contemporaine. Je dis tout cela pour les historiens de demain qui argueront du fait qu'ils

ne savaient pas ce qui se passait en Algérie depuis le début des années 1990" [Documents, literature, and testimonies exist and they will serve as the historical archive of this tragedy. Roughly 200 books were published in French on the topic in the last ten years, and a dozen fiction films were devoted to this significant moment of contemporary global history. I say this for tomorrow's historians who might claim that they did not know what was going on Algeria at the beginning of the 1990s] (2002). See also his *La Guerre invisible, Algérie, années 90* (2001b) and his analysis of what he fears might be an ephemeral "flambée de mémoire" [memory flare up] in France (2003b: 87).

11. The text is signed by Abdennour Ali Yahia, president of the Algerian League for the defense of Human Rights; Kamel Daoud, president of Algérie, droits de l'homme pour tous; Nasséra Dutour, spokesperson for the Collectif des familles de disparus en Algérie; Driss el Yazami, general secretary of the Fédération internationale des ligues des droits de l'homme; Malika Matoub, president of the Fondation Lounès Matoub; Robert Ménard, general secretary of Reporters sans frontières; Danielle Mitterrand, president of the Fondation France Libertés; Francis Perrin, president of the French branch of Amnesty International; Michel Tubiana, president of the Ligue française des droits de l'homme; and Nesroulah Yous, general secretary of Vérité et Justice pour l'Algérie.

12. On the different types of censorship (and therefore on the various tactics of opposition) available to Maghrebi intellectuals, see Gafaïti 1997. On the repercussions of the French decree of January 1961 on the film industry, see Stora 1996.

13. If his model is correct, the fragments cannot even be perceived as an unfinished puzzle or a "mosaic," as Mildred Mortimer (2001) puts it. The original binary pair (Algeria-France) has been "diffracted" but not "recomposed" (unlike the creolized Caribbean mosaic imagined by the authors of *Eloge de la créolité/In Praise of Creoleness* (Bernabé et al. 1993: 27/88).

14. We even know that it would have been possible to pay attention much earlier, as historians regularly remind us (Stora 1991 and Vidal-Naquet 1996).

15. Stora is alluding to the following films: Bertrand Tavernier's *La Guerre sans nom* (1992), Pierre Schoendoerffer's *L' Honneur d'un capitaine* (1982), Yves Boisset's *RAS* (1973), and Alexandre Arcady's *Là-bas mon pays* (1999).

16. When commentators insist on the multicultural composition of a given football team, when they point out that players do not all come from the previous colonial metropolitan center, their observations sometimes collapse the difference between the players' ethnic origins and their nationalities. On the field, spectators and journalists perceive a white, black, and brown (*blanc-black-beur*) team, which gives the impression that the national team is racially diverse. But the type of deterritorialization undergone by individual players is bound to be different for a Brazilian player who plays for an Italian team or for a "Beur" who plays for "Les Bleus" and was born in one of Marseilles' northern *banlieues* like "Zizou" (see Silverstein 2000: 34–39).

17. To describe the type of inner conflict that Zidane may have experienced, Bernard Philippe (2001) and Mustapha Harzoune (2003) even invoke the quintessentially French "Cornelian" debate.

18. Here, the word "politics" would have had the restrictive meaning that Rancière gives it.

19. Ali Benflis, head of the Algerian government, insisted (one is tempted to add

"naturally") that "L'année de l'Algérie en France est la manifestation de tous les Algériens sans exclusive" [the Year of Algeria in France is the expression of all Algerians without any exception] (*El Watan*, 19 January 2002). It is this type of statement that the boycott easily deprives of any performative success. The dialogue that will not take place would precisely bring to the same table Ali Benflis (the representative of "Algeria") and Kamal Nait-Zerrad (also a representative of "Algeria"). In *Libération*, Nait-Zerrad writes: "Quand toute une région est exclue, laissée à elle-même et aux forces de police, il est légitime et justifié de parler d'indécence de la part des autorités françaises" [When a whole region is excluded, abandoned, and at the mercy of the police, it is legitimate and justified to accuse the French authority of indecent conduct] (2003: 8).

20. For a similar, but differently articulated, position, see Amazigh Kateb's rejection of the boycott in terms that highlight the limits of performative statements: "Les gens qui boycottent l'année de l'Algérie en soutien à la Kabylie, ils ne la soutiennent qu'au moment où ils disent 'Je boycotte.' En fait, le boycott, c'est la sieste." [People who say that they are boycotting the Year of Algeria to support Kabylia only show their support when they state: "I boycott." In fact, to boycott is like taking a nap] (Kassa 2003: 101).

21. In 2003, an earlier version of the first part of this chapter appeared in French as "Farança-Algéries ou Djazaïr-Frances? Fractales et mésententes fructueuses" (*Modern Language Notes* [MLN] 118, no.4: 787–806). I wish to thank guest editors Françoise Lionnet and Dominic Thomas for coordinating the "Francophone Studies: New Landscapes" issue, as well as the journal's editorial board for granting me permission to reproduce my work here.

Chapter 2

1. Djebar's text thus constitutes a discrete contribution to the unresolved linguistic issue that haunts Maghrebi literature and to which chapter 3 is devoted. For a synthetic analysis of the difference between Djebar, Khatibi, Memmi, and Derrida, see Cooke's "In Search of Mother Tongues" in *Women Claim Islam*, 2001: 29–51.

2. The presence of several alphabets also haunts this discussion and complicates the issue. Even opacity can be idealized and exoticized. Rey Chow suggests, for example, that the keystone of Jacques Derrida's critique of Western thought is a stereotyped hypothesis about what Chinese writing is, or, rather, looks like. (2001)

3. Between sound and noise, melody and voice, a "vibration" resembles Balibar's fractal frontier, which transforms space into a labyrinthine chaos capable of questioning the distinction between the territory and the line of demarcation. In his study on "cultural mediators" (the social agents whose role is comparable to Djebar's characters), Thierry Fabre suggests that their work can be described as a "véritable mouvement vibratoire franco-algérien . . . [et] qu'ils donnent forme, donnent corps à une entité culturelle commune qui, avec eux, doit être appelée méditerranéenne" [genuine, vibrating franco-algerian movement . . . [and] that they give a shape and a body to a cultural entity that, like them, must be called Mediterranean] (1989: 42).

4. This could be an intertextual echo of a well-known passage from Khatibi's *Love in Two Languages*. At the beginning of the book, the author plays with the resemblance between the French word "mot" and "mort" [death] and displaces his anxiety onto

another pair of terms: the verb "se calma" (he calmed down) reminds him of the Arabic word "Kalima" or "Kalma," which means "word" (1983a: 11; 1990: 4)

5. I am borrowing and adapting the playful title of Bonnie Honig's article: "My Culture Made Me Do It." In this essay, she responds to Susan Moller Okin's concerns that feminism and multiculturalism may not be compatible (Honig in Cohen et al. 1999: 35–40).

6. Here, the country of residence determines the choice of name associated with Arabic, whereas writers reverse that logic, choosing a language over a national territory. As Jamel Eddine Bencheikh explains to Christiane Chaulet-Achour, "C'est le français que j'habite, ce n'est pas la France. En France, je ne me sens pas Français" [I live in French not in France. In France I do not feel French] (Chaulet-Achour 1995: 124).

7. An earlier version of this chapter appeared in a special issue of *Studien zur Literatur und Geschichte des Maghreb* devoted to Assia Djebar and coordinated by Pit Ruhe ("Moh et Titi: 'parler tout contre' dans *Oran, langue morte*," Würzburg: Verlag Königshausen und Neumann, 2001: 133–56). I also wish to thank Michael Dash and Francesca Sautman for organizing the conference on "Migration, Memory, Trace: Writing in French Outside of the Hexagon" held at New York University and CUNY Graduate Center in April 2001.

Chapter 3

1. For an analysis of the sociological, political, and cultural repercussions of the process of "arabisation" (sometimes translated as "arabicisation") in Tunisia, Morocco, and Algeria, see Grandguillaume 1983. Twenty years ago, he had already come to a conclusion that continues to be agreed upon by recent studies: namely that the reduction of the Maghreb's multilingual reality to a postindependence rivalry between two official languages fails to find adequate solutions or even correctly identify the problem. Arabisation has not put an end to the erosion and depreciation of spoken tongues. As for the impossible (and possibly unnecessary) opposition between French and Arabic, it mostly serves the interests of those who seek to represent the Maghreb as having to choose between modernity and archaism or between a colonial past and a more authentic indigenous culture.

2. In their 1989 *Eloge de la créolité/In Praise of Creoleness*, Jean Bernabé, Patrick Chamoiseau, and Raphaël Confiant peformatively brought into existence a type of "créolité" that is at the crossroads between cultural, historical, and linguistic trajectories. A creole community would speak and write Creole *as well as* French, without having to choose between two languages or to systematically reject French as the former colonial tongue, "Car la langue dominante idolâtrée ignore la personnalité du locuteur colonisé, fausse son histoire, nie sa liberté, le déporte de lui-même. Pareillement, l'idolâtrie par le colonisé de la langue dominée, si elle peut être bénéfique dans les premiers temps de la révolution culturelle, ne saurait en aucune façon devenir l'objectif principal ou unique des écrivains créoles d'expression créole" [For the dominant idolized language ignores the personality of the colonized speaker, falsifies his history, denies his freedom, and deports him out of himself. Accordingly, the colonized's idolizing of the dominated language, even though it might be beneficial in the early years of the cultural

revolution, should absolutely not become the primary or unique objective of Creole writers writing in Creole] (1993: 47/108).

3. For an analysis of the specific status of postindependence Moroccan Berber speakers, see Faiq 1999. Grandguillaume also regrets that in Algeria the politics of arabisation should be hostile to "les langues parlées, notamment le berbère, et [. . .] le français" [the languages people actually speak, Berber in particular [. . .], but also French] (1997). He concludes that "l'arabisation tend à exclure toutes les langues, sauf une: celle précisément que seul le pouvoir parle" [Arabisation, to put it bluntly, tends to exclude every language except one—the one spoken by the authorities and no one else] (1997). See also Dourari's 1997 study on the possibility of officializing various Berber languages in Algeria and Caubet 2004 on contemporary creations.

4. Unlike, for example, the issue of a common currency.

5. Hargreaves notes, for example, that when French is creolized from within the hexagon by minority writers, some cultural critics tend to dismiss their contribution as a lack of mastery and talent (2000: 41). Their reaction, however, is sometimes motivated by the fear that celebrating a so-called "banlieue language" will only reinforce economic and cultural alienation. What Begag calls "trafic de mots" [word dealing] (1997) evokes other forms of parallel economy that can either be celebrated as a creative form of resistance or mourned as the symptom of stigmatization and exclusion.

6. And as Gill reminds us, France's most active expansionist colonial period coincides with the moment when regional dialects were systematically suppressed with what she calls "staggering success" (1999: 124).

7. On Khatibi's concept of *bi-langue*, see Thomas Beebee's "The Fiction of Translation: Abdelkebir Khatibi's *Love in Two Languages*"; Mounia Benalil's "Trajets idéologiques de la bi-langue khatibienne dans *Amour bilingue*" [The Ideological Trajectories of Khatibi's bi-language in *Love in Two Languages*]; Réda Bensmaïa's "Traduire ou 'blanchir' la langue: *Amour bilingue* d'Abdelkebir Khatibi" [How to Translate or Whiten Language: Abdelkebir Khatibi's *Love in Two Languages*]; James McGuire's "Forked Tongues, Marginal Bodies: Writing as Translation in Khatibi"; and Zohra Mezgueldi's "Mother Word and French Language Moroccan Writing."

8. Here, the "two" of "l'entre-deux-langues" [in-between-two-languages], which Djebar prefers to "l'entre-langues" [the in-between languages] (1999a: 30) continues to refer to writing and speaking, but that duality does not exclude the presence of more than two languages. It is a space as unstable as Khatibi's *bilingua*.

9. This chapter focuses on his 1999 *Méfiez-vous des parachutistes*, but linguistic issues are also addressed in his other texts: see especially *De quel amour blessé* (1998) and the eighteenth chapter of *La Fin tragique de Philomène Tralala*, in which the first-person narrator is a fictional incarnation of Calixthe Beyala (2003: 77–92).

10. Maati Kabbal suggests that since the 1970s, a strong element of self-derision characterizes the new "élite de gauche, à la culture machrekienne mâtinée de cosmopolitisme, dont certains membres font partie de l'actuel gouvernement [et dont l']apparition favorisa l'éclosion d'une culture nationaliste et socialo-marxiste, qui se voulait l'antithèse de celle du *makhzen* (administration du pouvoir central)" [left-wing elite, whose Machrekian culture is cosmopolitan, whose members often belong to the current government [and whose] emergence helped to create a nationalist and socialist-Marxist

culture which was meant to be the antithesis of the culture of the *makhzen* (the central-ized administrative authorities)] (1999: 30).

11. In Khatibi's *La Mémoire tatouée*, the rare encounters with contemptuous para-troopers are always a cause of humiliation: "Un para défonça la porte, nous repéra, mes frères et moi. Les mains levées, poussés par la mitraillette. Arrivée dans un hangar et interrogatoire. J'hésitais à expliquer à un policier pourquoi je n'étais pas rasé, il me gifla et 'baisse la tête quand je te parle,' hurla-t-il" [A paratrooper kicked the door open, saw my brothers and me. Hands up, machine guns in our backs. A warehouse. Interrogation. I hesitated, not knowing how to explain to an officer why I had not shaved. He slapped me and yelled: "Lower your eyes when I speak to you"] (1971: 106). See also Philip Dine's chapter, "The Myth of the Paratrooper" (1994: 23–43).

12. See also Jacqueline Leiner: "mon effort a été *d'infléchir* le français, de le trans-former pour exprimer disons: 'ce moi, ce moi-nègre, ce moi-créole, ce moi martiniquais, ce moi-antillais'" [I attempted to bend French, to transform, to express, say: "my self, my black-self, my creole self, my Martinican self, my Caribbean self"](1978: xiv).

13. The web site of the real Lycée Lyautey in Casablanca is obviously aware of the potential contradictions of this patronage and presents the marshall as an "atypical colonizer" <http://www.lyceelyautey.org>.

14. Although variously spelled, Rolet, who reappears several times throughout Boileau's work, is always invoked as the archetypal crook. The real Charles Rolet is a historical character about whom a footnote in the Pléiade edition tells us: "Brossette dit: 'Charles Rolet, Procureur au Parlement, étoit fort décrié, et on l'appeloit communément au Palais, l'ame damnée. Mr le Premier Président de la Lamoignon emploïoit le nom de Rolet pour signifier un Fripon indigne: C'est un Rolet, disoit-il ordinairement.' La tra-dition veut que Rollet ait fourni des traits au Vollichon du *Roman bourgeois* de Furetière et du Drolichon des *Plaideurs* de Racine. Molière fit appel à lui dans le procès qui l'opposa à Lully" [Brossette writes: "Charles Rolet was a prosecutor at the Parliament. He had many enemies and was routinely referred to as 'one of the damned' at the Palace. Mr. Le Premier Président de Lamoignon often used Rolet's name to refer to a despicable crook: 'he is a Rolet,' people used to say." Tradition has it that Rollet was the model for Vollichon in Furetière's *Roman bourgeois* and for Drolichon in Racine's "The Suitors." Molière called him to the stand in his lawsuit against Lully] (Boileau 1966: 877, n. 11).

15. Generations of French children growing up on a steady diet of the famous an-thologists André Lagarde and Laurent Michard may have discovered the quotation in the introduction to Boileau's text (Lagarde and Michard 1967: 317).

16. For a study of the children's tactics, see Ronnie Scharfman 1988–1989: 8.

17. In another context, Eve Sedgwick writes: "Knowledge is not itself power, al-though it is the magnetic field of power. Ignorance and opacity collude or compete with it in mobilizing the flows of energy, desire, goods, meanings, persons. If M. Mitterrand knows English but Mr. Reagan lacks French, it is the urbane M. Mitterrand who must negotiate in an acquired tongue, the ignorant Mr. Reagan who may dilate in his native tongue" (1993: 23).

18. The words are borrowed from English but are used in ways that no longer necessarily reflect the original English meaning (see "parking" versus "parking lot," or "corner" used only as a technical sports term).

19. *"Laissons vivre (et vivons!) le rougeoiement de ce magma"* [Let live (and let us live!) the red glow of this magma] (Bernabé et al. 1993: 27/75).

20. It would be a mistake to assume that this is an exclusively Maghrebi issue. Globalization tends to generalize the phenomenon: "We have learned in our French department, for example, not to ask students what their mother tongue is. If they are immigrants or children of mixed marriages—who may have gone to high school in French and college in English and speak a third language at home—they won't know what to answer. We prefer to ask them which is their strongest language. And we hope that they won't say they're equally good in all of them. (This is almost always a bad sign, especially if they want to become translators)" (Simon 2002: 16). Simon's last remark raises a problem that Laroui does not talk about. It suggests that it might be desirable to allow a certain amount of disparity between the different languages in order to better move between them.

21. The portion of this chapter devoted to Laroui's novel appeared in *Présence Fran-cophone 55* (2000) as "De la bilangue de Khatibi à l'a-langue amère de Fouad Laroui: *Amour bilingue* ou *Méfiez-vous des parachutistes*" (91–110). I thank Patricia-Pia Célérier, guest editor of that issue, as well as the editorial board of the journal for the rights to reprint. I also thank Robert Dion, János Riesz, and Hans-Jürgen Lüsebrink for organizing the colloquium at the University of Saarbrücken where a first version of this work was presented in June 2000.

Chapter 4

1. In an interview granted to Patrick Loriot in 2000, the Algerian historian, Mo-hamed Harbi, suggests that the "Deafening silence" surrounding the history of torture in Algeria may have something to do with the fact that "en matière de répression l'Etat algérien indépendant apparaît comme le plus similaire à l'Etat colonial, même si les drames n'ont pas revêtu la même dimension" [in matters of repression, the independent Algerian state appears very similar to the colonial state, although tragedies were of a different order]. Also see Harbi 1992, 1998, and 2001. On the history of the "transition from French oppression to Algerian repression," see Erickson 1998: 105.

2. Gradually, narratives change, probably under the pressure of voices that insist that the past should be told differently, and not because of the passage of a supposedly neutral "time." Writing about Abane Ramdane, one of the leaders of the Algerian Revo-lution killed by fellow Algerians, Stora notes that in 1999, the new president, Abdelaziz Bouteflika, rehabilitated several historic names, announcing that, "the airport of Béjaïa (previously Bougie) would be named after Abane Ramdane" (2001b: 127). In *Le Blanc de l'Algérie*, Djebar writes about Ramdane's last moments, about his thoughts, his murderers' reactions, blaming herself and her generation for allowing silence to prevail for so long: "Qui, parmi nous, trente-cinq ans durant, a pensé écrire 'un tombeau d'Abane Ramdane': en berbère, en arabe ou en français? A peine, de temps à autre intervenait un constat de politologue, d'historien, de polémiste" (1995b: 151) [Who among us, for thirty years, thought of writing Abane Ramdane's *tombeau* in Berber, Arabic, or French? We barely had interventions by political scientists, historians, po-lemicists] (2003: 128).

3. See Benmalek's seemingly matter-of-fact suggestion that the Algerian reader has

become a "demanding reader" who no longer puts up with a "black and white" version of the Algerian War (2003b: 274).

4. It should be noted, of course, that Nora has been criticized for deliberately excluding Algeria from his own corpus. Many critics have regretted that Nora's monumental reflection on historical monuments should shy away from non-Hexagonal sites. Emily Apter points out that "even the most recent volumes [. . .] with their New Historical attention to the mystificatory components of national identity, clumsily justify their choice not to include Algiers or Montreal as *hauts lieux*, or psychotopographies worthy of revisionist nostalgia" (1999: 2). The exception, as Daniel Sherman notes in his "The Arts and Sciences of Colonialism" (2000), is Charles-Robert Ageron's article on the 1931 Colonial Exposition (1984). See also Bensmaïa 2003: 38–40.

5. In "Disorienting the Subject in Djebar's *L'Amour, la fantasia*," Zimra calls the exchange between Djebar and Fromentin a moment of "textual and intertextual intercession" (1995: 156).

6. See Françoise Lionnet's "Immigration, Poster Art, and Transgressive Citizenship: France, 1968–1988."

7. The night of October 17, 1961 has inspired quite a number of contemporary French novelists, among them Leïla Sebbar, *La Seine était rouge* (Paris: Arcantère, 1986); Didier Daeninckx, *Meurtres pour mémoire* (Paris: Gallimard, 1984); and Nacer Kettane, *Le Sourire de Brahim* (Paris: Belfond, 1985). For a study of texts directly related to the events and their lasting effects, see Donadey 2001a.

8. For historical accounts of Kabylia and, more specifically the 1871 uprising, see Mailhé 1995, Sicard 1998, Dessaigne 1988, and Lorcin 1999: 173–83.

9. Jacques Thobie, author of *La France coloniale de 1870 à 1914*, notes the surprising indifference of the *métropole*: "On aurait pu penser que les événements d'Algérie relatifs à la liquidation par les colons du régime militaire, puis à la révolte de Kabylie et à sa répression, eussent entraîné d'importantes répercussions dans l'opinion éclairée et la classe politique métropolitaine: ces affaires ne sont pas minces et de nature à engager résolument l'avenir. Les résonances en sont plutôt modestes" [We would have thought that the incidents involving the elimination of the military regime by the settlers and then the Kabylia insurrection and its repression would have had important repercussions within the enlightened circles of public opinion and among metropolitan politicians. Those issues are not trivial and they definitely have consequences for the future. And yet the reactions were rather muted.] (1991: 11). Historical novels now provide the reader with clearly diverging viewpoints. Earlier renditions such as *Les Cerises d'Icherridène*, the third book of Jules Roy's *Les Chevaux du soleil* (1967–1972), tended to privilege the point of view of the French military. *Les Cerises* is dominated by the voice of a narrator whose perspective is definitely closer to the main character's, Captain Hector Griès, than to the Kabyles. On the other hand, Benmalek's *L'Enfant du peuple ancien* (2000) [*Child of an Ancient People*] (2003c)—in which the two heroes, a European woman and an Algerian man, are deported to Australia together—clearly articulate the insurgents' or dissidents' point of view.

10. In the introduction to the 1996 English edition of *Les Lieux de mémoire* [*Realms of Memory*], Pierre Nora talks about the choice of his title: "I took it from ancient and medieval rhetoric as described by Frances Yates in her admirable book, *The Art of*

Memory (1966), which recounts an important tradition of mnemonic techniques. The classical art of memory was based on a systematic inventory of *loci memoriae* or 'memory places'" (xv).

11. In this example, the historical script has indeed changed, but it is already easy to see which parts of Lallaoui's constructions of the new relationship between France and its former empire will be further problematized by the next generation. Although Paris is decentered, although other parts of the world are linked to the colonizing logic, the constellation of destination and arrival points still forms a relatively Francocentric network that corresponds to the ghostly geography of the empire. Other more recent novels such as Claire Messud's *The Last Life* (1999) or Anouar Benmalek's *Ce jour viendra* (2003a) triangulate among Algeria, France, and the United States (or what Michael Dash has called, in a different context, the "Other" America [1998]) to become part of the picture, adding a new vantage point to their search for a new history).

12. Writing on the body is a highly charged symbolic gesture whose valence may change depending on the context. Sartre imagines Western education as a form of "branding" (1963: 7), a text cruelly and definitively inscribed on the body. The body will always carry the trace of the violence undergone by the colonized subject: a mark of uprooting rather than a symbol of belonging. Lallaoui seems keen on presenting us with a more nuanced perspective. In *La Colline aux oliviers*, writing on the body is not the exclusive province of the colonizer, nor is the sign thus produced reliable or dictatorial in its meaning.

13. For an analysis of the interconnection between gender and historiography in the Maghreb, see "Wild Femininity and Historical Countermemory" in Woodhull (1993: 50–87).

14. As if Lallaoui's reference to tattooing was an implicit homage to and rewriting of Khatibi's autobiography (Khatibi 1971).

15. An earlier draft of this essay was presented at the University of Cincinnati. I thank Michèle Vialet and Catherine Raissiguier for their hospitality. Another version appears as "Tattoos or Earrings: Two Models of Historical Writing in Mehdi Lallaoui's *La Colline aux oliviers*" in *Identity, Memory and Nostalgia, Algeria 1800–2000*, ed. Patricia Lorcin (New York: Syracuse University Press: forthcoming). I am grateful to the press for the right to reprint.

Chapter 5

1. In *Le Serment des barbares* (1999), Sansal imagines that the mysterious murder of an old man, eventually solved by the detective, is directly connected to his decision to tend his former European employers' abandoned graves. In the story, French *pieds-noirs*, whose ancestors or parents are buried in Algeria, are conned by criminals who promise them to care for their dead when, in reality, they take their money and use the coffins as hiding places. On the other side of the Mediterranean, the desecration of Jewish and Muslim burial sites is not a literary phenomenon. It is one of the cultural and political ghosts that haunts this chapter. In the 1990s, the exhumation of Felix Guermon in the Carpentras cemetery generated not only strong and emotional reactions, but also questions about how to cover and commemorate such events. Since then, desecrations

have been disturbingly episodic rather than exceptional. A report published in *Le Monde*, which only lists the most serious incidents, counted more than eighteen cases in many different French regions (see "Les principales profanations des cimetières juifs en France," *Le Monde*, 10 August 2004). During the same period, Muslim sites were also desecrated in Val-de-Marne in 2003 and in Alsace in 2004, and a few days before the publication of the article on the profanation of Jewish graves, *Le Monde* documented the alarming and increasing number of a attacks directed against Muslim sites (cemeteries and mosques). See "Chronologie des actes contre des cimetières et des lieux de culte musulmans" (*Le Monde*, 6 August 2004, <http://www.lemonde.fr>).

2. There are countless references to lost graves in postcolonial Franco-Maghrebi films or texts, regardless of the genre. They appear just as frequently in autobiographies (Halimi 1999) as in realistic fictions (such as Merzak Allouache's *Bab El Oued City*, where two *pieds-noirs* make sure to include a trip to the cemetery during a nostalgic visit to Algeria. Their effort to clean up the abandoned graves is slightly pathetic). In Bensmaïa's *Alger, ou, la maladie de la mémoire: l'année des passages* (1997) [*The Year of Passages*](1995) and in Benmalek's *Les Amants désunis* (1998) [*The Lovers of Algeria*] (2001), the protagonists choose a different tactic: they adopt a stranger's grave in order to be able to honor, in some indirect, translated, and crosscultural way, the memory of their missing dead. In Benmalek's story, a woman whose family was killed by the NLF systematically visits cemeteries in order to look for surrogate graves, and specifically for headstones bearing the names of Mehdi or Meriem, her own children's names.

3. The ghostly encounter is loosely related to another kind of haunted "logos," namely the "hauntology" that Derrida defines in *Specters of Marx*. But it is more than just a logos or the ghostly shadow of all ontological existence. It is one of those triangular collusions between language, protocol, and subjectivization that we now recognize as the signature of a specific kind of encounter. The difference here is that the prewritten script accounts for the fact that one of the protagonists cannot speak or hear. Instead, the encounter allows a subject to speak with and for a dead person, who, as a result, will not be reduced to silence.

4. The book is dedicated to three dead friends: Mahfoud Boucebci, M'Hamed Boukhobza, and Abdelkader Alloula. Alloula was involved in the theater and had directed plays in Arabic. Boucebci was a psychiatrist and a member of the "Comité pour la vérité sur l'assassinat de Tahar Djaout" [Committee for the Truth in Tahar Djaout's Murder]. Djaout, the writer, was killed in 1993. Boukhobza was a sociologist, the author of studies on the rural world and the agrarian revolution, as well as a book on the 1988 riots. Others were also killed, including journalists, teachers, priests (on the murder of Pierre Claverie, see Pérennès 2000), and raï singers, such as Cheb Hasni in Oran and Lounes Matoub. Like Djebar, Malika Mokeddem often dedicates her novels to dead authors. *L'Interdite* [*The Forbidden Woman*] is dedicated to Tahar Djaout, while *Des Rêves et des assassins* [*Of Dreams and Assassins*] is dedicated to Alloula: "Pour Abdelkader Alloula, illustre fils d'Oran et du théâtre algérien. ASSASSINE" [For Abdelkader Alloula, illustrious son of Oran and of Algerian theater. MURDERED]. On Mokeddem's work see Helm 2000 and Chaulet-Achour 1995 and 1998.

5. On the ethical issues raised by the question of whether the dead can "talk to us," especially when their testimony has to do with violence and survival, see Davis 2004. See

O'Riley 2004 on the value of "position and spectrality as strategic modes of historical recovery" (68). Also see his discussion of how other postcolonial theorists—Chambers 2001, Prakash 1997, Bhabha 1994—have linked haunting to postcolonial historiography.

6. By so doing, authors find a solution to the double constraint that literary analysts often impose on *literary* testimonies when they dismiss them as "mere" testimonies. Here is how Leïla Sebbar starts her review of Slimane Benaïssa's recent novel *Le Silence de la falaise* [The Silence of the Cliff]: "Pas un roman algérien de ces dernières années, qui ne cherche à expliquer la situation politique de l'Algérie à un moment particulier de son histoire. C'est ce qui fait, en général, leur faiblesse. Slimane Benaïssa, qu'on connaît en Algérie et en France pour son théâtre 'engagé,' n'échappe pas à cette tentation" [In the past few years, every single Algerian novel has tried to explain the political situation of Algeria at a particular historical moment. Generally, it is their weakness. Slimane Benaïssa, who is well known for his "committed" theater both in France and in Algeria, is no exception to the rule] (2001: 66).

7. In contemporary Western literature and Hollywood cinema, the ghost story is often a subgenre of the whodunit. The protagonist who is in contact with the ghost must become a detective: consider Jerry Zucker's, *Ghost* (1990) or Manoj Nelliyattu Shyamalan's *The Sixth Sense* (1999) for example. In Djebar's text, the goal is not so much to unmask the assassins (they are unimportant) as to allow the victims to speak again. After all, their murderers wanted to silence them. When Mokeddem dedicates *L'Interdite* to Djaout, she writes: "A Tahar Djaout. Interdit de vie à cause de ses écrits" [To Tahar Djaout; To his life forbidden because of his writings].

8. The book is structured by the number three (a symbol of mourning). The original edition contains three "processions" spread over four chapters: Procession 1 (103–23), Procession 2 (152–93), Procession 3 (216–31), and Procession 3 (a sequel) (240–55).

9. In the letter to Derrida that constitutes the last chapter of his 2001 book, Robert Young suggests that most of the people who were to be associated with the theses of poststructuralism were "so to speak, Algerians improper, those who did not belong easily to either side—a condition that the subsequent history of Algeria has shown in its own way characteristically Algerian, for the many different kinds of Algerians 'proper' do not belong easily to the Algerian state either" (414).

10. It should be noted that even the cause of Sénac's death is treated as a controversial issue by recent films, such as Abdelkrim Bahloul's 2003 *Le Soleil assassiné*, a moving and quasi-hagiographical biography that portrays the poet as a victim of state violence.

11. Zimra suggests that the deaths of those who were not directly killed by terrorists were "largement précipitées par la morbidité de cette plongée du pays dans la folie— Kateb Yacine fut l'un des premiers ainsi que Mouloud Mammeri" [in a large measure hastened by their country's morbid descent into madness—Kateb Yacine was one among the first to go, followed by Mouloud Mammeri] (1995: 826). Zimra's scenario is far from implausible, but Djebar's text has the added advantage of reuniting even those individuals that death separated.

12. In another genre, Rachida Krim's film, *Sous les pieds des femmes* [Under the Women's Feet], asks similar questions about the macabre perpetuation of violence across several generations—something that we read as a "repetition" that history often tries to explain by inserting it into one coherent, rational, or teleological narrative. Dina

Sherzer analyzes the series of flashbacks and conversations between Aya and Amin (a former lover) and points out that each voice interrupts the other so that the film both proposes and refutes the parallel between the violence of the Islamic Salvation Front (FIS) and that of the NLF: "By juxtaposing Aya's and Amin's past, as militants of the NLF in France, and their present, Aya as Algerian-French in France and Amin as Algerian living in Algeria, Krim shows the parallel between the fanaticism and the idealism of the 1958 revolution and the fanaticism of the present day FIS activists" (2001: 160).

13. See Salem 1997. The author analyzes the trajectory of migrants who only go back to Algeria after their deaths.

14. Caribbean and African-American literature often portrays slaves who believe that they will go (back) to Guinea when they die (even if their African land of origin is not Guinea strictly speaking). The myth endures long after the abolition of slavery and finds its way into twentieth-century novels such as Joseph Zobel's *Rue Cases-Nègres*, first published in 1950. See the conversation between José and Médouze, the old cane-cutter, who melancholically points out that when he goes back to Guinea after his death, he will not be able to take the child with him (1974: 58).

15. On the connection between death, passages, and trespassing (*trépas* in French), see Calle-Gruber 2001. About *Le Blanc de l'Algérie*, she points out that death is "ce 'dépasser en marchant' (*trespasser*) qui est un événement absolu; le pas de trop" (109) [the overstep (trespass) that is an absolute event; the step too many].

16. Benguigui's film is thus comparable to other contemporary autobiographical fiction and essays, such as Gisèle Halimi's *Fritna* (1999) and Hélène Cixous' *Les Rêveries de la femmes sauvages* (2000). The book version of *Inch'Allah dimanche* was produced by Albin Michel, Djebar's Parisian publisher.

17. I thank Leïla Ibnassi for pointing out that the song is in Berber.

18. On the effect on fragmentation in *La Nouba*, see chapter 5 of Réda Bensmaïa's *Experimental Nations: On the Invention of the Maghreb* (2003).

19. Similarly, readers of *So Vast the Prison* will know something about why and how *La Nouba* was made, even if they have not yet watched the film. Emily Tomlinson's reading of one of Djebar's earlier novels, *Les Alouettes naïves* (1967), suggests that other less explicit echoes between her novels can be read as the regular reappearance of the ghost of dead *moudjahidate*. She proposes that "*Les Alouettes* sets a precedent for the strange 'ghost story' that would constitute its author's response to another wave of horror, another 'civil war': 1995's catalogue of political disappearances and demises, *Algerian White*" (2003: 46).

20. On how Henri Rousso's theory of the interruption of the mourning process (based on memories of World War II) can be applied to women writing about the Algerian war, see Donadey 2001b.

21. On the ambivalence of the gaze in Djebar's work, see Zimra 1995, Mortimer 1996, and Prabhu 2002.

22. As Georges Bataille puts it "Ces os blanchis n'abandonnent plus les survivants à la menace gluante qui commande le dégoût. Ils mettent fin au rapprochement fondamental de la mort et de la décomposition dont jaillit la vie profuse" [The bleached bones no longer expose survivors to the oozing threat that triggers disgust. They put an end to the primeval connection between death and decomposition out of which the

profusion of life springs.] (1957: 63). See also Edgar Morin 1970, Mary Douglas 1994, and Julia Kristeva 1980.

23. The word appears in Cixous's *Les Rêveries de la femme sauvage*, a book in which Cixous stages the writing of loss as the loss of writing. Her text, as we are reading it, replaces a lost text and becomes the *mise en abyme* of the impossibility of ever completing the mourning process. The first pages, the author explains, are not the first pages, and we will never read them because, as Cixous adamantly insists, they got lost between the night when she wrote them and the morning when she looked for them. Written under the spell of a strange and incoercible *surgissement* [welling up] (2000: 9), they have mysteriously disappeared by the time she wakes up. Like some form of automatic writing or possession, the beginning of the text had "fait son apparition" [appeared] like a ghost in the middle of the night (9). The narrative never rationalizes the loss as a dream. The story is simply absent and inexorably present, like a haunting. On the relationship between death and departing see also Stevens 2002.

Chapter 6

1. I added markers of biological sex to preserve the obvious system of identification between the first person narrator and her animal *alter ego*, which, in French, is adequately reflected in the grammatical gender of words.

2. Within the fable, a third animal character plays the role of mediator. For the sea urchin and the jellyfish to meet, they need the intervention of an excluded third, a whale, who will help them connect.

For the opportunity to present earlier versions of this text on *N'zid*, I thank Seth Graebner and Stamos Metzidakis from the Washington University in Saint Louis as well as Draï Wengier, coorganizer of the 2004 Foreign Languages Graduate Student Conference, "Ex-Centric Texts, Exiled Selves," held at the University of Miami. A French version of this study came out as "Lectures mythophores des récits de l'origine dans *N'zid* de Malika Mokeddem" in *Présence Francophone* 62 (2004): 22–38. I thank the editorial board of the review for authorizing me to reprint.

3. In 1993, this drawing attracted my attention in a discussion of what it meant for Beur writers to be described as in between. At the time, I assumed that representational tactics provided an author with a choice: inbetweenness was a form of acrobatic performance, and it was up to the artist whether to view it as suffering or as physical skill (Rosello 1993). More than ten years later, though Plantu's acrobat still haunts me, I realize that I cannot read him in the same manner. Today, a comparison between several textual and visual renditions of the migrant's flexibility leads me to focus on the way in which different texts represent the same type of necessary flexibility, acknowledging that both suffering and acrobatic skill coexist and that compassion and admiration do not have to be incompatible.

4. In *A quoi rêvent les loups*, Khadra uses a different image to characterize the impossibility of crossing the space of suspicion between subjects. "Bridges" between individuals have collapsed, and Algeria has become an archipelago of solitudes. No ship, no special seat can provide a link between humans: "Sid Ali, le chantre de la Casbah, me disait que l'Algérie était le plus grand archipel du monde constitué de vingt-huit millions

d'îles et de quelques poussières. Il avait omis d'ajouter que les océans de malentendus qui nous séparaient les uns des autres étaient, eux aussi, les plus obscurs et les plus vastes de la planète" [Si Ali, the poet from the Casbah, was telling that Algeria is the largest archipelago in the world, made up of twenty million islands and a few extra specks. He had forgotten the oceans of misunderstanding that separate us from one another, and that those oceans are the darkest and deepest on the planet] (1999: 36).

5. In an interview granted to *Algérie Littérature Action* in 1998 and republished in *Chroniques de l'Algérie amère: 1985–2002* in 2003b, Benmalek talks about his grandmother: "J'ai parlé tout à l'heure de ma grand-mère trapéziste. C'est elle qui m'a inspirée le premier thème de ce livre: celui du cirque. Le thème du cirque, de ses errances et de ses dangers, est omniprésent dans ce roman. Peut-être est-ce inconsciemment une métaphore de l'existence humaine: quelques cabrioles risquées où la chute, inévitable, est la seule conclusion logique?" [I mentioned my grandmother who was a trapeze artist. She was the inspiration for the book's main theme: the circus. The circus with its endless wandering and its dangers is a recurrent theme throughout the novel. It may be an unconscious metaphor of human life: a few spectacular jumps and the inevitable fall at the end. Isn't this the only logical conclusion?] (2003b: 37).

6. *Les A.N.I du "Tassili"* came out in 1984 at the beginning of the decade during which so-called "beur" literature flourished (see Hargreaves 1995 and Vurgun, 2004). It was followed by two other novels: *Courage et patience* and more recently *Le Porteur de cartable*, which was turned into a television film (directed by Caroline Huppert) and aired in 2002 in conjunction with the Year of Algeria in France. That story is another good example of encounter between a young "Algerian" (who has always lived in Paris) and a young "French" boy repatriated just before the end of the war. Their friendship forces them to reinvent the roles that history tries to impose on them. Omar will begin by hating Raphaël, the *pied-noir* who moves into a flat that Omar has been coveting for many years. "Kicked out" of the imaginary paradise he has never had by the arrival of this stranger from "his" country (although he has never been there and although it is not technically a country yet), Omar finds in Raphaël an ironic and mythical alter ego. Like the narrative voice of Hélène Cixous' *Rêveries de la femme sauvage*, Omar understands that his encounter with Algeria is a form of Algeriance that can only be translated by poetry or humor. Neither Omar nor Raphaël can ever arrive or be in their native land.

7. On the third space in Tadjer, see Manopoulous 1996.

8. Three distinct episodes during which the narrator suffered from humiliating racist attacks are related but framed as monologues, each paragraph starting with "Je ne peux tout de même pas lui expliquer ce que j'ai ressenti lorsque. . ." [It is not as if I could explain to her how I felt when. . .] (170–71). Just as Anna gives up on the idea of climbing a tree to prove her point because the audience is inappropriate, Omar recognizes that he does not have the necessary tools or narrative skills to turn Nelly's question into a proper performative encounter that would transform her into a receptive auditor. The preconditions of a true dialogue can only be imagined in the novel as a whole, while these passages adequately stage the impossibility of a dialogue between the two characters.

9. Fethi Benslama adamantly refuses that the Algerian government's attempt to camouflage or disguise colonial monuments under a "peau de céramique algérienne" [skin

of Algerian ceramic] constitutes a positive reappropriation of a people's memory. He claims that this "déguisement monumental" [monumental disguise] drags "le désir légitime d'une restitution, dans un processus de confusion et de manipulation perverse de l'identité" [the legitimate desire for restitution into a process of confusion and perverse manipulation of our identity] (1995: 56).

10. An earlier version of this study on acrobats was published as "L'entre-deux et les acrobates," in *Migrations des identités et des textes entre l'Algérie et la France, dans les littératures des deux rives*, ed. Charles Bonn (Paris: L'Harmattan, 2004): 231–46. I thank the press for permission to reprint.

Conclusion

1. Rather than noticing that the subjects created by performative encounters belong in a universe of historically favored multiplicity that goes well beyond the duality of bilingualism or biculturalism, we may focus instead on the fact that parts of our collective imaginations are seeking singular ways of representing a relationship to the community that transcends the opposition between universalism—tactical or not—and culturalism or communitarism (Rosello 2003). Like the variables of Balibar's poetical and political equations, the subjects involved in performative encounters represent a chaotic series of fractals, an atotality that is not adequately formulated by the laws of (popular) arithmetic.

2. Thelja only briefly alludes to the battle during which the French forces (led by the Duke of Aumale) captured Abd-el-Kebir's *Smala* in May 1843. She wonders silently whether her friends know about the event.

References

Addi, Lahouari. 2003. "Un soutien aux démocrates." *Libération*, 9 January: 8.

Agence France-Presse (AFP) and Reuters. 2003. "La France et l'Algérie veulent 're-fonder' leurs relations." *Le Monde*, 17 January. Cited articles can be accessed online with a paid subscription to *Le Monde*'s archives. <http://www.lemonde.fr>

Ageron, Charles-Robert. 1984. "L'Exposition coloniale de 1931: mythe républicain ou mythe impérial?" *Les Lieux de mémoire*. Volume 1: *La République*. Ed. Pierre Nora. Paris: Gallimard, 1984. 561–91.

———. 1991. *Modern Algeria: A History from 1830 to the Present*. Trans. Michael Brett. London: Hurst.

———. 1997. *La Guerre d'Algérie et les Algériens: 1954–1962*. Paris: Armand Colin.

Ahmed, Sara. 2000. *Strange Encounters: Embodied Others in Post-Coloniality*. New York and London: Routledge.

Ajar, Emile. 1975. *La Vie devant soi*. Paris: Mercure de France.

Allouache, Merzak. 1995. *Bab el Oued City*. Paris: Seuil.

Amselle, Jean-Loup. 1990. *Logiques métisses: Anthropologie de l'identité en Afrique et ailleurs*. Paris: Payot.

Anzaldúa, Gloria. 1987. *Borderlands/La frontera: The New Mestiza*. San Francisco: Spinsters/Aunt Lute.

Apter, Emily. 1999. *Continental Drift: From National Characters to Virtual Subjects*. Chicago: University of Chicago Press.

Atwood, Margaret. 2002. *Negotiating with the Dead: a Writer on Writing*. Cambridge: Cambridge University Press.

Aussaresses, Paul. 2001. *Services spéciaux, Algérie 1955–1957*. Paris: Perrin.

Austin, John L. 1962. *How to Do Things with Words*. 2nd ed. Oxford: Oxford University Press.

Balibar, Etienne. 1998. "Algérie, France: une ou deux nations?" *Droit de cité*. Paris: Editions de l'aube.

———. 2001. *Nous citoyens d'Europe? Les Frontières, l'Etat, le peuple*. Paris: La Découverte.

Barbé, Philippe. 2001. "Transnational and Translinguistic Relocation of the Subject in *Les Nuits de Strasbourg* by Assia Djebar." *Esprit-Créateur* 41, no. 3 (fall): 125–35.

Barthes, Roland. 1981. *Le Grain de la voix*. Paris: Seuil.

Bataille, Georges. 1957. *L'Erotisme*. Paris: Minuit.

Baudrillard, Jean. 1993. *The Transparency of Evil: Essays on Extreme Phenomena*. Trans. James Benedict. New York: Verso.

Baussant, Michèle. 2002. *Pieds-noirs, mémoires d'exil*. Paris: Stock.

Beaugé, Florence. 2000. "Le Général Massu exprime ses regrets pour la torture en Algérie." *Le Monde*, 22 June.

Beebee, Thomas. 1994. "The Fiction of Translation: Abdelkebir Khatibi's *Love in Two Languages*." *SubStance* 23, no. 1: 63–78.

Begag, Azouz. 1989. *Béni ou le paradis privé*. Paris: Seuil.

———. 1997. "Trafic de mots en banlieue: du 'nique ta mère' au 'plaît-t-il?'" *Migrants-Formation* 108 (March): 30–37.

Begag, Azouz and Christian Delorme. 2001. "Energumènes ou energ-humains?" *Le Monde*, 13 October.

Belghoul, Farida. 1986. *Georgette!* Paris: Barrault.

Benalil, Mounia. 1998. "Trajets idéologiques de la bilangue khatibienne dans *Amour bilingue*" *Etudes Francophones* 13, no. 2 (autumn) : 93–103.

Benguigui, Yamina. 1996. *Femmes d'Islam*. Paris: Albin Michel.

———. 1997. *Mémoires d'immigrés: l'héritage maghrébin*. Paris: Canal + éditions.

———. 2001. *Inch'Allah dimanche*. Paris: Albin Michel.

Benmalek, Anouar. 1998. *Les Amants désunis*. Paris: Calmann-Levy.

———. 2000. *L'Enfant du peuple ancien*. Paris: Pauvert.

———. 2001. *The Lovers of Algeria*. Trans. Joanna Kilmartin. London: Harvill.

———. 2003a. *Ce jour viendra*. Paris: Pauvert.

———. 2003b. *Chroniques de l'Algérie amère: 1985–2002*. Paris: Pauvert.

———. 2003c. *The Child of an Ancient People*. Trans. Andrew Riemer. London: Harvill.

Benslama, Fethi. 1995. "La cause identitaire," *Intersignes* 10 (Spring): 47–68.

Bensmaïa, Réda. 1985. "Traduire ou 'blanchir' la langue: *Amour bilingue* d'Abdelkebir Khatibi." *Hors cadre* 3: 187–207.

———. 1995. *The Year of Passages*. Trans. Tom Conley. Minneapolis: University of Minnesota Press.

———. 1997. *Alger, ou, la maladie de la mémoire: l'année des passages*. Paris: L'Harmattan.

———. 2003. *Experimental Nations: On the Invention of the Maghreb*. Trans. Alyson Waters. Princeton, N.J.: Princeton University Press.

Bentahila, Abdelali. 1983. *Language Attitudes among Arabic-French Bilinguals in Morocco*. Clevedon: Multilingual Matters.

Berger, Anne-Emmanuelle. 2002. "The Impossible Wedding: Nationalism, Languages and Mother Tongue in Postcolonial Algeria." *Algeria in Other's Languages*. Ed. Anne-Emmanuelle Berger. Ithaca: Cornell University Press. 60–78.

Bernabé, Jean, Patrick Chamoiseau, and Raphaël Confiant. [1989] 1993. *Eloge de la créolité/In Praise of Creoleness*. Trans. M. B. Taleb Khyar. Paris: Gallimard.

Bernard, Philippe. 2001. "Du match France-Algérie au 17 octobre 1961." *Le Monde*, 26 October.

Bhabha, Homi. 1994. *The Location of Culture*. New York and London: Routledge.

Boileau, Nicolas. 1966. *Oeuvres Complètes*. Ed. Françoise Escal. Paris: Gallimard.

———. *The Works of Monsieur Boileau. Made English from the last Paris edition, by several hands*. Vol. 1. London, 1712. 3 vols. *English Short Title Catalogue: Eighteenth Century Collections Online*. Gale Group. <http://galenet.galegroup.com/servlet/ECCO>

Bongie, Chris. 1998. *Islands and Exile: The Creole Identities of Post/colonial Literature*. Stanford: Stanford University Press.

Bonn, Charles, and Farida Boualit, eds. 1999. *Paysages littéraires algériens des années 90: témoigner d'une tragédie?* Paris: L'Harmattan.

Butler, Judith. 1990a. *Gender Trouble: Feminism and the Subversion of Identity.* London and New York: Routledge.

———. 1990b. "Performative Acts and Gender Constitution: An Essay in Phenomenology and Feminist Theory." *Performing Feminisms: Feminist Critical Theory and Theatre.* Ed. Sue-Ellen Case. Baltimore: Johns Hopkins University Press. 270–83.

———. 1993. *Bodies that Matter: On the Discursive Limits of Sex.* London and New York: Routledge.

———. 1997a. *Excitable Speech: A Politics of the Performative.* New York: Routledge.

———. 1997b. *Theories in Subjection: The Psychic Life of Power.* Stanford: Stanford University Press.

Calle-Gruber, Mireille. 2001. *Assia Djebar ou la résistance de l'écriture.* Paris: Maisonneuve et Larose.

Caubet, Dominique. 2004. *Les Mots du bled.* Paris: l'Harmattan.

de Certeau, Michel. 1990. *L'Invention du quotidien.* Paris: Gallimard.

Césaire, Aimé. 1946. *Les Armes miraculeuses.* Paris: Gallimard.

———. 1982. *Moi Laminaire.* Paris: Seuil.

———. 1995. *Cahier d'un retour au pays natal/ Notebook of a Return to My Native Land.* Trans. Mireille Rosello and Annie Pritchard. Newcastle: Bloodaxe.

Chambers, Iain. 2001. *Culture after Humanism: History, Culture, Subjectivity.* London: Routledge.

Charef, Mehdi. 1989. *Le Harki de Meriem.* Paris: Mercure de France.

Chaulet-Achour, Christiane. 1995. "Place d'une littérature migrante en France." *Littérature des immigrations.* Vol. 2: *Exils croisés.* Ed. Charles Bonn. Paris: L'Harmattan. 115–24.

———. 1998. *Noûn: Algériennes dans l'écriture.* Biarritz: Atlantica.

Cherki, Alice. 2003. "Paris-Alger." *Panoramiques. Algériens-Français: bientôt finis les enfantillages?* 107–10.

Chow, Rey. 2001. "How (the) Inscrutable Chinese Led to Globalized Theory." *PMLA* 116, no. 1 (January): 69–74.

Chraïbi, Driss. 1970. *La Civilisation ma mère.* Paris: Denoël.

———. 1984. *Mother Comes of Age.* Trans. Hugh A. Harter. Washington, D.C.: Three Continents Press.

Cixous, Hélène. 1979. *Vivre l'orange.* Paris: Editions des femmes.

———. 1997a. "Mon Algériance." *Les Inrockuptibles* 115 (20 August–2 September): 71–74.

———. 1997b. *OR—Les lettres de mon père.* Paris: Editions des femmes.

———. 1997c. "Pieds nus." *Une enfance algérienne.* Ed. Leïla Sebbar. Paris: Gallimard. 53–63.

———. 2000. *Les Rêveries de la femme sauvage.* Paris: Galilée.

Clerc, Jeanne-Marie. 1997. *Assia Djebar: Ecrire, transgresser, résister.* Paris: L'Harmattan.

Cohen, Joshua, Matthew Howard, and Martha C. Nussbaum, eds. 1999. *Is Multicul-*

turalism Bad for Women? Susan Moller Okin with Respondents. Princeton, N.J.: Princeton University Press.

Colombani, Florence. 2003. "Festival Promesses algériennes à Clermont." *Le Monde*, 28 January.

Cooke, Miriam. 2001. *Women Claim Islam*. New York and London: Routledge.

Curnier, Jean-Paul. 1999. "La Nostalgie de l'immensité" (A conversation with Patrick Leboutte and Laurent Roth). *L'Image le Monde 1, Marseille Face à son image* (fall): 26–32.

Dash, Michael. 1998. *The Other America: Caribbean Literature in a New World Context*. Charlottesville: University Press of Virginia.

Dauge-Roth, Alexandre. 2004. "L'Intimité à l'épreuve de *L'Intrus* et de *L'Interdite*: la greffe comme (des)saisie de soi." *Esprit-Créateur* 44, no. 1 (spring): 27–37.

Davis, Colin. 2004. "Can the Dead Talk to Us? De Man, Levinas and Agamben." *Culture, Theory and Critique* 45, no. 1: 77–89.

Deleuze, Gilles, and Felix Guattari. 1980. *Mille Plateaux*. Paris: Minuit.

Deleuze, Gilles, Felix Guattari, and Claire Parnet. 1987. *Dialogues*. Trans. Hugh Tomlison and Barbara Habberjam. New York: Columbia University Press.

Dely, Renaud. 1998. "Zidane, icone de l'intégration." *Libération*, 10 July: 4–5.

Derrida, Jacques. 1972. "Signature Événement Contexte." *Marges de la philosophie*. Paris: Minuit. 365–93.

———. 1982. "Signature Event Context." *Margins of Philosophy*. Trans. Alan Bass. Chicago: Chicago University Press. 309–30.

———. 1992. *Given Time. I, Counterfeit Money*. Trans. Peggy Kamuf. Chicago: University of Chicago Press.

———. 1993. *Spectres de Marx: l'état de la dette, le travail du deuil et la nouvelle Internationale*. Paris: Galilée.

———. 1994a. *Politiques de l'amitié*. Paris: Galilée.

———. 1994b. *Specters of Marx: The State of the Debt, the Work of Mourning and the New International*. Trans. Peggy Kamuf. New York: Routledge.

———. 1996. *Le Monolinguisme de l'autre*. Paris: Galilée.

———. 1997a. *Adieu à Emmanuel Lévinas*. Paris: Galilée.

———. 1997b. *Monolingualism of the Other or The Prosthesis of Origin*. Trans. Patrick Mensah. Stanford: Stanford University Press.

———. 1999. *Adieu to Emmanuel Levinas*. Trans. Pascale-Anne Brault and Michael Naas. Stanford: Stanford University Press.

Derrida, Jacques, and Anne Dufourmantelle. 2000. *Of Hospitality*. Trans. Rachel Bowlby. Stanford: Stanford University Press.

Dessaigne, Francine. 1988. *Bordj bou Arreridj: l'insurrection de 1871*. Versailles: Editions de l'Atlantide.

Détienne, Marcel, and Jean-Pierre Vernant. 1970. *Les Ruses de l'intelligence: la mètis des Grecs*. Paris: Flammarion.

Dib, Mohammed. 1994. *L'Infante maure*. Paris: Albin Michel.

Dine, Philip. 1994. "The Myth of the Paratrooper." *Images of the Algerian War: French Fiction and Film, 1954–1992*. Oxford: Clarendon Press. 23–43.

Djaout, Tahar. 1984. *Les Chercheurs d'os*. Paris: Seuil.

———. 1999. *Le Dernier été de la raison*. Paris: Seuil.

Djebar, Assia. 1967. *Les Alouettes naïves*. Paris: Julliard.

———. 1969. *Poèmes pour l'Algérie heureuse*. Alger: SNED.

———. 1973. *Les Enfants du nouveau monde*. Paris: UGE.

———. 1980. *Femmes d'Alger dans leur appartement*. Paris: Editions des femmes.

———. 1992. *Women of Algiers in Their Apartment*. Trans. Marjolijn de Jager. Charlottesville and London: University of Virginia Press.

———. 1993. *Fantasia: An Algerian Cavalcade*. Trans. Dorothy Blair. Portsmouth: Heinemann.

———. 1994. *Far from Medina*. London: Quartet.

———. 1995a. *L'Amour, la fantasia*. Paris: Albin Michel.

———. 1995b. *Le Blanc de l'Algérie*. Paris: Albin Michel.

———. 1995c. *Vaste est la prison*. Paris: Albin Michel.

———. 1997a. *Les Nuits de Strasbourg*. Arles: Actes sud.

———. 1997b. *Oran, langue morte*. Arles: Actes sud.

✗ ———. 1999a. *Ces voix qui m'assiègent . . . en marge de ma francophon*ie. Paris: Albin Michel.

———. 1999b. *So Vast the Prison*. Trans. Betsy Wing. New York: Seven Stories Press.

———. 2002. *La Femme sans sépulture*. Paris: Albin Michel.

———. 2003a. *Algerian White*. Trans. David Kelley and Marjolijn de Jager. New York and London: Seven Stories Press.

———. 2003b. *La Disparition de la langue française*. Paris: Albin Michel.

Donadey, Anne. 2001a. "Anamnesis and National Reconciliation: Re-membering October 17, 1961." *Immigrant Narratives in Contemporary France*. Ed. Susan Ireland and Patrice Proulx. London: Greenwood Press. 47–56.

———. 2001b. *Recasting Postcolonialism: Women Writing Between Worlds*. Portsmouth: Heinemann.

Douglas, Mary. 1994. *Purity and Danger: an Analysis of the Concepts of Pollution and Taboo*. New York: Routledge.

Dourari, Abderrezak. 1997. "Pluralisme linguistique et unité nationale: Perspectives pour l'officialisation des variétés berbères en Algérie." *Plurilinguisme et identité au Maghreb*. Ed. Foued Laroussi. Rouen: Publications de l'université de Rouen. 45–53.

Erickson, John. 1998. *Islam and Postcolonial Narrative*. Cambridge: Cambridge University Press.

Fabre, Thierry. 1989. "Les intermédiaires culturels: vers une dialogique franco-algérienne." *Migrations Sociétés* 1, no. 5–6 (October-December): 27–42.

Faiq, Said. 1999. "The Status of Berber: A Permanent Challenge to Language Policy in Morocco." *Language and Society in the Middle East and North Africa*. Ed. Yasi Suleiman. Richmond: Curzon. 137–53.

Fanon, Frantz. 1959. *L'An Cinq de la Révolution Algérienne*. Paris: François Maspéro.

Faulkner, Rita. 1996. "Assia Djebar: Frantz Fanon, Women, Veils and Land." *World Literature Today* 70, no. 4 (Autumn): 847–55.

Felman, Shoshana. 1980. *Le Scandale du corps parlant: Don Juan avec Austin, ou la séduction en deux langues*. Paris: Seuil.

————. 1983. *The Literary Act: Don Juan with J.L. Austin, or Seduction in Two Languages*. Trans. Catherine Porter. Ithaca: Cornell University Press.

Feraoun, Mouloud. [1962] 1990. *Journal*. Reprint, Paris: Bouchêne, Alger.

Ferro, Marc. 1994. *Histoire des colonisations: des conquêtes aux indépendances XIIIe-XXe siècle*. Paris: Seuil.

Fuchs, Gérard. 1987. *Ils resteront: le défi de l'immigration*. Paris: Syros.

Gafaïti, Hafid. 1996. *Les Femmes dans le roman algérien: histoire, discours et texte*. Paris: L'Harmattan.

————. 1997. "Between God and the President: Literature and Censorship in North Africa." *Diacritics* 27, no. 2: 59–84.

————. 2001. *Cultures transnationales de France: des "Beurs" aux . . . ?* Paris: L'Harmattan.

————. 2002. "The Monotheism of the Other: Language and De/Construction of National Identity in Postcolonial Algeria." *Algeria in Other's Languages*. Ed. Anne-Emmanuelle Berger. Ithaca: Cornell University Press. 19–43.

Garcés, María Antonia. 2002. *Cervantes in Algiers*. Nashville: Vanderbilt University Press.

Gill, Hélène. 1999. "Language Choice, Language Policy and the Tradition-Modernity Debate in Culturally Mixed Postcolonial Communities: France and the 'Francophone' Maghreb as a Case Study." *Language and Society in the Middle East and North Africa*. Ed. Yasi Suleiman. Richmond: Curzon. 122–36.

Glissant, Edouard. 1969. *L'Intention poétique*. Paris: Seuil.

————. 1981. *Le Discours antillais*. Paris: Seuil.

————. 1989. *Caribbean Discourse*. Trans. Michael Dash. Charlottesville: University Press of Virginia.

————. 1990. *Poétique de la Relation*. Paris: Gallimard.

Gosnell, Jonathan. 2002. *The Politics of Frenchness in Colonial Algeria: 1930–1954*. Rochester: University Press of Rochester.

Grandguillaume, Gilbert. 1983. *Arabisation et politique linguistique au Maghreb*. Paris: Maisonneuve & Larose.

————. 1997. "Le Maghreb confronté à l'Islamisme: Arabisation et démagogie en Algérie." *Le Monde Diplomatique* (February). Trans. John Howe as "Demagogues and Arabisers." <http://mondediplo.com/1997/02/10algeria>

Grossberg, Lawrence. 1996. "Identity and Cultural Studies." *Questions of Cultural Identities*. Ed. Stuart Hall and Paul du Gay. London: Sage. 61–86.

Halimi, Gisèle. 1999. *Fritna*. Paris: Plon.

Hall, Stuart. 1996. "When Was the Post-colonial?" *The Postcolonial Question: Common Skies, Divided Horizons*. Ed. Iain Chambers and Lidia Curti. London: Routledge. 242–60.

Hamoumou, Mohand. 1993. *Et ils sont devenus harkis*. Paris: Fayard.

Harbi, Mohamed. 1992. *L'Algérie et son destin*. Paris: Arcantère.

————. 1998. *1954, La Guerre commence en Algérie*. Paris: Complexe.

————. 2000. "Du côté algérien: Cet assourdissant silence." Interview by Patrick Loriot. *Nouvel Observateur* 1884 (14 December). <Maghreb-France.fm/Nouvel%20Obs%20Algerie/ dossier_1884:dossier4.html>

———. 2001. *Une vie debout.* Paris: La Découverte.

Hargreaves, Alec. 1991. *Voices from the North African Immigrant Community in France: Immigration and Identity in Beur Fiction.* 1st ed. Oxford and New York: Berg.

———. 1995. *Immigration, "Race" and Ethnicity in Contemporary France.* London and New York: Routledge.

———. 2000. "Les minorités postcoloniales face à la francophonie." *Présence Francophone* 55: 33–47.

Hargreaves, Alec, and McKinney, Mark. 1997. *Post-Colonial Cultures in France.* London and New York: Routledge.

Harzoune, Mustapha. 2003. "Psychodrame autour d'un ballon rond." *Hommes et Migrations* 1244 (July-August): 54–64.

Helm, Yolande Aline, ed. 2000. *Malika Mokeddem: Envers et contre tout.* Paris: L'Harmattan.

Honig, Bonnie. 1999. "My Culture Made Me Do It" In Cohen et al. 35–40.

Hureau, Joëlle. 2001. *La Mémoire des Pieds-noirs.* Paris: Perrin.

Ighilahriz, Louisette. 2001. *Algérienne.* Presented by Anne Nivat. Paris: Fayard/Calmann-Lévy.

Kabbal, Maati. 1999. "Le Maroc en mutation: Une effervescence culturelle." *Le Monde diplomatique*, April: 30.

Kacimi-El Hassani, Mohamed. 1992. "Langue de Dieu et langue du je." *Algérie, trente ans: Les enfants de l'indépendance. Autrement.* Série monde, no. 60 (Mars): 115–19.

Kassa, Sabrina. 2003. "Année de l'Algérie: 'Le boycott, c'est la sieste.'" Interview with Amazigh Kateb. *Hommes et Migrations* 1244 (July-August): 97–101.

Kaye, Jacqueline, and Abdelhamid Zoubir. 1990. *The Ambiguous Compromise: Language, Literature, and National Identity in Algeria and Morocco.* London and New York: Routledge.

Kédadouche, Zaïr. 2002. *La France et les Beurs.* Paris: La table ronde.

Kepel, Gilles. 2000. *Jihad: expansion et déclin de l'islamisme.* Paris: Gallimard.

Khadra, Yasmina. 1997. *Morituri.* Paris: Baleine.

———. 1999. *A quoi rêvent les loups.* Paris: Pocket.

Khatibi, Abdelkebir. 1971. *La Mémoire tatouée.* Paris: Les lettres nouvelles.

———. 1983a. *Amour bilingue.* Montpellier: Fata Morgana.

———. 1983b. *Maghreb pluriel.* Paris: Denoël.

———. 1990. *Love in Two Languages.* Trans. Richard Howard. Minneapolis: University of Minnesota.

Kristeva, Julia. 1980. *Pouvoirs de l'horreur: Essai sur l'abjection.* Paris: Seuil.

Lacan, Jacques. 1973. *Le Séminaire, livre XI: Les quatre concepts fondamentaux de la psychanalyse.* Paris: Seuil.

———. 1975. *Le Séminaire, livre XX: Encore.* Paris: Seuil.

Lagarde, André and Laurent Michard. 1967. *Collection littéraire, XVIIème siècle.* Paris: Bordas.

Lallaoui, Mehdi. 1986. *Les Beurs de Seine.* Paris: Arcantère.

———. 1989. *20 ans d'affiches antiracistes.* Paris: Association Black Blanc, Beur.

———. 1996. *Une nuit d'octobre.* Paris: Editions alternatives.

————. 1998. *La Colline aux oliviers*. Paris: Editions alternatives/SEDAG.

Lallaoui, Mehdi, and David Assouline. 2001. *Un siècle d'immigrations en France*. Paris: Au nom de la mémoire.

Laronde, Michel. 1993. *Autour du roman beur*. Paris: L'Harmattan.

Laroui, Fouad. 1998. *De quel amour blessé*. Paris: Julliard.

————. 1999. *Méfiez-vous des parachutistes*. Paris: Julliard.

————. 2003. *La Fin tragique de Philomène Tralala*. Paris: Julliard.

Laroussi, Foued, ed. 1997. *Plurilinguisme et identités au Maghreb*. Rouen: Publications de l'université de Rouen.

Latour, Bruno. 1993. *We Have Never Been Modern*. Trans. Catherine Porter. London: Harvester Wheatsheaf.

Leiner, Jacqueline. [1942] 1978. "Entretien avec Aimé Césaire" in *Tropiques* 1, no. 5 (April 1941–42): i–xxxviii. Facsimile reproduction, Paris: Éditions Jean-Michel Place.

Levinas, Emmanuel. 1993. *Dieu, la mort et le temps*. Ed. Jacques Roland. Paris: Grasset.

————. 2000. *God, Death and Time*. Trans. Bettina Bergo. Stanford: Stanford University Press.

Lionnet, Françoise. 1989. *Autobiographical Voices: Race, Gender, Self-Portraiture*. Ithaca: Cornell University Press.

————. 1995. *Postcolonial Representations: Women, Literature, Identity*. Ithaca: Cornell University Press.

————. 1998. "Immigration, Poster Art, and Transgressive Citizenship: France, 1968–1988." *Borders, Exiles, Diasporas*. Ed. Barkan, Elazar and Marie-Denise Shelton. Stanford: Stanford University Press. 197–216.

Lionnet, Françoise and Ronnie Scharfman, eds. 1993. *Post/Colonial Conditions*. *Yale French Studies* 2, no. 83.

Lorcin, Patricia. 1999. *Imperial Identities: Stereotyping, Prejudice and Race in Colonial Algeria*. London: I.B. Tauris.

Lyotard, Jean-François. [1983] 1988. *The Differend: Phrases in Dispute*. Trans. Georges Van den Abbeele. Minneapolis: University of Minnesota Press. Originally published as *Le Différend*. Paris: Minuit.

Mailhé, Germaine. 1995. *Déportation en Nouvelle-Calédonie des communards et des révoltés de la Grande Kabylie: 1872–1876*. Paris: L'Harmattan.

Mammeri, Mouloud. 1952. *La Colline oubliée*. Paris: Plon.

Manopoulous, Monique. 1996. "Sofia ou le Néo-orientalisme tiers-espaciel dans les A.N.I. du 'Tassili' d'Akli Tadjer." *L'Ecriture décentrée*. Ed. Michel Laronde. Paris: L'Harmattan. 85–108.

Maoudj, Danièle. 1996. "Mon Désorient." *Confluences Méditerranée: Passions franco-algériennes* 19 (fall): 125–30.

Mazouz, Brahim. 2003. "Boycott des artistes kabyles de l'Année de l'Algérie en France." *L'Actualité*, 2 February. <http://www.algeria-watch.de>

McGuire, James. 1992. "Forked Tongues, Marginal Bodies: Writing as Translation in Khatibi." *Research in African Literatures* 23, no. 1 (Spring): 107–16.

Meisami, Julie Scott. 2003. *Structure and Meaning in Medieval Arabic and Persian Poetry: Orient Pearls*. London: Routledge.

Mellal, Arezki. 2002. *Maintenant ils peuvent venir*. Arles: Actes sud.

Memmi, Albert. 1969. *Le Scorpion ou la confession imaginaire*. Paris: Gallimard.

———. 1973. *Portrait du colonisé*. Paris: Payot.

———. [1955] 1984. *Agar*. Paris: Gallimard.

———. 1990. *The Colonizer and The Colonized*. Trans. Howard Greenfeld. London: Earthscan.

Messud, Claire. 1999. *The Last Life*. New York: Harcourt Brace.

Mezgueldi, Zohra. 1996. "Mother Word and French Language Moroccan Writing." *Research in African Literatures* 27, no. 31 (autumn): 1–14.

Mignolo, Walter. 2000. *Local Histories, Global Designs: Coloniality, Subaltern Knowledges, and Border Thinking*. Princeton, N.J.: Princeton University Press.

Miller, Christopher. 1990. *Theories of Africans: Francophone Literature and Anthropology in Africa*. Chicago: University of Chicago Press.

———. 1998. *Nationalists and Nomads: Essays on Francophone African Literature and Culture*. Chicago: University of Chicago Press.

Milon, Alain. 1999. *L'Etranger dans la ville*. Paris: PUF.

Mimouni, Rachid. 1982. *Le Fleuve détourné*. Paris: Robert Laffont.

Moatassime, Ahmed. 2000. "Arabo-francophonie et enjeux géolinguistiques en Méditerranée." *Présence francophone* 55: 49–62.

Mokeddem, Malika. 1993. *L'Interdite*. Paris: Grasset.

———. 1995. *Des Rêves et des assassins*. Paris: Grasset.

———. 1998. *The Forbidden Woman*. Trans. K. Melissa Marcus. Lincoln: University of Nebraska Press.

———. 2000. *Of Dreams and Assassins*. Trans. K. Melissa Marcus. Charlottesville: University Press of Virginia.

———. 2001. *N'zid*. Paris: Grasset.

de Montaigne, Michel. 1952. *Essais*. Paris: Les Portiques.

Morin, Edgar. 1970. *L'Homme et la mort*. Paris: Seuil.

Mortimer, Mildred. 1996. "Reappropriating the Gaze in Assia Djebar's Fiction and Film." *World Literature Today* 70, no. 4: 859–66.

———. 2001. *Maghrebian Mosaic: A Literature in Transition*. Boulder: L. Rienner.

Moss, Jane. 1999. "Postmodernizing the Salem Witchcraze: Maryse Condé's I, Tituba, Black Witch of Salem." *Colby Quarterly* 35, no. 1 (March): 5–17.

Nagy-Zekmi, Silvia. 2002. "Tradition and Transgression in the Novels of Assia Djebar and Aïcha Lemsine." *Research in African Literatures* 33, no. 3: 1–3.

Nait-Zerrad, Kamal. 2003. "Faut-il boycotter l'Année de l'Algérie en France?" *Libération*, 9 January: 8.

Nancy, Jean-Luc. 2000. *L'Intrus*. Paris: Galilée.

Nora, Pierre. 1996. "From *Lieux de mémoire* to *Realms of Memory*." *Realms of Memory*. Trans. Arthur Goldhammer. New York: Columbia University Press. xv–xxiv.

———, ed. 1984. *Les Lieux de mémoire*. Paris: Gallimard.

———, ed. 2001. *Rethinking France*. Trans. Mary Trouille. Chicago: University of Chicago Press.

Nouchi, Franck. 2003. "La voix de Depardieu et la foi de Saint Augustin." *Le Monde*, 9 February.

O'Riley, Michael. 2002. "Translation and Imperialism in Assia Djebar's *Les Nuits de Strasbourg.*" *French Review*, 75, no. 6 (May): 1235–49.

———. 2004. "Place, Position, and Postcolonial Haunting in Assia Djebar's *La Femme sans sépulture.*" *Research in African Literatures* 35, no. 1 (spring): 66–86.

Ouary, Malek. 2000. *La Robe kabyle de Baya.* Saint Denis: Editions Bouchène.

Ounali, Habib. 1970. "La langue des étudiants." *Cahiers CERES-Série linguistique* 3 (November): 167–213.

Pérennès, Jean-Jacques. 2000. *Pierre Claverie, un Algérien par alliance.* Paris: Cerf.

Philippe, Bernard. 2001. "Du match France-Algérie au 17 octobre 1961." *Le Monde*, 26 October.

Prabhu, Anjali. 2002. "Sisterhood and Rivalry in-between the Shadow and the Sultana: A Problematic of Representation in *Ombre sultane.*" *Research in African Literatures* 33, no. 3: 69–96.

Prakash, Gyan. 1997. "Postcolonial Criticism and Indian Historiography." *Dangerous Liaisons: Gender, Nation, and Postcolonial Perspectives.* Ed. Anne McClintock, Aamir Mufti and Ella Shohat. Minneapolis: University of Minnesota Press. 491–500.

Pratt, Marie-Louise. 1992. *Imperial Eyes.* New York and London: Routledge.

Rancière, Jacques. 1995. *La Mésentente: politique et philosophie.* Paris: Galilée.

Riahi, Zohra. 1970. "Emploi de l'arabe et du français par les élèves du secondaire." *Cahiers CERES-Série linguistique* 3 (November): 99–165.

Rosello, Mireille. 1993. "The 'Beur Nation': Toward a Theory of 'Departenance.'" *Research in African Literatures* 24, no. 3: 13–24.

———. 2002. "Remembering the Incomprehensible: Hélène Cixous, Leïla Sebbar, Yamina Benguigui and the War of Algeria." *Remembering Africa.* Ed. Elisabeth Mudimbe Boyi. Portsmouth: Heinemann. 187–205.

———. 2003. "Tactical Universalism and New Multiculturalist Claims in Postcolonial France." *Francophone Studies: Postcolonial Issues.* Ed. Charles Forsdick and David Murphy. London: Arnold. 135–44.

Roux, Michel. 1991. *Les Harkis: Les oubliés de l'histoire, 1954–1991.* Paris: La Découverte.

Roy, Jules. 1967–1972. *Les Chevaux du soleil.* Paris: Grasset.

———. 1982. *Etranger pour mes frères.* Paris: Stock.

Saadi, Nourredine. 2003. "La mémoire du vent." *Panoramiques: Algériens-Français: bientôt finis les enfantillages?* 170–72.

Saadi-Mokrane, Djamila. 2002. "The Algerian Linguicide." Trans. Whitney Sanford. *Algeria in Other's Languages.* Ed. Anne-Emmanuelle Berger. Ithaca: Cornell University Press. 44–59.

Salem, Nadia. 1997. "Algérie, pays de l'ultime retour." *Le Livre du retour. Récits du pays des origines.* Ed. Sonia Combe. Collection mutations, no. 173. Paris: Editions Autrement. 83–98.

Sansal, Boualem. 1999. *Le Serment des barbares.* Paris: Gallimard.

———. 2000. *L'Enfant fou de l'arbre creux.* Paris: Gallimard.

———. 2003. "Souvenirs d'enfance et autres faits de guerre." *L'Algérie des deux rives.* Ed. Raymond Gozier. Paris: Mille et une nuits. 37–56.

Sartre, Jean-Paul. 1938. *La Nausée*. Paris: Gallimard.

———. [1948] 1985. "Orphée noir." *Anthologie de la nouvelle poésie nègre et malgache de langue française*. Paris: PUF. vii–xliv.

———. 1963. Preface to *The Wretched of the Earth* by Frantz Fanon. Trans. Constance Farrington. Paris: Présence Africaine. 7–31.

———. 1964. *Qu'est-ce que la littérature?* Paris: Gallimard.

Schalk, David. 1991. *War and the Ivory Tower: Algeria and Vietnam*. New York: Oxford University Press.

Scharfman, Ronnie. 1988–1989. "Maghrebian Autobiography or Autoportraiture? Abdelkebir Khatibi's *La Mémoire tatouée*." *Revue Celfan/Celfan Review* 8, nos. 1–2: 5–9.

Searle, John. 1969. *Speech Acts: An Essay in the Philosophy of Language*. Cambridge: Cambridge University Press.

———. 1977. "Reiterating the Differences: A Reply to Derrida." *Glyph* 1: 198–208.

———. 1979. *Expression and Meaning: Studies in the Theory of Speech Acts*. Cambridge: Cambridge University Press.

Sebbar, Leïla. 1982. *Shérazade, brune, frisée, les yeux verts*. Paris: Stock.

———. 1997. *Enfances algériennes*. Paris: Gallimard, collection haute enfance.

———. 2001. Review of Slimane Benaïssa's *Le Silence de la falaise*. *Magazine Littéraire* 401 (October): 66.

———. 2003. *Je ne parle pas la langue de mon père*. Paris: Julliard.

Sedgwick, Eve. 1993. "Privilege of Unknowing: Diderot's *The Nun*." *Tendencies*. Durham: Duke University Press. 23–51.

———. 2003. *Touching Feeling: Affect, Pedagogy, Performativity*. Durham and London: Duke University Press.

Serres, Michel. 1991. *Le Tiers instruit*. Paris: François Bourin.

Sherman, Daniel. 2000. "The Arts and Sciences of Colonialism." *French Historical Studies* 23, no. 4 (fall): 707–39.

Sherzer, Dina. 2001. "Maghrebi-French Directors Behind the Camera: The Cinema of the Second Generation." *Studies in Twentieth Century Literature* 26, no. 1: 144–71.

Sicard, Christian. 1998. *La Kabylie en feu: Algérie, 1871*. Paris: Sud.

Silverstein, Paul. 2000. "Sporting Faith: Islam, Soccer, and the French Nation-State." *Social Text* 18, no. 4: 25–53.

Simon, Sherry. 2002. "Crossing Town: Montreal in Translation." *Profession*. New York: Modern Language Association: 15–24.

Sperl, Stefan and Christopher Shackle, eds. 1996. *Qasida Poetry in Islamic Asia and Africa*. Leiden & New York: E. J. Brill.

Spivak, Gayatri. 1992. "Acting Bits/Identity Talks." *Critical Inquiry* 18 (summer): 770–803.

———. 1994. "Responsibility." *Boundary 2* 21, no. 3 (fall): 19–64.

Stevens, Christa. 2002. "Hélène Cixous, auteur en 'algériance.'" *Expressions maghrébines* 1, no. 1: 77–91.

Stora, Benjamin. 1991. *La Gangrène et l'oubli*. Paris: La Découverte.

———. 1995. "Mémoires comparées: femmes françaises, femmes algériennes. Les écrits des femmes, la guerre d'Algérie et l'exil." *L'Ère des décolonisations: actes du colloque d'Aix-en-Provence.* Ed. Charles-Robert Ageron and Marc Michel. Paris: Karthala. 172–93.

———. 1996. "Censures pendant la 'non-guerre' d'Algérie dans le cinéma français." *Revue d'histoire maghrébine* 2, no. 83–84: 725–32.

———. 2001a. "Décloisonner les mémoires autour de la guerre d'Algérie." Interview by Eugénie Barbez. Institut National de l'Audiovisuel (INA) colloquium: *Regards croisés sur la guerre d'Algérie,* 17 November. <http://www.ina.fr/voir_revoir/algerie/itv_stora.fr.html>

———. 2001b. *La Guerre invisible, Algérie, années 90.* Paris: Presses de Sciences Po.

———. 2002. "L'Algérie d'une guerre à l'autre." *Enseigner la guerre d'Algérie et le Maghreb contemporain* in *Actes de la DESCO.* Université d'été, October 2001. © Ministère de l'Education nationale, direction de l'Enseignement scolaire, *Eduscol,* April. <http://www.eduscol.education.fr/D0033/algerie_acte08.htm>

———. 2003a. "L'absence d'images déréalise l'Algérie." Interview by Juliette Cerf and Charles Tesson. *Cahiers du cinéma*: Special issue, "Où va le cinéma algérien?" (February): 7–17.

———. 2003b. "Guerre d'Algérie: 1999–2003, les accélérations de la mémoire." *Hommes et Migrations* 1244 (July-August): 83–95.

Tadjer, Akli. 1984. *Les A.N.I. du "Tassili."* Paris: Seuil.

———. 2000. *Courage et patience.* Paris: Jean-Claude Lattès.

———. 2002. *Le Porteur de cartable.* Paris: Jean-Claude Lattès.

Taleb Ibrahimi, Khouala. 1995. *Les Algériens et leur(s) langue(s).* Alger: Editions El Hikma.

———. 1997. "L'arabisation, lieu de conflits multiples." *Elites et questions identitaires.* Ed. Mustapha Madi. Algiers: Casbah Editions. 39–61.

wa Thiong'o, Ngugi. 1986. *Decolonising the Mind: the Politics of Language in African Literature.* London: J. Currey; Portsmouth, N.H.: Heinemann.

———. 2000. "Europhonism, Universities, and the Magic Fountain: The Future of African Literature and Scholarship." *Research in African Literatures* 31, no. 1: 1–11.

Thobie, Jacques. 1991. *La France coloniale de 1870 à 1914.* Paris: Armand Colin.

Tillion, Germaine. [1960] 1961. *France and Algeria: Complementary Enemies.* Trans. Richard Howard. New York: Knopf. Originally published as *Les Ennemis complémentaires.* Paris: Minuit.

Tomlinson, Emily. 2003. "Assia Djebar: Speaking to the Living Dead." *Paragraph* 3: 34–50.

Treille, Alcide. 1876. *L'Expédition de Kabylie orientale et du Hodna, mars-novembre 1871: notes et souvenirs d'un médecin militaire.* Paris: J. B. Baillère.

Tribalat, Michèle. 1998. "Ce jour est magique, il incarne l'idéal du creuset français." Interview by Dominique Simmonot. *Libération,* 10 July: 5.

Urbain, Jean-Didier. 1989. *L'Archipel des morts: Le sentiment de la mort et les dérives de la mémoire dans les cimetières de l'Occident.* Paris: Plon.

Vidal-Naquet, Pierre. 1996. "La guerre d'Algérie: Bilan d'un engagement." Interview with Bernard Ravenel. *Confluences Méditerranée: Passions franco-algériennes* 19 (fall): 145–50.

————. 2001. "Il faut prendre ce livre pour ce qu'il est, les Mémoires d'un assassin." *Le Monde*, 2 May.

Vurgun, Sibel. 2004. "ANI tu es, ANI tu resteras." *Migrations des identités et des textes entre l'Algérie et la France, dans les littératures des deux rives*. Ed. Charles Bonn. Paris: L'Harmattan. 65–75.

Wahbi, Hassan. 1995. *Les Mots du monde*. Agadir: Publications de la faculté des lettres et sciences humaines.

Waltzer, Michael. 1997. *On Toleration*. New Haven and London: Yale University Press.

Williams, Patricia. 1991. *The Alchemy of Race and Rights*. Cambridge: Harvard University Press.

Woodhull, Winnifred. 1993. *Transfigurations of the Maghreb: Feminism, Decolonization and Literatures*. Minneapolis: University of Minnesota Press.

Yacine, Kateb. 1956. *Nedjma*. Paris: Seuil.

Yee, Jennifer. 2001. "The Colonial Outsider: 'malgérie' in Hélène Cixous's *Les Rêveries de la femme sauvage*." *Tulsa Studies in Women's Literature* 20, no. 2 (fall): 189.

Young, Robert. 2001. *Postcolonialism: An Historical Introduction*. London: Blackwell.

Zimra, Clarisse. 1995. "Disorienting the Subject in Djebar's *L'Amour la Fantasia*." *Yale French Studies* 87: 149–70.

Zobel, Joseph. [1950] 1974. *Rue Cases-Nègres*. Paris: Présence africaine.

Index

Mireille Rosello teaches comparative literary and cultural studies at Northwestern University. Her most recent publications are *Postcolonial Hospitality: The Immigrant as Guest* and *Declining the Stereotype: Representation and Ethnicity in French Cultures*.